PRINCETON
A Love Story

PRINCETON
A Love Story

Terry Fong

CORNER
TREE
PRESS

Canadian copyright registration
1154501

Cam Shaw, cover designer
Cam Shaw, front cover and back cover photographer
David Moratto, interior book design

Corner Tree Press
www.cornertreepress.com

Printed on 100% 55 lb. recycled PCW offset natural web cream paper.

First edition.
Printed in Canada.

ISBN 978-1-9995104-0-4 (paperback)

For Princeton.
You may not be with me
the way you were before,
but I also know you never really left.

And for those who choose
to adopt an animal and save a life.
Princeton's was my life to save.
There are countless others
that need saving too.

Author's Note

THE CONTENTS OF this book are written from memory. Locations, people, and events are represented as well as I can remember them. I apologize in advance to the reader and to those mentioned in this book if my memory is even poorer than I think it is and some details are a little off.

Contents

Prologue

I DON'T KNOW where to begin. I've never really thought of myself as a writer. But I've noticed many writers mentioning the same thing: write about what you know. So I suppose I'll start there. I know I had a dog named Princeton. A dog who lived to nearly eighteen years of age and occupied approximately one-third of my life. I know I loved him more than anything I've ever had or anyone I've ever known. I know he was my constant companion, rarely leaving my side for all the years we were together. I know I was also his travel companion in later years, he and I seeing much of Western and Northern Canada together. And although I miss him terribly, I know that my feelings of sadness and emptiness will eventually be replaced by the wonderful memories I have of him. More than anything, however, I know there will never be another dog like him. A dog who, in the last five years of his life, demonstrated a tremendous courage and determination. Lastly, I know that the many others who met Princeton and were inspired by him also continue to miss him greatly. Princeton was that sort of dog—a dog who touched the hearts of many and remained in their thoughts long after he continued on his way. This is our story.

A Dignified Dog

It all started with a dog named Gypsy. Or maybe I should say that it started with my getting reacquainted with a dog named Gypsy. In the fall of 1997, after being away for several years, I purchased the farm I had been raised on. It was a poultry farm, started by my parents in 1972 and successfully operated by them for twenty-five years. When I was younger and living on the farm, I never considered that I would one day take it over. I suppose like many others growing up on a farm, I felt that my future would be much brighter the farther away I was from the place. I enjoyed growing up in the country very much, but the appeal of farming was lost on me. Being allergic to chickens didn't add to my enthusiasm either. But when I did return to the farm, I immediately rekindled my affection for the big Newfoundland dog named Gypsy who lived with my parents.

Gypsy was originally found by my sister (who had the good sense to stay away from farming after she left) in a ditch eating out of a discarded McDonald's bag. We all thought she was less than a year old at the time and decided she would be a welcome addition to the family. I can't recall who named her, but she became known as Gypsy. She grew into a big, loveable, and loyal farm dog. New-foundlands are known as water dogs because of their instinctual

Five-day-old chicks.
—Photograph by author

love of water. Show a Newfoundland dog a puddle of water, and they'll soon be splashing around in it. The farm is alongside a river, and we'd often see Gypsy swimming around in it while my sister and I hollered frantically for her to stop and return home. She was there for me when I returned to the farm, accompanying me while I did my chores or watching me silently as I worked on my new home.

Poultry farming is a lot of work. I'm still in the profession today, always telling myself and others, "Probably not for much longer." That I've been saying the same thing for several years hasn't motivated me to abandon farming, however. Mine is an average-size farm, capable of producing up to thirty thousand chickens every eight weeks. For a one-person operation, it can be pretty demanding. Each growing cycle is approximately six weeks long, followed by two weeks of cleaning, disinfecting, repairing barns and equipment, and preparing for the next flock.

The growing cycle starts when the chicks, only a few hours old, arrive at the farm and I place them inside the barns. At such a young age, they're extremely cute but also extremely fragile. The barns must be heated to about 35°C when the chicks arrive, and I follow strict lighting and environmental protocols to ensure they're comfortable and can begin eating and drinking. For the first few days, they are under almost constant supervision. In addition to providing a suitable environment, I need to constantly monitor and adjust the equipment and machinery. A faulty boiler or furnace, an improperly working exhaust fan, or a mechanical failure involving feed or water systems can have catastrophic consequences. As the chicks grow and mature, they still require constant supervision and ongoing adjustments to their environment. When not in the barns, I'm usually hauling feed or performing general maintenance. It's not a nine-to-five, five-days-a-week sort of job; it's an in-the-barns-every-few-hours, seven-days-a-week sort of job. It's not uncommon for me to be working in the barns throughout the entire day and then having to address a mechanical failure at 1:00 a.m., repairing it, and then having to perform regular checks and maintenance a few hours later.

When the chickens are ready for market, they are loaded onto specially designed trailers and shipped off farm to be processed. After that the cleaning component begins. Standing in chicken shit, a wash hose draped over your shoulder while you're encased in a vinyl suit, washing twenty-four thousand square feet of poultry barns is far less glamorous than it sounds. When that's completed I disinfect the barns and prepare new bedding. I also repair and adjust the water and feed equipment, and the entire process repeats itself once more.

Regardless of the work involved, it's something I enjoy and will probably continue doing for some time despite how much complaining I do. It also gives me a sense of pride knowing that my farm is recognized for producing a quality product and, most importantly, for following very strict animal welfare protocols.

There are numerous benefits to being a farmer, or in my case, a chicken farmer. I'm my own boss, and my successes or failures are generally of my own making. My commute to work is an approximately six-hundred-foot walk from my home. And best of all, I can have a dog. A companion who keeps me company as I go about my day. Gypsy was that sort of dog. But one day she left and never returned. In her later years, she was never one to wander off the farm, so if she chose to leave, the reason had to have been important to her. I remember looking for her for days, but deep down I knew she was gone forever. Gypsy must have been about fourteen years old and had become a tired old dog. Some animals choose to go away on their own when death comes for them, preferring to pass away on their own terms. I knew that Gypsy had simply decided to leave us one day to die on her own. She left me with many wonderful memories, and although it would have been nice to have been with her when her time came, I respect and understand why she chose to leave.

It was difficult not seeing Gypsy around the farm. She wasn't the type of dog to wait for me outside the barns or follow me around, but she was always a welcome sight, whether she was sleeping under a tree or lying on the grass outside my home. She was missed. In time, I started to think about getting another dog. The type or breed didn't matter to me as long as the dog was on the larger side and capable of living outdoors.

I've always believed that the perfect dog is the dog who needs a home. I can't imagine ever getting an animal from a breeder, preferring instead to go the adoption route. Plenty of wonderful dogs who need a home are often overlooked simply because they're not of a particular breed or type. Many of these dogs never get a home. They never get the chance to be loved. And the people who pass them over are missing out on a special opportunity to receive the love only a dog who has known hardship or abandonment can give. I understand there will always be those who will only consider a purebred or a particular sort of dog, but that preference is something I've never been comfortable with. Thousands of cats and dogs are euthanized each year in Canada simply because they're unwanted, and I've always felt that it's better to save one of these animals instead of purchasing from a breeder.

I also preferred an adult dog. Puppies and kittens are cute and cuddly and tend to be adopted quickly, leaving the adults sitting alone in their kennels wondering why they were left behind. I was also aware that entirely black dogs and cats often have a harder time finding a home than their multicoloured counterparts, so I preferred a dog with a completely black coat. In short, I was prepared to adopt any dog, but I liked the idea of giving a home to one who would have the most difficulty finding one.

Princeton was approximately a year old when I first saw him. It was early winter of 1999. He was the first dog available when I decided to adopt. He was black with a tiny bit of white on his chest. The info card on his cage stated that he was a cross between a black

Lab and a border collie. I found him in a pet store offering animals available for adoption from the local humane society. His info card also said his name was Prince, and in bold, capital letters, that he was *extremely intelligent*. To me he looked more bored than anything. A floor associate informed me that he was the last of a family of dogs brought to the humane society by one individual; all of his brothers and sisters had found new homes. The humane society had been unsuccessful in trying to place him, so they sent him to this particular store to see if he would have better luck. The associate also said that the staff found him remarkably well behaved and very intelligent. I would discover later that yes, he was intelligent, but well behaved? Well, no. There was a hold on him for twenty-four hours, as someone else had an interest in him. Even though he didn't seem all that outgoing or even interested in me, something about him intrigued me. And he seemed to be a hard luck case, which appealed to me even more. I left my name, and the staff promised to phone me within twenty-four hours to let me know if he was still up for adoption.

The next day the store staff contacted me to inform me that Prince's adoption hadn't gone through and he was mine if I wanted him. I stopped by after lunch to find him sitting in his cage, still looking bored and very much in his own little world. But I could tell he recognized me from the day before. I spoke his name and he immediately came forward, his brown eyes filled with the intelligence I hadn't seen earlier.

I walked closer to his cage and said to him, "Do you want to go home with me? Do you want to be a farm dog?" Looking at me inquisitively and cocking his head to one side, he let me know his answer.

I told a store associate I wanted to adopt him, and she began working on the adoption process. While waiting, I found a nice red collar I thought would go well with his black fur. After Prince was officially mine, the staff let him out of his cage and I put the new collar around his neck. He would wear the same collar for the rest of his life. It would be removed only for the surgeries, treatments, and X-rays that would happen frequently later in his life.

After paying the adoption fee, I led Prince to the back of my truck, where I had placed a large animal crate in the bed. He showed little emotion but was remarkably well behaved as we crossed the parking lot. From my limited knowledge of border collies, I expected him to be rambunctious and outgoing; Prince showed neither of these qualities. It was when we arrived at my truck that I decided his new name would be Princeton instead of Prince. I wanted him to have a connection to his past, but I really didn't like the name the store staff had given him. I thought "Princeton" had a dignified tone to it, and it suited his regal bearing. After all, such a supposedly intelligent dog deserved to have a dignified name. My newly acquired dignified and intelligent dog then pissed all over me as I lifted him into the crate.

2

Life on the Farm

SOON PRINCETON ARRIVED at his new home—a home we would share for almost seventeen years. Upon his arrival he didn't seem enthused, not moving for several minutes after I had lifted him from his crate and placed him onto the ground. For the first few days, he didn't do much of anything except follow a few steps behind me. For a dog approximately a year old, I expected him to be much more, well, puppy-like. Instead he behaved like a much older dog. He didn't play, didn't bark, and followed directly behind me, stopping when I stopped and moving again when I moved. If I left him alone, he would stay there until I returned. He had obviously had a lot of training and knew some basic commands; perhaps this was why the staff at the pet store thought he was very intelligent.

When I tried to play with him by throwing a stick, he clearly wanted to chase after it, but after moving a few steps toward it, he would sit down and look at me. Princeton had never been allowed to play. Someone must have trained him at a young age to be very obedient. To be a working dog. I suppose there's nothing wrong with that, but I expected (and wanted) him to be a little more outgoing—a dog not afraid to have a little fun and to enjoy and thrive in his surroundings. This was, after all, a farm. He had lots of room to roam around and do what he wanted. I realize dogs need to be trained for both their benefit and that of their human companions, but I felt Princeton had missed out on his puppyhood. I told him this several times as we wandered around the farm together for the first few days. I told him that as long as he didn't hurt anything, chase cars, or leave the property, he could do whatever he wanted. In retrospect, this probably wasn't a good idea.

When Princeton finally came out of his shell, he did it in a big way. A week after he arrived at the farm, he discovered he really could do what he pleased. He could bark. He could run. He could play. Unfortunately, he also thought his newfound freedom included ignoring my wishes entirely. If he wanted to chase a car coming up the driveway, he did. If he thought a cat looked intriguing, he considered himself free to investigate kitty a little further. Leaving the property to visit the neighbours? No problem. Hurtling himself down the embankment toward the river because he'd heard something and wanted to investigate it? Absolutely. Most of this involved my chasing after him and screaming his name as he ignored me. More than once I longed for that overly disciplined dog who had come home with me a few weeks before. He decided his life was so much better now that he didn't need to practise all that training he'd received earlier.

His determination to do his own thing was really apparent when I introduced him to chickens for the first time. I'm often in the barns about six times a day to make sure the chickens are fine and all equipment is working properly, and a couple of weeks after his arrival, I thought I would show Princeton where I disappeared to from time to time. The first time he entered a barn with me, the chickens were only about two weeks old. Observing the grin that appeared on his face, I knew I had made a mistake. Princeton, being part border collie, was bred to be a working dog, and most of their duties involved herding things. Sheep, cattle, goats, and other types of farm animals are often rounded up by border collies and kept secure under their watchful gaze. Princeton thought chickens should be too.

Chickens do not like to be stressed. Chickens like to eat, drink, eat, shit, peck things they find in their bedding, and then eat some more. They like security and rarely take the effort to move more than a few feet at a time. They do not like a woolly, monstrous-looking black creature bearing down on them and deciding where they should be, especially when this creature is barking loudly. Chickens become stressed when things like this happen. They begin making lots of noise and start running in all directions. Princeton, naturally, took their response as a personal insult and began to bark louder and herd them with even greater authority. Adding to the chickens' stress was the monstrous creature's human companion, their once trusted caregiver, chasing after the seemingly deaf beast, both of them tripping over feed and water lines. Princeton ran down the entire length of a 150-foot barn, barking and shifting from one direction to another in a vain attempt to move a chicken or group of chickens to what he felt was a more appropriate location. It didn't work. What it did do was force thousands of chickens to plaster themselves to either side of the barn, stepping over each other and clucking frantically. When Princeton was satisfied with his work, he confidently strode to where I was, looked up at me, and waited for me to praise him for his outstanding performance. He had been a *good* dog. It would be a long time before he was allowed to enter the barns again with chickens present.

Instead Princeton spent the next several months tied up outside any barn I had to enter. If he wasn't tied up, he often wouldn't be there when I came back out. My formerly well-trained and obedient dog had decided he could bugger off wherever he wanted to if I wasn't around. After all, he had a lot of making up to do for his lost puppyhood. But Princeton, though very disobedient, was very happy. You could see it on his face. He was in constant awe of his surroundings and had chosen to experience all he could.

Unfortunately, he often felt that nine acres was not enough space to appreciate all that life had to offer. He would wander off the property, eventually returning with a satisfied expression and his fur all muddy and matted. During the nights, I chained him to his doghouse, reasonably confident he wouldn't escape. If he did ever escape and became lost, I hoped the small dog tag I'd purchased for him, engraved with his name and mine, along with my phone number, would help bring him home.

Early one morning I walked out of my house and there was no Princeton—only a chain, one end still attached to his doghouse and the other lying on the grass. How he'd managed to break free I'll never know. Before I had time to think of how to go about looking for him, the phone rang in my house.

"Um, uh, do you have a black dog that may be missing? I think his name is Princeton or something like that," said the voice at the end of the line.

"Yes. Yes, I do," I replied, assuming the worst.

"Well, we're out flying our aircraft and there's a dog here with a tag with this name and phone number on it."

This concerned me immediately for two reasons: one, Princeton had indeed wandered off, and two, why the hell was he at the airport? It's about ninety kilometres from my farm. Thankfully, the caller went on to explain that he and a few others were at an abandoned gravel pit about five kilometres away flying their radio-controlled model aircraft. Princeton had suddenly appeared while one pilot was taxiing his plane for flight, and he tried to chase it. Luckily, the man managed to get it airborne before Princeton got a hold of it. Princeton then retreated to the trees, only to be seen again when another pilot landed his aircraft and Princeton darted out from his hiding place to chase it. Unfortunately, this aircraft hadn't fared as well as the previous one. I hopped into my truck and drove to the gravel pit to retrieve him and prevent any further aviation tragedies. Princeton and I would need to discuss that there wasn't a need to herd aircraft, even if he thought they looked like chickens.

Upon my arrival I discovered Princeton tied with a piece of string to a tree, intently watching all the model aircraft taking off and landing. He was amused by the entire thing and, surprisingly, wasn't in much trouble with the model aviators. All was forgiven. As I would discover in the years that followed, people almost always forgave Princeton for his indiscretions.

As he grew more confident, he became even more outgoing. He was obviously very happy and comfortable in his new surroundings. As the weeks and months continued, Princeton became more obedient and took his farm duties more seriously. Finally, I stopped tying him up outside the barns, as he understood that he was to remain waiting outside the door until I returned. As I went about my day, Princeton understood what I had to do and what was expected of him. He was still a free spirit, but he was beginning to understand that he had responsibilities. He had an occupation. A duty. To watch over the farm and to be a companion. Over time Princeton began to take pride in what he did, with an enthusiasm and carefree manner I came to appreciate and respect. He had found his calling, and I was glad to have him with me.

One habit Princeton refused to abandon, however, was eating interesting things he found in chicken manure. Most of these things were either dead chickens or parts of dead chickens. During the course of a growing cycle, I might expect to lose 3 to 4 percent of a flock to such things as heart attacks and other growth-related ailments. Removing these dead birds is just one component of daily operations, and once I come out of the barns, I dispose of them immediately. Every so often I miss one, as it becomes buried within the bedding, hidden from sight. The overlooked chicken eventually decays and becomes part of the manure. When I've sent the chickens away to be processed and the barns are waiting to be cleaned, it's impossible to know where these lost carcasses are. Well, impossible for me. For Princeton, not at all. Apparently, Labs have a tremendous sense of smell, and if a decaying carcass was hidden somewhere in the manure, Princeton would find it.

Princeton *loved* to find these. A decaying carcass was a prize. As I worked inside the barns preparing the equipment to be washed, I always had to keep a watchful eye on him and make sure he didn't find and dig up a lump of something that was once a chicken. If he did find one I had overlooked, he'd dig it up while I wasn't looking and run out of the barn with it. I would run after him, foolishly believing he understood the words "Drop it!" and "That's disgusting!" Apparently, he understood these words about as well as I understood his fascination for decaying chickens. Chasing him across the yard and yelling at him only made him run faster, until he disappeared into the tree line. He'd reappear later, a smile on his face and a smell on his breath that would make most people gag.

On at least two occasions, Princeton had to visit the veterinarian because he'd eaten a decaying carcass. His tummy would be upset, and the vet would prescribe some really expensive canned dog food for a few days until he felt better. The really frustrating part was knowing that Princeton always restrained himself among all the dead chickens I brought out of the barns each day. I'd make a small pile before disposing of them, and he'd sit there guarding them, knowing he wasn't supposed to touch them.

A few unfortunate incidents aside, Princeton became very comfortable with his surroundings and farm life in general. He took an active part in the daily operations and went about his duties with real enthusiasm. If he didn't see anything worth chasing, he'd wait patiently outside each of the barns while I was inside taking care of the chickens. Whether it was 35°C or −35°C, or there was bright sunlight and scorching temperatures or blizzard conditions and two feet of snow, he would patiently wait for me to exit one barn and continue on to the next. He loved being a farm dog, and I think that having a sense of purpose and responsibilities benefited him later in life when he was facing his challenges. And I loved having him around. I've never disliked doing my chores, but his presence made them so much more enjoyable. It was rarely a bad day if he was at my side. For nearly seventeen years I would go to work with my best friend.

Around this time Princeton began to be noticed and appreciated by others. Even people who didn't really like dogs found something about him to like. He was always smiling and looking friendly and intelligent. He was outgoing around people but never needy or clingy. He also carried himself with dignity, and people appreciated and admired him for that. As I grew closer to him, I wanted to take him everywhere with me. I decided it was time for Princeton to learn how to ride in a pickup truck.

I don't recommend dogs ride in the back of pickup trucks, as many are killed or injured if the truck becomes involved in a collision or accident. Even without an accident, a dog can jump out and get hit by another vehicle. For short rides around the farm, however, or to the neighbours' or the feed mill, I thought it would be okay for Princeton to ride in the back of a pickup truck. Considering how intelligent he was, I expected him to know that jumping out of the truck would be a *very bad thing*. The first time he rode in the back, he did very well. I opened and lowered the tailgate of the truck, and he jumped right in. After I closed it, I walked away and called for him several times to see if he would try to jump over the tailgate or sides of the truck. He didn't. He just sat there, leaning up against the cab and waiting for me to take him to the places I had gone whenever I left him behind. I then took him around the block, and he stuck his head out over the side of the truck, smiling and enjoying the scenery.

For the next few days, we took several short trips around the area, which Princeton loved. I refused to take him on the highway or into the city, instead going no farther than a coffee shop located on the outskirts of town. Princeton really enjoyed the ride to the coffee

*Princeton's old F-150. He would spend much
of his life riding in its passenger seat.*
—Photograph by author

shop, probably because I would give him a treat when we were there for being such a good boy. Neither of us knew it then, but these short rides would begin a daily tradition lasting over sixteen years.

In Canada we have a chain of coffee shops called Tim Hortons. Established in 1964, it's a franchise most everyone knows and many have come to identify as uniquely Canadian. Princeton would wait by the endgate of the truck each morning, wanting to go for a ride. I was still uncomfortable with taking him too far, so the Tim Hortons a few kilometres from our home was our destination. Soon we were doing this each morning and occasionally in the afternoon as well. We'd always go through the drive-thru, and I would order a coffee for myself and a Timbit for Princeton. He'd eagerly await his treat, which I'd toss into the truck box from inside the cab. For those unfamiliar with a Timbit, it's basically a little ball of dough covered with spices and sugar or a sugary glaze. Princeton loved them. Eventually, the staff of the drive-thru stopped charging me for the Timbit, as they looked forward to Princeton's daily visit.

As we continued these daily trips, it became clear that he also wanted to go with me whenever I left the farm for other reasons. Each time I had to go somewhere other than Tim Hortons, I'd leave him behind, usually confined to the deck of the house with the gate closed. He'd peer through the slats of the deck, his eyes full of sadness as I drove away. The truck we were using for our coffee runs was new, and as it was a regular cab, I didn't want Princeton up front with me because he was often stinky from mucking around on the farm. Since winter was approaching and I didn't want him in the truck box in the cold either, I bought an older Ford F-150 so he could ride in the cab with me. Soon he was going with me wherever I went. If I had to go somewhere he wouldn't be welcome, he still went with me, sitting in the cab for however long it took me to complete my business.

Whenever Princeton and I went somewhere together, he'd sit up front and stare out the windshield, fascinated by everything around him. A few incidents made me aware of how intelligent he really was. One morning we were travelling somewhere and I had to stop suddenly for a red light. Princeton unfortunately went sailing off the front seat, hitting the dash with a furry *whump* before ending up on the floor of the truck. I felt terrible and looked to see if he was all right. He looked up at me, an expression of "What the fuck?" on his face. It happened again a few days after that and once more about a week later.

A couple of days after that, I had to brake suddenly for a car that lost control in the snow and spun out in front of me. Princeton, surprisingly, remained seated and continued looking through the windshield. About a week after that, someone pulled in front of me, causing me to slam on the brakes. Although the sudden braking caused him to move toward the edge of the seat, he didn't hit the dash or end up on the floor. I was curious as to why he hadn't ended up on the floorboard as he had before. Once we were under way and clear of everyone, I decided to brake suddenly to see what Princeton was doing to avoid falling. What I discovered amazed me. Princeton, while looking ahead, sensed when I suddenly moved my foot from the accelerator to the brake pedal and pushed himself hard against the back of the seat. Even more amazingly, if I slowly moved my foot he would remain where he was, not expecting an emergency stop. Very intelligent? Absolutely.

3

Vagabonds and Misfits

P RINCETON'S FIRST EXPOSURE to cats (that I know of) was Kaiser. Kaiser had lived a few kilometres from the farm at a nearby golf course. When the course closed for the season, he was unceremoniously kicked out on his ass and told to fend for himself, eventually finding his way to the farm. He lived in the shop for a while before migrating to my parents' house, close to my own, where he lived the rest of his life before succumbing to cancer in 2012. The other cat on the property was Sierra, a black-and-white little girl who had her own distinctive attitude. I adopted her in 1997 before I moved to the farm. She generally hated everyone except me. Let's just say she had a few unresolved emotional issues she needed to work through. Although Princeton rarely saw Sierra or Kaiser, he never acted in a threatening way toward them. He treated them with mild interest and, although he accepted that each had their place on the farm, never considered them part of his crew.

The first real member of Princeton's crew was Boris. Boris was a fluffy, long-haired grey cat I discovered behind one of my barns one morning. He was in pretty rough shape, weighing only slightly over five pounds. One of the few disadvantages of country living is the many irresponsible pet owners who grow tired of their furry friends and think it's fine to drop them off in the country rather

Boris would become the first member of Princeton's animal crew.
—Photograph by author

than take them to an animal shelter. They wrongly think that some-how the animals will find their way to the welcoming arms of rural homeowners and live out their days being cared for and peacefully roaming the countryside. This seldom happens, especially for cats. Cats go feral after a while and cannot be captured. They are forced to fend for themselves against predators and vehicles and, during the winter, find themselves trying to survive −35°C temperatures. Most of them die, usually horribly.

Boris was such a drop-off, stolen from his original owners by a neighbour who didn't care for him and thought he should give country living a try. After rescuing him I brought him to the veter-inary clinic to get him back on his feet. The veterinarian checked him over and sent him home with antibiotics, worm medication, and a big bag of expensive cat food. As Boris recovered I discovered he was a pretty interesting cat. The best way to describe him was as singularly focused. If he wanted something, he wanted it now; there was no compromising with Boris. He also had six toes on each of his front feet and could wrap his paw around most things you passed to him. At his maximum weight of nearly twenty pounds, his front feet measured nearly three inches across, and his ability to use his extra toes to his advantage was one of the most memorable things about him. After Boris had recovered I found his original owners and learned how he'd arrived at the farm. They still loved him very much and were delighted to take him back. They contacted me a few weeks later, however, and told me that Boris (whose original name was Rigatoni) was no longer happy with *them*. He obviously missed me and the country lifestyle. Would I take him back? Take care of him and love him? Okay.

Boris and Princeton arrived at the farm at nearly the same time. They were comfortable with each other, if not entirely close friends. The two of them would sometimes walk along together, Boris stop-ping from time to time to use his big mitts to smack any butterfly, bee, or fly that dared to intrude into the airspace above him. Up

Kosomo, along with Boris, lived in the shop for several years, both of them getting along well with Princeton.
—Photograph by author

until Boris's passing in 2014, I never saw them quarrel except for when Princeton took offence when Boris stuck one of his mitts into Princeton's food bowls.

The second cat of Princeton's crew was a big black behemoth named Kosomo. He arrived in 2001 and is still alive today. He lived in my shop for many years with Boris before being adopted by my parents a couple of years ago. Kosomo is usually very gentle but is prone to mood swings in which he feels it necessary to beat the crap out of something. Unfortunately, this was often Boris when the two of them lived together. I have no idea why Kosomo would suddenly become violent, but he never had a problem putting the occasional hole in poor Boris if he wanted to. Kosomo was another drop-off, abandoned by his previous owners. When he arrived he was feral, and I couldn't catch him for about seven months. When I finally did catch him, it was because he had a badly infected laceration from the bottom of his chin to his lower abdomen and was feeling very sick. He was dying. Off to the veterinarian he went, where he was hospitalized for a few days. During his stay the staff found a tattoo in his ear, and when they tried to contact his owners, they discovered that the phone was disconnected and they had moved away. They had left no forwarding address with the veterinary office that had done the tattoo. Kosomo and Princeton got along in the same way Princeton and Boris got along: their relationship was one of mutual respect. The three would often wander around until one of the cats got bored and decided to do something else. They may not have been really close to one another, but each respected the boundaries of the others.

The third member of the crew was Barnie. She was different from Boris and Kosomo for two reasons. First, Barnie was not a drop-off, and second, she and Princeton were openly affectionate toward each other. The story of how Barnie arrived at the farm begins with a friend inviting me to meet up for dinner one evening. While driving my truck toward downtown, I saw a small orange cat

Barnie, seen here looking through her barn window after a rainstorm, would eventually become Princeton's best animal friend.
—Photograph by author

run across the street a few cars in front of me. A car made direct contact with her and sent her tumbling out from underneath the car. Another car then ran over the unfortunate little cat, again sending her tumbling out from beneath the vehicle. Neither of the two cars stopped as the cat lay twisted and unmoving on the street. I did stop, however. I expected her to be dead, but I feel that it's a lousy thing to accidentally run over a cat and leave her behind without checking to see if she needs help. I steered my truck over both lanes, stopping traffic in both directions. Everyone sat in their vehicles, pretending to look away as I walked toward the twisted pile of orange fur. I lifted it up and brought the corpse to the side of the street. The little pile of fur wasn't a corpse but a frightened, badly injured cat who needed help. I never made it to dinner that evening.

The next morning, Barnie, as that little orange cat became known, went to see the veterinarian. He phoned later on to tell me that she needed stitches and a couple of teeth removed, and was suffering from parasites. He also informed me that she definitely had the look of a homeless street cat. Before ending the conversation, he asked, "Do you want me to spay her while she's here?" Okay. "A full round of vaccinations?" Sure. I had now given up trying to budget for all of these critters. I had accepted that something beyond my control was forcing me to spend all my hard-earned money on these wayward animals who had somehow become my responsibility. Barnie returned after an extended hospital stay during which I maxed out my credit card.

I went back to where I had first scraped her off the street and spent the afternoon knocking on doors to see if anyone was missing a little orange cat. If they were, they weren't prepared to admit to it. After a week of browsing the Animals Lost section in a few local publications and checking in with local animal shelters without success, I realized Barnie probably didn't have a home. I spent another week trying to find her one, but no one wanted her. I finally accepted that Barnie's place was with me on the farm. I would lock

Princeton's nemesis, the goat.
—Photograph by author

her in an empty barn at night and let her out during the day. This
is how she became known as Barnie. In exchange for my generosity,
she would take care of any mouse problem in her barn and the
others surrounding it. So far she has kept up her end of the bargain
in exemplary fashion—probably too well. She kills not only mice
but also innocent little birds. And frogs. And gophers. And snakes.
And anything else she considers to be an intruder. Basically, Barnie
gets up in the morning and decides what lives and what dies.

Barnie hates most everyone except me. If anyone else tries to
pet her, they usually find themselves drawing back a bloody hand.
Probably because I saved her, she's very affectionate toward me,
always rubbing against me until I pick her up in my arms; then she
starts drooling with delight. Barnie also loved Princeton, rubbing
against his legs and following him around. More often than Boris
or Kosomo, Barnie would join me and Princeton as we did chores
around the farm. If I was inside a barn, Barnie would often wait outside with Princeton. Whenever I was working on a piece of equipment or machinery, Princeton would watch me from a few feet away
while Barnie lay on top of whatever I was working on and looked
down at me. She would only leave me and Princeton if she saw
something that, in her opinion, needed to die. Or if she saw Boris
or Kosomo off in the distance and decided she should slap them
around a little, just so they wouldn't forget who was really the boss.
To this day Barnie misses Princeton. She still follows me around but
often goes to the places where Princeton would sometimes sleep or
spend time alone. After a few moments she returns, but as the day
goes on, she continues to look for her friend.

Of all the animals on the farm, the only one Princeton truly hated
was a goat. Your basic, run-of-the-mill goat—or more appropri-
ately, as I eventually discovered, a Boer goat. How the goat showed
up at the farm isn't that much different from how any other creature
arrives on the property. She just did. She wandered onto the farm
from wherever she came and decided she liked it here. This was in

2006. She's never left. I don't think she has any desire to. During the day she wanders around doing what goats do—a lot of eating and not much else. Sometimes she chases cars that come up the driveway, usually frightening their occupants. Other times she's content to wander around and eat the flowers and the leaves off the trees. She doesn't seem to serve any real purpose. At night she goes into the horse barn, eats hay, drinks water, licks a salt block, and sleeps. I've never wanted to own a goat and still don't, but I've accepted that this thing is probably mine until she dies. No one knows how old she is, but she's been happily wandering around the property for twelve years, so I assume she's getting up there in age.

When the goat showed up, she wasn't in very good shape. She was emaciated and had several scabs and scratches on her body. A vet-assistant friend came out and took a look at her and agreed that yes, she was a goat. I drove around the area, asking if anyone had lost their goat. No one had, or so I was told when whoever I asked realized that it was a serious question. The county bylaw offices didn't care, nor did the local animal shelters. I had two choices: ship her off to some sort of goat farm or allow her to live here. I truly believe that Princeton never forgave me for choosing the second option. From the outset the two hated each other. At first Princeton treated her as some sort of novelty, probably expecting she would soon be on her way. Eventually, he realized she would be staying but continued to think she served no real purpose and would become a liability. As far as he was concerned, if I wanted her, she was my baggage.

It was the goat who drew first blood. One morning while she was walking behind me and Princeton, she suddenly ran up and head-butted him in the ass. It was hard enough that poor Princeton tripped and landed hard on his face. I immediately yelled at the goat and slapped her on her behind, which led to what I guess is the typical goat response of rearing up and attempting to butt me. What an ungrateful little bitch. As Princeton and I walked toward the barns, we kept looking over our shoulders to make sure she wasn't trying to repeat her sneak attack.

In time I discovered that the goat was pleasant if Princeton wasn't around. She needed to understand, however, that he was the boss. Not anyone else, not even Barnie, had more authority than Princeton over the farm animals. The goat would have to learn to keep her evil ways in check, and if she didn't, she wouldn't be around much longer.

A few days later she tried to head-butt Princeton again, but he was too quick for her. He easily got out of her way and trotted quickly up to the barn we were walking toward. Once at the door he turned around and lay down, waiting for me to join him. I continued walking to the barn while the goat followed. When I had almost reached Princeton, he got to his feet and started walking toward me. As I walked up to him, a nearly inaudible growl emanated from him. I looked behind me and saw that the goat had stopped in her tracks. Princeton stood beside me, continuing to growl softly. I took a few more steps toward the barn and, looking behind me, watched the goat take another step forward.

I rarely ever saw Princeton attack something. But that day he did. Princeton lunged at the goat and grabbed her by the neck with his jaws, and the two of them fell to the ground. He released her and grabbed her again before she had the opportunity to stand. The goat, now on her side, started bleating and kicking. Princeton released his grip and she got to her feet. She made a half-assed attempt to kick him with her back legs, which he avoided easily; he then started barking at her. The goat ran off, bleating and continuing to kick at something that wasn't there. Soon Princeton turned around and walked back toward me. When he reached me I hugged him and told him he was a *good* dog.

In the years that followed, Princeton and the goat still had their occasional grievances with each other, but nothing as severe as the day of the Great Battle. If the goat was aggressive toward Princeton,

When I first saw Kona, the remnants of the leash placed on him by his previous owners was with him.
—Photograph by author

it was usually a half-hearted attempt, kicking at him from a few feet away. They ultimately learned to respect each other, and if they found themselves occupying the same piece of real estate, it was the goat who would move away first. And later, when Princeton had his disability or was moving slower because of his advanced age, they had already chosen to ignore each other completely.

From the time I adopted Princeton, Kona was the only dog who ever lived with him. He was a very large, very handsome purebred Alaskan malamute who lived with us for too little time. I still miss Kona and regret not having met him sooner so I could have given him the life he deserved. Kona came into our lives starting with a phone call from a neighbour, informing me that a homeless dog had moved into a roadside ditch a couple of kilometres from the farm. Apparently, this dog was guarding the discarded deer carcass some ignorant hunter had left in a ditch and was using it as a source of food. Interested to find out more about him, I loaded Princeton into the pickup and drove to where my neighbour told me he could be found.

Sure enough, a huge, woolly malamute was sitting in the ditch beside the remains of a recently skinned deer. He was a beautiful dog. I imagined that he was at least eighty or so pounds, and he resembled a large wolf. He looked confident, regal even, like the type of dog who would never surrender what he considered his. But his eyes filled with sadness and terror as I got out of the truck; he quickly turned and ran off into the trees. I let Princeton out of the truck, and we inspected where he was living. It looked as if he had been there for some time, as the late-fall grass was flattened where he had been sleeping. The discarded remains of the deer looked adequate for now but probably wouldn't be much good to him within a few days. I felt sorry for the big malamute and wanted to help him in any way I could, but first I had to find out more about him.

I discovered that Kona (my friend Emily gave him his name) was a purebred Alaskan malamute and only a few years old. He had been rescued by a couple living near Edmonton from a community in the Northwest Territories. His early life had been filled with hardship, for he was beaten and abused by the people he trusted to take care of him. His rescuers knew he deserved better and took him away from the only life he had ever known. Kona's rescuers, living in the city, would take him for outdoor walks in the area around the farm. It was during one of these walks that he escaped. Since he had been abused and beaten for nearly his entire life, he was very much frightened of everyone, including those trying to help him. After repeated attempts to get Kona back, his saviours had to give up and let him decide for himself what he wanted to do. He chose to stay around the area, hunt for his food, take shelter where he could, and hope no one would bother him.

The next morning, after chores, Princeton and I drove to the ditch to see Kona. We had brought doggy kibble, fresh water, and two rubber bowls. As I drove into the ditch, Kona watched us with suspicious eyes and ran into the woods when I got out from the truck. I placed the two bowls on the ground and filled each with water and food and, in a gentle voice, told Kona to come eat. After waiting for a few minutes and not seeing him, I decided to return home. The following evening I returned with more food and water and filled the empty bowls. Although he ran off when he saw me, I was glad he had eaten the food I'd left for him earlier.

This went on for about two weeks, and I began to wonder if Kona would ever make any progress. By the third week, however, he seemed a little more at ease, only running a few feet from me when I arrived to feed him. I was now letting Princeton out of the truck when we went to feed Kona, but he took very little interest in the malamute. Princeton would wander around, sniff at what was left of the deer remains, lift his leg, piss where Kona had slept last, and wander back to the truck. He had chosen to treat Kona as an interloper, our visits nothing more than an inconvenience for him. As the days became shorter and colder, I wondered how Kona would survive a cold Alberta winter with only me to care for him.

Word of what we were doing began to circulate. A few others were also stopping by to give Kona treats. Tom, my neighbour who had originally discovered Kona and hoped I could do something for him, managed to secure a doghouse from another neighbour. They moved it into the ditch and filled it with straw. Kona was setting himself up pretty well. Not only was he having two regular meals and numerous treats throughout the day, but he had also secured himself a sweet insulated doghouse filled with fresh straw. Kona loved his new house and soon took to lying on its flat roof whenever it was sunny, obviously basking in the sun's rays on his thick fur. He was also becoming more confident whenever he saw me. He'd bark a greeting and stand beside his bowls as I filled them. He still wouldn't let me touch him, but the fear he'd had in his eyes when I first met him was slowly diminishing.

Everyone in the community seemed to accept that we had a big Alaskan malamute living in a ditch. He wasn't hurting anyone, and people would often see him throughout the day walking through the fields. Mostly, however, he was content to stretch out on the roof of his doghouse and watch the traffic go by. Unfortunately, many of the drivers would stop by the farm to inform me of a big, majestic, wolf-like thing lying on top of a doghouse. I appreciated the concern but found myself answering the same questions over and over again. Yes, I'm aware of that. No, I don't think he's in any danger. Yes, you can have him if you can catch him. Yes, he can live here if he wants to. No, I don't think he wants to. It got so annoying having to answer the same questions from everyone that I wrote out a two-page synopsis about Kona and why he was there and how he was being cared for. I put these pages in plastic sleeves, along with my phone number, and nailed them to Kona's doghouse. Except for a few overly concerned individuals, this really cut down on the visits from passing motorists.

By late winter, however, I received a visit from a county official. Although sympathetic to the situation, the county didn't really feel comfortable with a homeless dog living in a ditch, content to spend his days watching traffic. I completely understood their reasoning but was concerned about what would happen to Kona if anyone tried to catch him. He was only just learning to trust people. I convinced them to let me try to trap Kona on my own. They agreed, even offering me the use of a large trap, which was essentially a cage an animal walked into, the door sliding closed behind it automatically. Still skittish, Kona refused to enter the trap regardless of the food I placed in it. After a couple of weeks, he still hadn't entered the trap and I was becoming discouraged. One day, however, a county officer showed up and told me Kona was in the cage! The officer had stopped by earlier that morning and placed a piece of Ukrainian sausage in the trap. Driving by later, he saw Kona lying in the cage and the sausage gone. I went down with my pickup, and four of us loaded the crate with one very distressed-looking malamute into my truck.

After returning home, I placed a leash on Kona, slowly opened the cage door, and escorted him into an old dog run I had. The run was constructed of a heavy-duty chain-link fence secured to steel poles set into a concrete grade beam. There was no way he would get out of that. I now had the opportunity to work with him, hopefully getting him to the point where he could be adopted by a loving family. Kona really deserved that. Two days later he escaped by chewing through the chain link. When I drove to the ditch to see if he was there, he greeted me with a friendly howl.

Once again the cage went back to the ditch with another piece of Ukrainian sausage. A day after that the same four guys loaded the cage into my truck. This time Kona didn't go back to the farm; he went directly to the veterinarian. He was put under anaesthetic, neutered, given a thorough checkup with a complete array of inoculations, and microchipped. I took him back to the farm, opened the door to the cage, and told him that this was all I could do. I knew that Kona would never be completely tame. Placing him in a pen or tying him up would be a terrible experience for him. Although I believed he was a gentle dog, he had been abused and beaten too severely to ever be entirely trusting of people. Kona would never truly be happy unless he was allowed to do as he pleased. I had tried my best. He leaped from his cage and ran off toward the road, never looking back. Take care of yourself, Kona.

Two days later he showed up at the farm. Drove down to the ditch to get his doghouse. Same four guys.

Although Kona would stay at the farm for some time, he never allowed me to touch him. If he was sleeping somewhere and was awakened by my approaching, he would get up, walk a few feet, and lie down again, continuing to watch until he was satisfied I was far enough away. Although I consider his time spent with me and the rest of the farm crew far too short, I do believe that, at least for a while, he knew he had a home.

So this was Princeton's crew. He, the gentle but undisputed leader; Barnie, the muscle and second-in-command; Boris and Kosomo, the two independent shop cats; the goat, Princeton's nemesis; and Kona, the shy and confused malamute. Each of them interacted with one another as best they could. It wasn't always easy and they had plenty of disagreements along the way, but everyone generally got along well enough that no one got their feelings hurt too badly or lost a body part (except for Princeton, but not because of the other animals).

Although I loved them all, Princeton was always the one I was closest to. Not only was he my best friend, but he was also involved in nearly everything I did. If I was working around the farm, he was beside me. If I was hauling feed, he would be in the semi truck cab staring down at everyone around us. He'd sit alongside me as I drove for parts, looking through the windshield, watching my leg from the corner of his eye to see if I was about to make any sudden stops. When I had a business meeting or presentation, if allowed he would accompany me into the office of the person I was meeting.

In time, if I were somewhere off farm and he wasn't with me, the first thing people would often ask was "Where's Princeton?"

When the farm had evolved to the point where it had to become a corporate entity, there was only one name to consider: Black Dog Farms Inc. Without Princeton's constant companionship, making the long and often arduous days a little easier, the farm wouldn't have gotten to where it was. One of my proudest moments was when the company name, combined with a silhouette of Princeton, was applied to the door of the newly acquired Peterbilt semi truck. I think Princeton liked the logo too. I'd watch him while we were stopped in traffic. He'd look through the passenger-side window and down at whoever was looking up at him; they knew he was the "Black Dog" displayed on the door. Not only was Princeton a working dog, but he also had corporate responsibilities as well.

4

The Vessel

I'D ALWAYS LIKED camper vans, especially the ones built on an extended chassis and with a raised roof. To me they represent freedom and adventure. They aren't overly large or bulky, allowing you to find and experience places off the beaten track. For years, whenever I wanted to get away and I didn't have any chickens in the barns, I took solitary motorcycle trips. I love travelling by motorcycle and always thought that a van represented the same sort of freedom but was a little cozier and with a few more amenities. The only bad thing about taking a bike trip was knowing I'd be leaving Princeton behind for several days in the care of friends or family. He knew when he was about to be left behind, his eyes full of sadness when I started to fill the luggage cases on the motorcycle. As much as I loved my motorcycle journeys, it was time to start looking for a van—one that would allow Princeton to experience and enjoy the same things I had when I was travelling. It was time for us to get out on the road together.

I had a few conditions when I started to look for a camper van. It had to be based on a one-ton chassis. It also had to be an extended version. Princeton and I wanted to be cozy but not cramped. It needed to have a stove, fridge, and flushable toilet. We were travellers but wanted at least some amenities. And it had to be a Ford.

Princeton and I were Ford guys. Finally, it had to be in reasonable condition. It turned out to be a frustrating search. First, it seems most older camper vans were based on a half-ton chassis. I knew we would eventually be travelling to some remote locations, so I needed to find a van with a heavier chassis for increased ground clearance and the ability to carry lots of supplies and equipment. But by far the hardest thing was to find one in reasonable condition; most were in rough shape.

Sounds easy enough, doesn't it? Good body. Decent mechanicals. Serviceable camper stuff. It wasn't. I've restored cars through the years, and I've learned that everyone has their own interpretation of "good shape." Apparently, this also extends to camper vans. I've always thought of a vehicle as being in good condition if it's basically serviceable and not something soon destined for the scrap heap. In addition to the rust, dents, and poorly maintained mechanicals, there were often filthy carpets, broken cabinetry, leaky plumbing, and appliances that didn't work. Perhaps the most disgusting things were the holding tanks for the black (toilet) and grey (wash) water, which hadn't been emptied since the last time the van had been used. Several vans were covered with auto club decals and stickers from roadside attractions that had gone out of business years ago. Others had tinfoil covering the windows. These particular vans tended to give off a creepy child-molester vibe I didn't think was suitable for our future adventures. The ones I found in outstanding condition were priced accordingly, their owners obviously knowing exceptional vans were tough to come by.

Almost a year went by without much success, and I was becoming discouraged. I'd either have to settle for a van that wasn't in the best shape and restore it, or be prepared to spend a lot more money than I wanted to. This all changed one afternoon when I was having lunch with my friend Connie. She knew I was looking for a good camper van and asked how my search was going. I told her it wasn't.

"That's too bad. I should see if my cousin wants to sell hers," Connie responded.

"Huh?" I replied, wondering why the hell she hadn't told me this before.

"A van. A big camper van. Just like you want."

"Well, do you think she'd sell it?"

"Probably. Let me go see her first. She's a little eccentric."

It turned out she *did* want to sell it. Connie went over to her cousin's house that evening to inquire about the van and check the overall condition.

"It's really big. Has a nice bed too. It's blue and silver and it's a Ford. Seems pretty good," she told me over the phone when she got home that evening.

Connie gave me her cousin's phone number and I called her immediately, and she confirmed everything Connie had told me. She explained further that she and her husband had purchased the van a number of years ago so they could travel around Canada and the US when they retired. The van had done some travelling but was now parked in her driveway, unused because of some health issues her husband was experiencing.

The next evening I loaded Princeton into the pickup and we were off to look at the van. When I pulled into the driveway, I was happy to see an extended version sitting on a heavy-duty chassis. After telling Princeton to stay in the truck for the time being, I went to meet Connie's cousin, who was standing at the back door of her home. After the introductions were made, she tossed me the keys and told me to give it a good once-over.

The first thing I looked for was the manufacturer's tag. It indicated it was an E-350, or a one-ton van chassis. It also identified it as an extended length model. The body of the 1991 van was in good shape, with only a dent on the hood and some surface rust behind the rear wheels. The raised roof portion was faded and would need

Seeing Poseidon for the first time.
—Photograph by author

to be repainted. Sliding open the big side door revealed an interior in surprisingly good shape. The carpet and linoleum were quite clean. Connie's cousin had told her that all the appliances worked, but the water pump would need to be replaced because the van hadn't been winterized the winter before and the pump had frozen and cracked. Almost comically, the toilet was located directly across from the refrigerator. You could sit on the toilet, open the fridge door, and grab yourself something cold to drink. It also had a good-sized furnace to keep you warm and toasty when the temperatures got chilly. A little microwave was also included. All in all, both the interior and exterior of the van were promising.

Mechanically, it wasn't too bad, but some things needed repairs. The intake manifold would need to be pulled off and resealed, as there was a coolant leak. The front tires were worn, and the front brake discs would need to be resurfaced and new brake pads installed. Both batteries were missing, as was the spare tire. The fuel gauge didn't work. The van would also benefit from a good tune-up and having all the fluids drained and replaced.

Overall, I was impressed. It would need some work, but at least everything was easily repairable. Depending on the price, it was the one Princeton and I were looking for. I had seen similarly equipped vans from the early nineties go for about $10,000 to $12,000 if they were in great shape. This van wasn't quite there yet but could have easily been in that category if I was prepared to spend a few thousand dollars and a few weeks working on it. I was prepared to make an offer. It turned out I didn't have to.

"Looks good. It needs some repairs, but I can do that," I said to Connie's cousin. "How much do you want for it?"

"Thousand bucks," she replied. "I just want it gone."

Okay.

A few days later the big van went to its new home. From this point on it would be affectionately referred to as Poseidon. I thought of the name while driving back to the farm. I'd like to say that the van's name was influenced by the Greek god Poseidon, protector of the sea and all its aquatic creatures, but instead it was inspired by the movie *The Poseidon Adventure*—the original version of 1972, not the crappy remake that followed years later. In the original version a ship is struck by a tidal wave while travelling from New York to Greece. It capsizes and a small group of people try to make their way to the bottom (now the top) of the ship in an attempt to be rescued.

The name came to mind when, driving the van home, I encountered some severe crosswinds. The van, being the extended version with a raised roof, didn't care much for this. It became a large flat billboard. Because of the van's high centre of gravity and a steering response best described as theoretical, the wind had no problem pushing me onto the shoulder as I drove down the highway. This was accompanied by a very disturbing feeling that the van could end up on its roof at any moment. Turning the steering wheel to get off the shoulder and back onto the highway only made this sensation worse. This uneasy feeling reminded me of *The Poseidon Adventure*, which I had watched a few weeks earlier. Over time I learned to adapt to the van's specific handling quirks, but it would always be called Poseidon.

I started working on Poseidon a few weeks after I brought it home, deciding to take care of the mechanical issues first. After installing a new oil pressure sending unit to correct a falsely reading oil pressure gauge, I directed my attention to resealing the intake manifold to repair the coolant leak. Sounds easy enough. It wasn't. The job requires at least some basic knowledge of mechanics, but it's generally straightforward enough not to be a difficult chore. What I hadn't expected was the difficulty of accessing the engine. I don't know if you have worked on an older van before, but accessing the engine requires removing several things surrounding it and the patience and dexterity to get your hands and tools into tiny places. Probably due to packaging constraints, vans have everything built around their mechanicals. Lift the extremely short hood and you're greeted by not much more than a big air filter box and twin batteries. Removing the air filter box is required for accessing anything on the engine, and even then, most of the engine is tucked beneath the front cowl. Removing the "doghouse" cover located in the interior of the van to access the rear of the engine doesn't help much either, as most of the engine is covered in sensors that are traditionally installed on a firewall, and installation brackets used to install the engine when the van was being manufactured are left in place.

After only a few hours of yelling and cursing, I was finally able to remove the intake manifold from the engine. Boris and Kosomo had taken up residence inside the van while it was parked in the shop, and both watched in amusement as I cursed and yelled at no one in particular that I was going to burn the goddamn thing to the ground. Princeton lay outside the van, not quite understanding what all the yelling was about, but he understood enough to realize Dad should probably be left alone. Eventually, I reinstalled the intake on the engine, replaced spark plugs and injector O-rings, and put everything back together. It only took an entire weekend.

After that little chore was completed, I turned my attention to the broken water pump. In addition to the pump were a couple of cracked water lines needing replacement because the van hadn't been winterized before it was parked for the season. Winterizing involves dispersing any water left in the lines and water pump by running a non-toxic antifreeze through the entire water system to protect it from freezing temperatures. I also needed to replace the valve to flush the toilet because it had been frozen too. I was relieved to discover that the water pump wasn't damaged as I'd thought: instead I only needed to replace a broken electrical wire.

After checking that the stove, fridge, and furnace worked properly, I installed a roof vent with an electric fan and thermostat. I realize that no one should ever leave an animal in an enclosed vehicle for any length of time, but sometimes Princeton would have to remain in the van while I picked up things we needed on our trips. The new fan would keep the interior of the van from getting excessively hot. Once the interior reached a preset temperature, the electric fan in the vent would automatically turn on and the excess heat would be exhausted through the top of the van. This actually worked quite well for short periods if the exterior temperatures weren't too warm.

I then inspected the electrical wiring of the camper component of the van and added a couple of ground straps for good measure. Lastly, I pulled the wheels off, repacked the bearings, had the rotors resurfaced, and installed new brake pads. Then it was off to the tire store for an alignment and two new front tires.

Having sorted out the mechanicals and living quarters, I sanded the area behind the rear wheels down to bare metal to remove the surface rust. I sanded down the entire raised roof and repaired any cracks in the fibreglass. A body and paint shop repaired the dent in the hood and repainted it, along with the roof and behind the rear wheels.

After I did a complete cleaning and replaced some vinyl flooring, the van was finally finished. Poseidon looked great and was fully sorted, ready to hit the open road the following summer. Unfortunately, any trips I had planned would have to wait. In less than a year, something would happen to Princeton that neither of us was prepared for—something that would define Princeton as a dog and further solidify the relationship we already shared.

5

A Battle Begins

THE EVENING OF June 29, 2011, when Princeton was twelve, was when everything changed. It would mark a new chapter for both Princeton and me, the beginning of a journey filled with both happiness and hardship. As difficult as the journey was at times, I still don't have any regrets. I can unequivocally claim that Princeton didn't either.

It all started with a yelp from Princeton; he had landed on the grass after jumping off the deck to catch up with me as I walked to the barns for an early-evening check on the chickens. He limped toward me, favouring his right rear leg. When he caught up to me, I ran my hand up and down the leg. There were no noticeable cuts or abrasions but a small bump, warm to the touch, just below the knee. My initial thought was that he had injured it by running into something, probably causing the swelling and discomfort he was now experiencing. He was, after all, a farm dog, so these things happen. What concerned me most of all was the bump, which felt like bone and not swollen tissue. Rather than wait until morning, I phoned the veterinary clinic I usually dealt with, Park Veterinary Centre, to inquire if Princeton's regular veterinarian, Dr. Kwantes, was still in the clinic. He had gone home for the evening, but an associate, Dr. Rodriguez, thought it would be a good idea if I brought him in that evening.

Although Princeton had never been a patient of Dr. Rodriguez, she was aware he was a regular client of the clinic. She gave him a complete examination and performed an X-ray on his right rear leg. His physical exam came out fine, and Dr. Rodriguez remarked on how healthy he seemed for a twelve-year-old dog. The X-ray, however, revealed some soft tissue swelling and a slight change in bone structure where the lump was. She went on to explain that the lump could be a bruised bone, an infection, or, in the worst-case scenario, an osteosarcoma. Dr. Rodriguez prescribed some anti-inflammatories and an antibiotic and suggested that Dr. Kwantes see Princeton in a few days.

Dr. Kwantes was the one-time proprietor of Park Veterinary Centre, located in Sherwood Park. He'd been Princeton's primary veterinarian since 2000, when I first brought him in to be neutered and for a routine health check. He usually saw Princeton once a year, except when I had to bring him in for the occasional unexpected problem, like eating decaying chickens found in chicken manure. When he didn't indulge in these indiscretions, Princeton was the picture of doggy health. This was about to change very quickly.

A few days later Princeton seemed to be feeling better. He wasn't limping as much, and the swelling appeared to have lessened. Nonetheless, he went back to the clinic to see Dr. Kwantes for more tests and X-rays. Princeton's blood work and urinalysis were both fine, and the X-rays, this time of his entire body not including the leg, were clear. Dr. Kwantes and I discussed having a biopsy performed if the swelling didn't go down, but at the time he didn't think that cancer was a likely diagnosis. He recommended sending Princeton home to continue with the anti-inflammatories and antibiotics and coming back for another check in a couple of weeks.

Princeton took his medication and happily continued with his farm duties and chasing coyotes. He wasn't favouring his leg as much as before, but the swelling continued to be there. He appeared to be in less pain than before, but I didn't know if it was because he was feeling better or just becoming accustomed to the pain. After another veterinary visit two weeks later, Dr. Kwantes decided that the swelling, although not increasing, hadn't decreased either, and he suggested that a biopsy of the lump and the surrounding area would be the best way to determine what was bothering Princeton.

In late July Princeton went in for his biopsy. Hopefully, the results would yield some answers as to why the lump and inflammation had not gone away. Although the lump didn't really behave like a traditional osteosarcoma, the antibiotics and anti-inflammatories hadn't helped much, and everyone was becoming concerned as to what the problem could be.

When I picked Princeton up a few hours later, he was fine. He'd had to be under an anaesthetic for the procedure, but it hadn't bothered him. It would take a few days to get the results back, but Dr. Kwantes assured me he would phone me immediately when he received them. Princeton happily went out to the truck, either not aware or not caring about the agonizing wait I would have to endure for the next few days.

While I waited for Dr. Kwantes's call, I spent a lot of time online, researching the various bone diseases and cancers that afflict dogs. I generally discount or ignore most "information" I read online but managed to find several good sources offering plenty of information about different types of cancer and the treatments available. I was surprised to discover that many dogs will eventually develop cancer, and most forms of it offered a poor prognosis. Osteosarcoma seemed to be a particularly bad cancer, with many dogs succumbing to the disease rapidly. Also helpful were a number of forums and online groups in which pet owners came together to share information and their experiences of animals with similar diseases.

I spent hours learning the correct terminology and preparing questions to ask Dr. Kwantes. This was something I'd started doing when my cat Sierra was diagnosed with renal failure and would continue to do until Princeton's death. Whatever was bothering Princeton, I believed that one of the best ways I could help him was by being as knowledgeable as I could and preparing myself for anything. I remained hopeful, however, that he wasn't suffering from anything too serious and convinced myself I shouldn't become too concerned until I knew the biopsy results.

Inconclusive. After three days of waiting, the results yielded nothing specific. All they could determine was that the lump, or lesion, could be a result of trauma, infection, or cancer—basically what we'd first discussed a month ago. All anyone knew for sure was that Princeton had a lump on his leg, causing him some discomfort. The only positive was that the lesion wasn't behaving as most osteosarcomas do. It hadn't increased in size, and there was no evidence of metastasis. Usually, osteosarcomas grow rapidly and spread quickly to other parts of the body, commonly the lungs. None of this meant it wasn't cancer, but I had hoped the biopsy would determine unequivocally if Princeton was suffering from osteosarcoma. And if it wasn't cancer, why wasn't the bump responding to the antibiotics and anti-inflammatories? Feeling even more worried than before, I asked Dr. Kwantes what direction we should be taking. He recommended a new antibiotic and to continue the anti-inflammatories and pain medication, and he scheduled Princeton to return for another X-ray of the leg and physical examination.

Two weeks later Princeton was back at the clinic for his checkup and X-ray. The lump was still the same size. Walking in with him, I sensed that this visit would be different from the others. For nearly two months everyone involved with Princeton's case had tried to determine why a lesion had suddenly appeared on the leg of an otherwise healthy dog, and they were perplexed as to why none of the medications had failed to reduce it. We had performed X-rays, a biopsy, and multiple blood panels. He had been prescribed multiple antibiotics and anti-inflammatories, but none of them had made a difference. The biopsy had revealed a lesion resulting from the proliferation of bone cells but offered nothing definitive. No less than five veterinarians had studied Princeton's biopsy results, with no consensus about what the lesion was or how to treat it. I had made it very clear to everyone involved that I was prepared to do whatever was necessary to give Princeton the best quality of life, regardless of how old he was. He was otherwise healthy, and his eyes still had the same fire I had first seen over a decade ago. Considering none of the medications had worked, and regardless of the biopsy not yielding a definitive answer, only one diagnosis was left to consider: osteosarcoma.

The lump on Princeton's leg had grown by a millimetre. As Princeton lay on the floor between us, Dr. Kwantes and I discussed the X-ray results in one of the examination rooms. We were both frustrated, especially knowing that if the lump was cancerous, it needed to be treated as such immediately. Although it wasn't behaving like a typical osteosarcoma and the biopsy had failed to provide any answers, Dr. Kwantes now felt that Princeton was most likely suffering from bone cancer. He recommended removing Princeton's entire leg and having it analyzed. If the results came back positive for osteosarcoma, then Princeton would be a good candidate for chemotherapy treatment, which would need to be immediate and aggressive. But he went on to explain that, even with these treatments, Princeton would eventually succumb to the disease. Chemotherapy isn't considered curative when treating canine osteosarcoma but is used instead to slow the progression. Even if the disease was treated aggressively, Princeton would likely have only about a year to live.

The alternative was to continue to keep him on a regimen of antibiotics, pain medication, and anti-inflammatories, and hope that he was suffering from something other than osteosarcoma. If Dr. Kwantes was correct in his diagnosis, however, Princeton would survive only about two to three months on such a regimen. Having familiarized myself with osteosarcoma during the last several weeks and having learned how aggressive it could be, I accepted Dr. Kwantes's recommendation. Although it was a difficult decision, I wanted to give Princeton every possible chance of survival. If the leg didn't yield any signs of cancer after it was analyzed, then at least he wouldn't be suffering from any more pain.

Osteosarcoma is a bone cancer that is usually highly aggressive and quickly metastasizes, or spreads, to other parts of the body. Until researching it, I only knew it was the cancer first diagnosed in Terry Fox, the British Columbia native who, at eighteen, had his leg amputated, followed by aggressive chemotherapy. Terry Fox was a hero, known throughout Canada and other parts of the world for his attempt to run across Canada after his amputation to raise cancer awareness. Tragically, he never completed his journey, passing away when the cancer spread to his lungs. Since then yearly runs held in his honour in Canada and other countries have raised awareness of all types of cancers and raised in excess of $650 million for cancer research.

In dogs osteosarcoma is the most common form of bone cancer, generally attacking larger breeds in middle to later stages of life. Smaller dogs are also candidates for osteosarcoma but less commonly. It isn't really known why some dogs develop this form of aggressive cancer, but one theory is that dogs with a previous abrasion or bump may be more predisposed to it than others. Generally, the cancer grows from the inside of the bone outward, with many dogs not showing any symptoms or even discomfort until the lump on the bone becomes apparent. Other dogs will display few or no symptoms until the bone breaks. In many cases the cancer metastasizes, usually to the lungs. A biopsy is recommended to make a definitive diagnosis of osteosarcoma, but in rare instances, such as Princeton's, results are inconclusive.

Overall, the prognosis is not good, with most dogs succumbing to the disease in about a year, even with the most aggressive treatments. It's expected that X-rays will show evidence of the disease having spread to the lungs. It's generally accepted, however, that even if metastasis isn't apparent in the X-ray, the disease is still there on a microscopic level. Some studies have concluded that metastasis has occurred 90 percent of the time once the initial diagnosis is made.

Treatments to shrink the tumour, such as radiation therapy (without amputation), tend to have a poorer success rate when compared to amputation alone, with most dogs surviving only a few months after diagnosis. Amputation without chemotherapy usually allows a survival time of about four to six months. If metastasis isn't noticeable in the X-ray, chemotherapy is recommended immediately after amputation and usually consists of four to six treatments. A minimum of four is thought to have some therapeutic effect, and six is considered most effective. This form of treatment, amputation plus chemotherapy, tends to yield the best results, with most dogs surviving up to a year. In some instances, however, dogs can live comfortably for longer than that; one study found that slightly over one-fifth of dogs that had undergone amputation and chemotherapy survived up to two years. Although not accepted by all veterinarians, some evidence suggests that a holistic approach benefits dogs suffering from osteosarcoma as well. It relies on Chinese herbs and formulations and is practised by veterinarians who have received additional training in holistic medicine. This approach is not considered curative either but supports the dog's immune system and increases the benefits of chemotherapy.

After receiving Dr. Kwantes's recommendations, Princeton and I did what we usually did when faced with a problem, or in this instance, a life-threatening disease: we talked about it. After leaving the veterinary clinic, we drove to Tim Hortons for a coffee and a Timbit. We then drove around for an hour as I explained to him what he was facing and what we were going to do about it. I carefully explained the treatment options available and the one I wanted him to take. Princeton sat alongside me, looking at me often. I knew he was paying attention because of the solemn quality in my voice. I told him that I loved him and would always do what was best for him. I said that the battle ahead wouldn't be easy, but he was tough and would prove everybody wrong. And that's exactly what he did.

6

A Tough Old Mutt

THE LEG. HIS GODDAMN LEG. That's what I kept thinking about as I sat with Princeton the morning of his surgery. We were in the reception area of Park Veterinary Centre, and I didn't know what I should do about his leg. At the end of the day Princeton would be returned to me, a different dog, at least physically, from what he was now. He would be in pain he had never experienced before, and that would just be the beginning. He would need to learn to walk again, to go pee. Would he run again? Would he still be able to jump into the truck? Would my loyal, graceful friend be able to do the things he had done up until a few weeks ago? These are the things I should have thought about instead of obsessing about what I should say to his leg. That's right, as utterly fucking stupid as it sounds, I couldn't stop wondering if I should say something to a part of him that would no longer be there in a few hours. Should I say goodbye to it? Run my hand along it for the last time and thank it for everything it had given to Princeton for the last twelve years? Curse it? Hate it for developing something that might rob us of our relationship together? In the end, just before he was taken away by one of the veterinary staff, I stroked it for the last time and, after thanking it for its many years of dutiful service, said it had to go so the rest of Princeton could continue to live.

I held Princeton's nose up to mine and, looking into his gentle brown eyes, told him that I would see him again. That he would be fine and his farm would be waiting for him and he still had work to do. As the nurse escorted Princeton to the back of the clinic, I watched him walk away from me with four legs for the last time. I went home and waited for the call from Dr. Kwantes.

While Princeton was having his surgery, I was building a ramp—one leading from the lawn up to the deck of my house. I've always handled adversity by losing myself in my work, and I suppose that constructing a ramp was no different. There are five steps going from the ground to my deck, and not knowing if Princeton would be able to use them again, I decided this was something he needed. I worked mechanically, not allowing myself any satisfaction from what I was doing. It was beginning to turn out well, especially once the surface was covered with outdoor carpet so Princeton would have a good grip while walking on it. Every so often I'd look up and expect to see him there, looking at me as I worked, only to remind myself that he was still at the clinic. I would then wonder how he was doing. *Is he out of surgery yet? Is he frightened?* What I found myself thinking most about, however, was how dull things were without him and how much I missed him. When I finished the ramp, I drove back to the clinic to see if Princeton was out of surgery yet. Dr. Kwantes had promised to phone when he was finished, but I couldn't wait any longer.

When I returned to the clinic, Princeton was still in surgery. I desperately wanted to see him, touch him, and tell him that the worst was over and he would soon be back home. Finally, the staff informed me that the operation was over and Dr. Kwantes would soon come out to talk to me. I was placed in an examination room and waited for him to arrive. He came in and assured me everything had gone well and that Princeton, even at his advanced age, had gone through the surgery like a champ. The anaesthetic hadn't bothered him, and he was expected to recover without any complications.

The entire leg would be sent out to a lab for further analysis and, with so much bone and tissue to work with, they would likely achieve a definitive diagnosis. Whatever the findings, I felt relief knowing that whatever was causing Princeton pain was now gone, and once the amputation site had healed, he shouldn't have any further discomfort. I asked if I could see him and was told that it would be best to wait for an hour or two, as he needed to be monitored to ensure there were no complications and to allow the staff to move him to a recovery kennel.

At last, I was escorted to the recovery kennel to see him. He was on his side, lying on a soft pad and still groggy from the anaesthetic. I stroked his head and told him that he was a tough old mutt and I'd be back in a few hours to take him home. As he lay there breathing heavily, his unfocused eye looking up at the ceiling, I continued to wonder if I had made the right decision.

Dr. Kwantes wanted me to pick Princeton up that evening, as close to closing as possible. Knowing he would need to be laid flat when I picked him up, I decided to drive Poseidon to bring him home. While restoring the big van for me and Princeton to travel in and camp comfortably, I never imagined that one of its most important journeys would be to bring him home after a major surgery. When they brought him out to the reception area, my heart sank. I had never seen him look more terrible. Not because of his missing leg but because his eyes were full of sadness, despair, and pain. His once luxurious black fur was matted and dull, and a large bandage was wrapped around the rear part of his abdomen. He was still experiencing the effects of the anaesthetic leaving his body and couldn't stand without being supported.

One of Princeton's favourite receptionists, Amanda, helped me carry him to the van and place him inside. I could tell she was upset seeing him like this too. She was one of many who would become close to Princeton as the years went by; he made numerous friends in both the veterinary community and during our travels in later years. After we placed him gently inside the van, she explained how to assist him in walking while he was recovering and what signs would indicate he was experiencing any hardships due to his surgery. Princeton, quietly whimpering, never moved from where he lay behind me as I drove him home.

When we arrived back at the farm, I decided that Princeton would be the most comfortable where he already was. I could lie on the couch slightly above him and monitor him throughout the night. So it was that night, the day of Princeton's amputation, that we spent our first night in Poseidon together—parked in front of my house and only a few feet from the ramp I had built earlier. As I lay in my sleeping bag, I gently stroked Princeton's head as he continued to whimper and moan. He had been given pain medication at the veterinary clinic and couldn't have any more until morning. I had placed him on a camping mattress covered with towels and hoped he wasn't too uncomfortable. He urinated at times, his pee leaking onto the towels, which had to be changed throughout the night. As the night went on, I continued to stroke Princeton's head and, talking to him softly, reassured him that he was going to be fine. A few hours later he was noticeably more alert, so I took him outside the van to see if he could urinate. As I supported his chest with one hand and his hindquarters with the other, Princeton managed to pee a little. Not wanting him to overdo it, I carried him back to the van and placed him inside. Two hours later we did the same thing, but this time he tried to walk a couple of steps before I carried him back to the van. Although I didn't expect to get any sleep, I drifted off shortly before sunrise. I awakened about two hours later, sunlight flooding into the van and Princeton's face a few inches from mine. He had pulled himself up and was resting his head on the couch where my face was. His eyes were bright and clear. Princeton, the tough old mutt, was going to be fine.

Over the next two days, Princeton continued to improve. His enthusiasm returned and he was in a lot less pain. We lived together in the van, I helping him as best I could and he learning how to be a three-legged dog, or as I was told later, a "tripawd." I continued sleeping on the couch alongside him, taking him outside every few hours for a pee break. By the second day he could stand on his own but needed assistance to walk, and on the third he was learning how to move around by using his front legs as before and hopping with his remaining rear leg. He could only do this for short periods at a time but was becoming stronger each time he walked.

The pee thing he learned very quickly. The first time he attempted to urinate on his own, he ended up on his ass, a "What the hell?" look on his face. I don't know whether he tried to put his weight on the missing leg while lifting his other one to pee or he just happened to fall, but obviously something didn't go right. I helped him back up, and this time understanding that what he did before wasn't going to work, he positioned his feet like points on a triangle, squatted, and then peed. From this point on until near the end of his life, this was how Princeton urinated. Pooping was much the same, except he would shift some of his weight rearward so he could squat close to the ground.

After the third night in the van, I decided it was time for Princeton to use his new ramp. I had shown it to him during his periods of exercise and his potty breaks, but other than giving it a quick once-over, he was completely disinterested in it. I brought him to the bottom of the ramp and, while supporting him underneath his groin, gently walked him up the incline and onto the deck. Princeton hopped to his doghouse, looked inside, sniffed around the deck and, concluding that everything was more or less as he had left it, hopped by me. Before I could grab him, he tried walking down the steps. He did surprisingly well, only tumbling over when he reached the last step. He hadn't hurt himself, so I decided to take him up the ramp again and then help him walk down it, hoping he'd understand that he no longer needed to use the stairs. Going up wasn't a problem, but going down was. The ramp didn't have guardrails, so instead of walking down it, he jumped off it. He landed with an *oooooof*, his legs giving way underneath him, but he seemed fine enough. This was going to take longer than I thought. I had to check the barns and decided that we'd try again when I returned.

When I got back to the house, I saw he was on the deck. Good. He'd learned to walk up the ramp by himself. When he saw me approaching, he got up from where he was and trotted down the steps. This time he didn't fall. Even better. I climbed the steps to the deck, went to the ramp, and called for him to come join me, wanting to see how he climbed the ramp on his own. He walked up the steps instead.

For the next few years, Princeton rarely used the ramp I had made him. To him, nothing had changed and the steps were the proper way to gain access to the deck. The only one who appreciated the ramp was Boris, who thought it could possibly save some time during his journey from the shop to the house. Letting Boris out of the shop in the morning after I fed him was usually followed by his running down to the house for a second breakfast. He'd run across the lawn, gallop up the ramp, jump from the top of it, and pile into the door. I was glad someone had a use for it.

Over the next few days, Princeton continued to heal and adapt to being a tripawd. The amputation site healed quickly, and he didn't require any further pain medication after a few days of being at home. He improved upon his weird bounce-walk, and by the end of the week, he was walking up to the barns with me when I did chores. Each morning he'd come yawning out of his doghouse, bounce down the steps, lower himself into his triangular squat position, and do his business. He'd then wait for me to catch up, and we would walk up to the barns for a quick inspection. Satisfied everything was fine, he'd run back to the house and wait for me to lift him into the truck so he could go get his Timbit. Everything was back to the way it was, and except for the missing leg and his odd way of moving around, Princeton was back to his regular routine less than two weeks after his surgery. By the end of the second week, he was noticeably more active than he was before the surgery, obviously feeling much better now that the pain he'd experienced from the lump was no longer present.

Another noticeable difference was the way he interacted with other dogs. Animals have always adapted amazingly well when an illness or injury makes them physically different from their counterparts. They aren't self-conscious about their physical differences, and they aren't ridiculed or mocked by other animals. I live with a cat named Murray who has been blind since birth; I adopted him when he was just a tiny kitten. He has no idea he's different from other cats, and his disability hasn't stopped him from living a full and meaningful life. Some cats, however, are uncomfortable around him, not because he's blind, but because, as a result of his blindness, he doesn't behave like a normal cat. The same was now true of Princeton. Now three legged, he had no idea he was different from other dogs but had to change his way of getting around. It was this new way of walking and running, and not the missing leg, that made other dogs aware that something about him was a little different. Before his surgery Princeton would run up to other dogs, hoping to make a new friend, but now he bounced up to them instead. Many were unsure of this bouncing black dog moving toward them. The introductions took a little longer now, Princeton's new friends spending a little extra time checking him out, but soon everything worked out and everyone was happy.

One afternoon shortly after Princeton's surgery, Dr. Kwantes contacted me to discuss the findings on the amputated leg sent to the lab for evaluation. The results, while not surprising, were disappointing. The lump on Princeton's leg was a high-grade osteosarcoma, the cancer highly aggressive and metastasis likely. This was the worst news we could have received. In light of this new information, knowing that Princeton's leg had been amputated was of some comfort, but this was only the beginning of his battle.

Princeton a few weeks after his amputation.
—Photograph by author

After my call with Dr. Kwantes, I walked out onto the deck to find Princeton. He was rolling around on the grass, playfully barking at no one. Although a senior, he had yet to show any signs of slowing down. If anything, he was happier and livelier now that the painful leg had been amputated. As he continued enjoying himself out on the grass, I once again reminded myself that I would do all I could for him. As long as his fire burned brightly, he would receive the best care possible to battle the disease threatening to extinguish the flame inside him.

Princeton and I had an appointment with Dr. Kwantes the following day to discuss treatment options. Princeton, eager to show everyone how well he was getting around, confidently walked through the door of the veterinary clinic and, with a painful-sounding *thump*, ended up on his ass a few steps later. He tried to lift himself up, slipped, and once again fell to the floor. He had learned the hard way that you need to consider the obstacles when you only have three legs. One of these obstacles is a highly polished concrete floor. Great to have in a veterinary clinic, where you need to clean up little accidents, but not so great if you're a fifty-five-pound, elderly three-legged dog who thinks if he didn't have a problem before, he shouldn't have one now. Amid the horrified gasps of people waiting in the reception room and those behind the counter, I lifted Princeton off the shiny floor and onto the carpeted runner in front of the reception desk. Immediately, Laura, a staff member, came out from behind the desk and spent several minutes fussing over him. This would begin a tradition that continued until the day she moved overseas.

For the remainder of his life, Princeton would become the focus of the women behind the reception desk whenever he arrived at Park Veterinary Centre. Usually, Laura and Amanda spent the most time with him. After that it was Shayna. I guess there was something about a furry black Lab–border collie cross, greying around the mouth and chin and with warm brown eyes and three legs, that made the ladies grow soft. Each time he arrived he was fussed over and pampered, and they usually took him behind the desk before his appointment so he could visit with them. And for the next few years, he would be with them a lot. Princeton would sit there, taking in all the love and affection his girlfriends offered him. He learned quickly that all he needed to do was walk through the doors and park his ass on the carpet in front of the reception desk, and the love and treats would soon appear. He always had a way with the ladies.

After Princeton's little love affair with Laura, we were placed in an examination room to speak with Dr. Kwantes. He inspected the amputation site and remarked that it was healing nicely. We then discussed the options available to ensure Princeton would have at least another year of life, and more importantly, that whatever life remained would be comfortable. We talked about the types of chemotherapy drugs available, where they were administered, and the advantages of each particular drug. He recommended taking another X-ray of Princeton's lungs to determine if the cancer had spread, although we assumed that metastasis had already occurred at a microscopic level. I stressed that even if the X-rays revealed the cancer had spread, we would continue on with the chemotherapy. Dr. Kwantes mentioned that if lung metastasis was noticeable on the X-ray, surgical intervention might be an option. The chemo drug we decided on was carboplatin, as it had shown some success in battling osteosarcoma and had fewer side effects than other drugs, especially on the liver. Evidence also suggested that it could destroy microscopic cancer cells present in the lungs. Dr. Kwantes thought that he could administer the drug instead of sending Princeton to an oncology centre in Calgary, approximately 350 kilometres away. Princeton, lying on a mat, stared at us as we discussed him, his disease, and what we could do for him.

For weeks I had educated myself about canine osteosarcoma. I knew full well that the prognosis for Princeton, even with the most aggressive treatments, wasn't good. But as I looked at him now, sitting on his mat and looking at Dr. Kwantes and me as we discussed his future, I couldn't accept that he would be with me for only a year longer, two at the very most. This was Princeton we were talking about, and he still had things to do. *We* still had things to do together. Princeton was fortunate to have always had an unflappable, can-do attitude, and it was this that would make him a survivor. He never felt sorry for himself or relented on anything he felt was right. And he was a tough old bugger. Whether he was chasing a coyote off the property or waiting outside a barn door in −35°C temperatures, he never complained or failed to get the job done. As I carried him back out to the truck, I felt more confident than ever that Princeton would overcome the challenges in front of him. I decided that the best I could do for him was to accept the hand he'd been dealt and to support him in any way I could. If I was unwavering in my commitment to him, he would take care of the rest.

7

East Meets West

A<small>S</small> P<small>RINCETON</small> <small>WAITED</small> for his first chemotherapy session, several friends and acquaintances offered various opinions about how I was going to help him battle his cancer. Many felt, as I did, that a pet deserves everything you can offer them, especially when they're faced with a serious illness. They believed that what I was doing for Princeton was the proper thing to do. Others commented that they would never have gone through with the amputation and certainly wouldn't have considered the chemotherapy. When I asked why, they replied that it was ludicrous to spend a substantial amount of money on a dog who was getting on in years. Their attitude indicated that a pet is basically a consumable item and is easily replaced by another. Others felt that it was unfair to Princeton to put him through any procedure that could potentially make things more difficult for him, including amputation and chemotherapy. They felt that it would be in Princeton's best interest if he was treated with painkillers and then euthanized once the cancer metastasized or the leg simply fractured. I realized that many of the people whose views I didn't agree with really did have Princeton's welfare in mind when sharing their opinions, but I remained steadfast in the commitment I had made earlier to him. He was part of my family, and I had made the decision to carry on with further treatments based not only on the opinions of professionals and my research, but also on my knowledge of what Princeton would want and what he was capable of.

One incident in particular stands out when I recall everything I did for Princeton as he got older. I was walking into a PetSmart with him to pick up some things. He was very old then, around seventeen, but still active and loved going places. Taking him to PetSmart often meant he had to remain inside the entrance because of the evil, shiny concrete floors, but he was fine with that. Two women were exiting the store as we were walking through the parking lot. Both saw Princeton, smiled, and starting walking toward him. Princeton, always the gentleman, knew they wanted to meet him and hopped toward them. One of the women dropped to her knees and embraced him. She looked up at me and asked how old he was.

"Seventeen," I replied.

As she continued to hug him, she said something to him I've never forgotten: "You're not disposable." From the manner in which she said it, I could tell she understood something important: although Princeton was old, crippled, and nearing the end of his life, he had found someone who would do everything he could for him until there was nothing left to do.

No, Princeton, you were never disposable.

Because of this, we decided on chemotherapy. In simple terms, chemotherapy is a drug or combination of drugs given to a patient to kill cancerous cells. Cancer is basically unwanted cells in the body that begin to divide without stopping and, if malignant, spread into healthy tissue. In most living organisms existing cells normally divide and form new cells to take the place of old or damaged ones. This is how we age. With cancer, however, this process goes awry. Certain cells do not die as they become old or damaged, and as their cellular divisions become more frequent, the cells themselves become increasingly abnormal. This abnormal growth eventually forms a tumour, which invades normal tissue and bone. Chemotherapy works by stopping the rapidly occurring divisions of these rogue cells. Not all chemotherapy drugs attack all forms of cancer, however, and not all patients react to chemo in therapeutic ways. Sometimes a combination of drugs needs to be administered with other cancer-killing agents, such as radiation therapy. Unfortunately, there are side effects of chemotherapy because the treatments kill healthy cells in addition to cancerous ones. In short, it's not a precise science, and although we have made tremendous headway recently, a complete cure of all cancers has yet to be achieved.

The chemotherapy drugs used for animals are generally the same ones used for humans. Animals typically respond quite favourably to chemo drugs, usually suffering fewer side effects compared to people. The reason for this is that the regimen used for animals is intended to extend their lifespan, whereas for humans the intent is curative. Animals are also probably not aware they are battling cancer, instead suffering only the physical effects of the disease.

The carboplatin Princeton would be using is a drug used to battle, among others, ovarian, lung, and brain cancers in humans. It's given intravenously and seems to be relatively well tolerated by dogs, working particularly well to combat metastasis in the lungs after the original source of the osteosarcoma has been surgically removed. The side effects are mostly lethargy and gastrointestinal upset. And no, Princeton's fur didn't fall out. It generally doesn't with animals because the dosage is often less than that given to humans. I don't really know why this was so important to people, but it was something almost everyone asked about when told he was taking chemotherapy drugs. For some people it seemed to be of greater importance than if the chemotherapy was working. Princeton wouldn't have cared if his fur had fallen out, and other than being concerned about his being chilly sometimes, I wouldn't have cared either.

In early September Princeton received his first round of chemotherapy. The hope was to administer the full six treatments, with blood work two weeks after each dosage and again on the day of each round. The day of his first treatment, Princeton confidently hopped through the entrance of the veterinary clinic, and after I carried him to the reception desk, he spent a few moments visiting with Laura and Amanda. He was a little confused as to why he couldn't have a treat, not understanding that he had to have an empty stomach for his chemotherapy. I took a seat while Princeton's girlfriends took him behind the desk so he could continue to visit with them while they worked. Soon after, we were placed in an examination room, and Dr. Kwantes gave Princeton a physical examination and took his blood to achieve a baseline. After he was judged healthy enough for his first round of chemo, I carried Princeton to the back of the clinic and placed him in a caged area where the doctor would give him his treatment. Telling him that I loved him and would be back soon, I left him to face the next hurdle in what would become a truly remarkable journey.

The chemotherapy treatment itself wouldn't take very long, but Princeton would need to remain at the clinic for an hour or so after it was completed to ensure there were no immediate side effects. I returned within a couple of hours to see how he was doing. Laura took me to the back, where Princeton was resting comfortably in his kennel. The treatment just finished, he appeared to be fine. But what was on the door of the kennel caused me some concern. Printed in large letters were very clear instructions: "Do Not Touch." Dr. Kwantes came up and told me that he had just completed the chemotherapy and I couldn't touch Princeton for a while. He was also wearing a surgical mask, gloves, a hat, and what appeared to be a rubber apron. *Okay ... what the hell did you do to my dog?* I wondered. He then instructed me on how to limit my exposure to the chemotherapy drugs he'd given Princeton for the next forty-eight hours.

Dr. Kwantes explained that chemotherapy drugs are a hazardous material and I would need to take special precautions to protect myself and others whenever the drugs were administered to Princeton.

In addition to not getting too close to him for a couple of days, it was especially important not to handle Princeton's feces or urine without gloves. This wouldn't be a problem. Princeton was a farm dog and did his business where he wanted. I didn't care where he shat as long as I didn't step in it, and I had yet to spend any time handling it. He also shouldn't be around children. Again, not a problem. Hopefully never. The doctor also said that his stool might look a little runny for the next few days. And that his appetite might be a little off and he might sleep more than usual. An hour later there were no goodbye hugs from the staff for Princeton as I hurriedly carried him from the clinic and out to the truck. He was now apparently a walking, breathing biohazard. I placed him into the passenger side of the cab and, once inside the truck, shoved him as close to his door as I could. I made sure he stayed there for the ride home.

Princeton never had *any* issues whatsoever after the first round of chemo. Once at home he ran off somewhere, probably looking for the goat to purposely introduce her to the fascinating world of hazardous material. They still weren't getting along, and unwavering in his opinion that she should return to where she came from, he undoubtedly wanted to share his toxicity with her. He returned a few minutes later, bounced onto the deck, and waited by his food bowls. In addition to not having had breakfast that morning, he hadn't had his Timbit or any of the treats he usually got from his girlfriends. After being fed, he jumped off the deck and hopped away. For the remainder of the day, he continued doing his regular Princeton stuff. During the days that followed, he never suffered any of the reported side effects. He didn't sleep any more than usual and was still very active. When I could find it, his poop looked fine. The morning after his first treatment, he was once again sitting beside me as we made our way to Tim Hortons. I preferred to have a toxic dog beside me to not having one at all.

When someone is on chemotherapy, blood work needs to be performed regularly to determine if the drug is having a harmful effect on the body, since chemotherapy attacks perfectly normal cells that comprise living bone and tissues. It's frequently blood work that determines if any adjustments are required to a specific chemotherapy regimen. With Princeton, the values we were mostly concerned with were white blood cells (WBCs), red blood cells (RBCs), and platelets, all manufactured in bone marrow. WBCs are responsible for battling infections, and a decreased WBC count can lead to serious consequences, especially for a dog Princeton's age. RBCs contain hemoglobin, which carries oxygen around the body. If Princeton's RBC count dropped too low, he would suffer anemia, his various body tissues deprived of oxygen. Platelets are responsible for controlling bleeding, both inside and on the body. If Princeton experienced a declining number of platelets, he would bleed uncontrollably if he hurt himself. All of these blood cells are produced in bone marrow, which is often damaged by most chemotherapy drugs, including carboplatin. Fortunately, bone marrow repairs itself very quickly, usually soon after the chemotherapy drug is withdrawn or modified. Princeton would need to be monitored very closely for any changes so adjustments could be made to his treatment.

In Princeton's case the doctor did blood work two weeks after each chemo session to establish a trend; we would see whether certain values either remained static or decreased the longer he was exposed to the drug. Dr. Kwantes also took a small panel the day of each chemotherapy session and compared the results to the blood work of two weeks before. Low values wouldn't necessarily mean the end of chemo treatments, as bone marrow repairs itself and eventually restores blood cells to the appropriate level, but changes might need to be made to the chemotherapy regimen. Sometimes future treatments are delayed until blood values improve. In other instances chemotherapy needs to be stopped altogether if blood values don't return to pre-existing levels, or if other medical issues independent of the chemo drug result in bone marrow suppression and poor blood cell production.

In addition to Princeton's not showing any side effects from chemotherapy, his blood work results fell within specified parameters. I think everyone was a little surprised by this, especially considering his age. Only the blood work after the fifth chemo session caused some alarm: Princeton's WBC count was low. On the day of the sixth session, it hadn't increased to the level where Dr. Kwantes felt comfortable giving him his last chemotherapy injection. Princeton seemed to feel okay, but considering his age, Dr. Kwantes didn't want to risk Princeton's not being able to fight off an infection if he were unfortunate enough to get one. The doctor suggested that blood work be repeated in two weeks, and if the WBC had increased to a satisfactory level, he could administer the final chemotherapy injection. After two weeks he took another blood sample, and the values were perfect so he gave Princeton the last round of chemo.

In addition to the standard treatments for osteosarcoma, Princeton had also been receiving another type of treatment. One August afternoon I was driving home with him after picking up some parts, and an advertisement on the radio caught my attention. It was for the Edmonton Holistic Veterinary Clinic, and they were offering alternative treatments for animals suffering from various ailments or age-related issues. Although I had never considered alternative forms of medicine, preferring to embrace conventional methods, the advertisement appealed to me nonetheless. Admittedly, if Princeton hadn't been suffering from a disease that would almost certainly kill him, I probably wouldn't have been interested at all. But wanting to allow him every opportunity to extend his life, I made a point to call and set up an appointment when we arrived home. At that time Princeton had just recently completed his surgery and we were preparing to start the chemotherapy treatments, and anything that could increase his chances of survival couldn't hurt. I set up a consultation the following week with a Dr. Marshall.

My first visit to the holistic clinic would be without Princeton. Being completely unfamiliar with holistic medicine, I intended to see first what they could offer him. If I was comfortable with Dr. Marshall and thought Princeton could benefit from her methods, I would bring him in for an assessment. The clinic was very attractive and inviting, with numerous Chinese artworks on the walls. What made it different from most other veterinary clinics I had visited was that it was devoid of any unnecessary clutter. When you enter most veterinary clinics, you're immediately exposed to "prescription" pet foods, novelties, and an assortment of toys, all for sale and usually expensive. There was nothing like that at all in this clinic. It was orderly and calming. I don't know if the appearance of the clinic had anything to do with the type of medicine they practised, but I liked it immediately. I was offered a seat in the reception area and told that Dr. Marshall would be available shortly.

After I had waited a few minutes, a staff member escorted me to an examination room, and Dr. Marshall appeared soon after. She turned out to be a very pleasant woman who had received her degree in veterinary medicine in the United States, practising there for some time before exploring other modalities and deciding to practise in Canada. I was immediately comfortable with her, and since she's now provided five years of care to several of my animals, I can claim her to be one of the most caring and knowledgeable veterinarians I have ever worked with. She embraces and practises all facets of veterinary medicine but prefers to follow a holistic approach, using Chinese herbal medicines and similar remedies.

Because of my personal biases, I was expecting Dr. Marshall to suggest abandoning conventional treatments and adopting a regimen based entirely upon holistic medicine. If she had, I would have politely thanked her for her time and left the clinic. Instead she recommended continuing with chemotherapy and stated that the amputation of Princeton's leg was absolutely necessary. She explained further that what she offered worked in conjunction with conventional treatments. One approach, whether conventional or holistic, was not enough to battle a deadly disease like osteosarcoma. In her opinion, conventional and holistic medicine would complement one another to allow Princeton the best chance of battling his cancer. Her treatments would have few if any side effects, but some would need to be scheduled so as not to interfere with any of Princeton's chemotherapy treatments. In addition to boosting his natural defences and helping him overcome some side effects of chemotherapy, she could also offer treatments that would slow down the rate of metastasis, specifically to the lungs. At the end of the appointment, she wrote down what we had talked about, outlining the specific medicines and protocols to be used, allowing me to do further research on my own before deciding whether I wanted her assistance or not.

I spent the next few days researching holistic veterinary medicine. As to be expected, some of the information I found online was merely opinion, but after familiarizing myself with the products Dr. Marshall wanted to prescribe to Princeton, I discovered some evidence that using specific Chinese formulations and acupuncture could benefit sick or injured animals. Many of the remedies Dr. Marshall suggested had been used in traditional Chinese medicine for several centuries. With few side effects, the treatments worked by supporting the immune system, allowing the body's natural defences to combat cancers and other deadly diseases. They were particularly important during cancer treatment, working to boost an immune system weakened by chemotherapy drugs. Other formulations, particularly those containing various mushroom extracts, appeared to possess cancer-fighting properties, attacking cancer cells. Some aspects of traditional Chinese medicine have been embraced and practised in Western Europe and North America for many years now. Less skeptical than before, I decided to take Princeton to see Dr. Marshall for an evaluation.

When Princeton and I entered the Edmonton Holistic Veterinary Clinic together, he was, of course, enthusiastically greeted by the receptionists up front. Everyone agreed he was a handsome old boy with a great personality. Princeton appreciated their affection but was mostly interested in the dried liver treats they kept on the counter. When Dr. Marshall met Princeton for the first time, it was love at first sight for each of them. During the years that followed, I could tell she really cared for him, and she often told me that she had never met a dog with so much resilience and determination—a dog who would never give in to anything, all the while retaining his wonderful disposition and gentle personality.

The first visit included a complete physical examination and some acupuncture, followed by medications to both support Princeton's immune system and prevent the osteosarcoma from metastasizing to his lungs. Except for his osteosarcoma, he was very healthy, Dr. Marshall said, especially considering his age. He would need to come back regularly for checkups and adjustments to his medication, but considering the liver treats up front, I didn't think Princeton would have a problem with that. When the appointment was nearly finished, I asked Dr. Marshall what her expectations were. Without hesitating, she replied that Princeton would overcome his cancer. She could tell he was a survivor.

One of the most important things for me when choosing to offer Princeton holistic treatments was that Dr. Kwantes and Dr. Marshall would work together. Each offered different modalities, but I wanted to give Princeton every opportunity I could to help him defeat his disease. I informed Dr. Kwantes of Princeton's additional treatments, and he and Dr. Marshall agreed to work together to ensure that neither the conventional nor the Chinese approach would infringe on the other. Not only that, but Dr. Kwantes always sent the results of Princeton's blood work and X-rays to Dr. Marshall following his checkups. Princeton now had the support of two veterinarians, each of them committed to helping him as best they could. In time, however, each would claim it was the indelible spirit of Princeton himself that would help him the most.

Princeton's battle with osteosarcoma had begun on June 29,

2011, and by early 2012, just over six months later, he had gone through a major surgery to remove one of his legs, six rounds of aggressive chemotherapy, numerous blood tests and X-rays, and holistic treatments. He had received the best care available, and time would tell if any of it had made a substantial difference.

8

A New Lease on Life

THROUGHOUT THE FALL, Princeton remained his active and happy self during his chemotherapy and holistic treatments. While most dogs his age are content to sleep and relax during their later years, Princeton was revelling in a second puppyhood. Two incidents in particular reminded me that he wasn't prepared to let his recent amputation and ongoing treatments get the best of him. It all started late one afternoon when I walked out of my house and he wasn't on the deck. For about twenty minutes I walked around the property calling his name, but he didn't appear. This wasn't anything out of the ordinary for Princeton, as he sometimes buggered off on his own to do his own thing, reappearing only when he wanted to or decided he was hungry.

An hour went by and still no Princeton. It was now early evening, and I was concerned that something bad had happened to him. I walked the entire property, calling out his name and looking in the barns and outbuildings on the off chance I had accidentally locked him inside one of them. Nothing. Becoming even more concerned, I turned my attention to the river embankment that runs along the west side of the property. It's very steep and runs approximately one hundred feet down to the river itself. Princeton hadn't been down there for almost a year, and I didn't think he'd go down on his own now, especially since he was missing a leg. But as I stood at the edge of the embankment and called out for him, I saw the trees rustle slightly, close to the river's edge. Barely visible, standing among the trees, was Princeton. I couldn't see him very clearly, but what I did see of him convinced me that he wasn't worried about the situation he was in. "What the hell are you doing down there?" I asked him. Choosing not to reply, he continued to look up at me, waiting for me to come and get him.

Retrieving Princeton was not going to be an easy task. Going up or down the steep embankment involves taking small lateral steps while hanging on to small bushes for support. If you're at the bottom of the embankment, it takes about ten minutes to climb to the top. This is without carrying a fifty-plus-pound dog. The only thing I could do was go down after him, tie a rope around his chest, and have someone carefully pull him up while I pushed him from behind. My parents live fairly close by, and they came over to assist with the retrieval of my displaced mutt. I tied one end of the rope to a support at the top of the embankment, tossed the remainder of the rope down the embankment toward Princeton, and began my slow and careful descent to rescue him.

Once I was at the bottom, Princeton greeted me enthusiastically but didn't seem concerned about the predicament he had placed us in. In fact, he turned and started to hop toward the river, glad to have someone accompany him as he explored farther. Instead I grabbed him, told him how stupid he was, and checked him over. Other than his fur being a little matted, he seemed fine. I tied the rope around his chest behind his front legs and yelled to my parents to begin slowly pulling him up while I shoved him from behind.

And slow the process was. We'd stop often to rest, because, well, two of us were old, another was old and missing a body part, and I was still suffering from a previous injury. It took nearly twenty minutes, but with one final shove of Princeton's ass, he tumbled over the top edge of the embankment and was immediately greeted and fussed over by my mother, reaffirming his belief that he had done nothing wrong and that retrieving him was no problem whatsoever. I, meanwhile, lay on the grass, out of breath and very much aware that I'd have trouble walking for the next few days. Turning my head, I saw Princeton bouncing off toward home. It was late and time for dinner. A week later he did the same fucking thing.

This time I saw it happen. Princeton was always very territorial. As far as he was concerned, this was his farm, and he had the right to decide who was welcome and who wasn't. The goat wasn't welcome, of course, but he begrudgingly accepted that there was nothing he could do about her. He *could* do something, however, about the coyote we saw walking across the lawn one afternoon. With a loud woof he started chasing after it, and I started chasing after Princeton. The coyote, much more frightened of Princeton than he of it, took off, ran to the same place where we had pulled up Princeton a week earlier, and leaped gracefully off the edge of the embankment. Princeton, still in hot pursuit, took a not-so-graceful leap off the edge as he attempted to catch up to the coyote. When I reached the edge of the embankment and looked down, I saw Princeton smiling back up at me. He was fine and obviously proud of himself. He was, in his mind, a *good* dog. The coyote was nowhere to be seen.

"Hi, Dad! Better get the rope!"

I wasn't happy with Princeton. I was still sore from pushing him up the embankment the week before and didn't feel like doing the same thing again. I didn't care if he was proud of himself, and I wasn't in any hurry to bring him back up. Maybe if I let him stay down there for a while, he'd realize he hadn't been a *good* dog but a *bad* dog for not listening to me. I took my time getting the rope, deciding to check the barns and perform a few other chores before going back to the embankment and beginning the arduous task of bringing him up the hill. When I arrived back to where I had seen him earlier, he wasn't there. Calling out for him didn't make him reappear. He was gone.

The anger I had earlier was immediately replaced by panic. Where did he go? What had happened to him? I now felt like a complete asshole for abandoning him and started thinking the worst. How could I have left him where he was? I had visions of him falling into the river or a group of coyotes descending upon him. I ran alongside the embankment, yelling out his name, desperately wanting to see him reappear from wherever he was. But there was no sign of him. It had been about half an hour since I witnessed him taking flight over the edge, and obviously he was no longer where I had seen him last. Before going down the hill to look for him, I first had to go to the shop to retrieve a flashlight, as it would be getting dark soon. Running back to the embankment, I happened to look toward my neighbour's field and saw a little black dot. It was bouncing.

There was no way it could be Princeton. The only place he could have a chance of getting up from the river was nearly a kilometre north, where the distance from the river to the top of the embankment is only about forty feet. Although it's still quite steep, a four-legged dog might have a chance. But Princeton? As the bouncing black dot got closer, I could see it was definitely him. He had decided he wasn't going to wait for me to pull him up and walked along the river's edge for nearly a kilometre until he arrived at a location he thought he could climb. Somehow, he had managed to do just that and was now on his way back home, weaving among my neighbour's horses. A few minutes later Princeton plopped himself at my feet, breathing heavily, his fur full of mud and debris. Other than being tired, he appeared quite pleased with himself. He was, once more, a *good* dog. After a few minutes of his resting and my apologizing profusely, he got up and hopped toward the house. It was, after all, time for dinner. Watching him head toward home, I realized that this old and disabled mutt wasn't going to let any of life's challenges stop him, and I was just along for the ride.

The winter that followed was mostly uneventful. There were, thankfully, no further incidents of Princeton launching himself off the edge of the embankment. I think he had recognized that the effort wasn't worth it, considering all the work he had to do to get back home. If it was nice outside, Princeton and his loyal gang of followers walked around the property together until someone got their feelings hurt, sending each of them their separate ways. Princeton still had his occasional disagreements with the goat, but these were usually short-lived and ended with Princeton being the victor. He and Barnie continued to get along the best, the two of them usually together as they waited for me inside the entrance rooms of the poultry barns while I did my chores. Kona was still as timid as ever, and although he sometimes disappeared for a day or two, he seemed to have finally found peace and acceptance. I was pleased that he finally had a loving home and someone to care for him.

Princeton had completely adapted to his three legs and, although approaching thirteen years of age, was just as active as he'd ever been. He had some difficulty learning to walk on ice, but he quickly learned a technique that allowed him to have as much traction as possible. Every so often, if he was moving too quickly, he'd slip and go skidding along the ice, but he would jump back up and continue on his way as if nothing had happened. It was about six months since the lump on his leg had first been discovered, and although I still believed that he would live well past the expected survival time of other dogs afflicted with osteosarcoma, it was difficult not to think of how much time had passed and wonder how much time we had left together. Princeton and I had always been close, but because of the challenges of the previous six months, the bond between us was stronger than ever. We had come to depend on each other, and it was him I leaned on when there was a death in our animal family.

On January 20, 2012, my little cat Sierra died after battling kidney disease for a year. She was seventeen, having spent most of her life with me after I adopted her when she was eight weeks old. The night Sierra was euthanized, Princeton and I took a long walk along the road in front of the farm. I remember it being very cold, and the winter winds had formed snowdrifts across our path. I walked silently, thinking of the past seventeen years I'd had with Sierra, of the relationship we'd shared and how much I was going to miss her. Princeton, very much aware of my sadness, hopped alongside me. Usually, when we walked together on this particular road, he was slightly ahead, showing me the way, or off in the distance, investigating whatever captured his attention. That night, however, he understood we were on no ordinary walk, and although I rarely spoke to him, he continued to hop beside me. If I stopped, so did he. He wouldn't look up at me, wondering when we were going to start again; instead he looked ahead and waited patiently for me to take another step.

After a very long, very lonely walk, we returned home. I had difficulty entering my house because Sierra's body was inside, waiting for when I would drive her to the animal crematorium the next day. Princeton, who had never entered my house before, followed me inside and quietly lay down on the floor as soon as he was past the doorway. He stayed there until morning, sleeping on some blankets I laid down for him. He did the same the following two nights, not returning to his doghouse until Sierra's ashes were returned to me three days after her death.

That winter was also when we met someone who would eventually become a good friend to both of us. His name was Des, and he operated a hot dog cart in various locations throughout the city. One of his more regular locations was next to the parking lot of an auto parts/equipment store Princeton and I sometimes visited. Often Des would be there, rain or shine, freezing cold or blistering heat, cheerfully selling his hot dogs to a surprisingly large number of customers. One Saturday we checked it out. When Princeton and I approached his cart, we were greeted with an enthusiastic "Hi there, fellas! What'll it be?" I decided on a jalapeno dog for me and a plain dog for Princeton. While we were waiting for our hot dogs to be cooked (agonizing for Princeton), Des asked why Princeton was missing a leg. During the past few months, I had discovered that almost everyone Princeton met wanted to know what had happened to him. Des was no different, but his response was different from most. Instead of expressing sympathy as many others did, Des thought it was pretty incredible that Princeton's leg was missing because it meant he could go on enjoying his life. Princeton's lost leg wasn't so much a result of the disease he was battling as it was a symbol of moving forward and embracing more life to come. After we received our hot dogs, Des made his way out from behind his cart to stroke Princeton's head and scratch his muzzle. Princeton concluded that someone who offered not only excellent food but also affection had to be a decent guy. It's fair to say we both liked him immediately.

This one visit to Des's cart started a tradition that would last over four years. Each Saturday Princeton and I would drive into the city for a couple of hot dogs. Regardless of how busy we were, I always made time for our weekly hot dog run. After a few weeks I only needed to utter "hot dog" to Princeton and he'd run for the truck and wait patiently by the passenger door. When we arrived for our lunch, Princeton would bounce up to Des's cart and park himself in front of it, usually butting in front of the other customers. During all the years we visited Des's cart, I rarely heard anyone complain about Princeton's queue jumping. Des would always acknowledge him in the same way: "Princeton! How's my little buddy?" As our hot dogs were being cooked, I'd then explain to the other customers why he was missing a leg. Most people were impressed with Princeton's story, and if he was lucky, he'd receive the occasional offer from someone to buy him another hot dog. Princeton always thought it rude not to accept their generous offer. After he ate his hot dog(s), he would move behind Des's cart and watch him intently as he served his other customers. Our lunch completed, we'd return to the farm, Princeton undoubtedly looking forward to the next Saturday.

Des never once charged me for Princeton's hot dog. I don't know if hot dogs are bad for dogs, but considering how many Princeton ate throughout the years and how long he lived, I don't think they did him any harm, and he got so much joy from our Saturday afternoon lunch breaks. As the years went by, we all became good friends, and in August of 2015 Princeton sat beside me and watched Des say his wedding vows to his lovely soon-to-be wife, Beryl. Afterwards Princeton dined on something else Des had prepared for him. This time it wasn't hot dogs but a feast of lamb and chicken.

Toward the end of the winter, in March, Princeton was scheduled for an X-ray and blood work to determine if the amputation, chemotherapy, and holistic treatments had been successful in preventing the cancer from spreading to his lungs or elsewhere. Although he was behaving normally and I remained confident he would beat the disease, I was nonetheless apprehensive about what the tests might reveal. It had been about nine months since the osteosarcoma had first appeared, and I knew all too well that the average lifespan of a dog afflicted with his disease and having received the same treatments was only a year—three short months away. Upon doing the physical examination, Dr. Kwantes determined that Princeton was healthy, but it would be the X-ray and blood work that would confirm how well the treatments had worked so far. After the blood was taken and I had carried Princeton into the X-ray room, I returned to the reception area and waited for the preliminary X-ray findings. Dr. Kwantes came out half an hour later to tell me that the X-ray looked fine at first glance —nothing indicated the cancer had spread to Princeton's lungs or anywhere else. It would take a day or two to get the blood results back, and the doctor would need to study the X-rays in greater detail, but everything was good so far.

A few days later the results of the blood work came back from the lab, and all values were well within the normal range. In fact, the results failed to show any of the age-related issues you would expect in a dog Princeton's age. Dr. Kwantes had also looked at the X-rays more closely, confirming that there were no signs of metastatic disease. Princeton was doing even better than most people expected.

That spring, however, didn't bring all good news. Kona, the lonely and timid malamute, left one morning and never returned. He would sometimes disappear for several days, but he always returned, usually announcing his return by howling as he sauntered up the driveway. I had no idea what Kona did while he was away, but when he returned he didn't seem any different from when he left. Although the farm was his home, in many respects he was still wild and never completely comfortable around people, and maybe his leaving from time to time was something he had to do to make himself feel at peace. When at the farm he was content to follow me and Princeton at a distance or sleep in his doghouse, but he still couldn't be touched or petted. Despite his timidity he was a wonderful dog, and I was happy that he considered the farm his home and the other animals part of his clan. I would have liked to have known him before he was abused and taken him in and cared for him, giving him all the love and friendship a dog like him deserved. Kona's situation was one of the most tragic I had ever seen in an animal. He truly didn't have a mean bone in his body, yet he was so poorly treated when his life began that his heart just broke, and he decided never to offer it to anyone ever again.

When he left for the final time, I wasn't that worried at first, as I had gotten used to him leaving for a few days each month. When he didn't return after the third day, I went looking for him, calling out his name, even returning to the ditch where I had first met him. Princeton walked with me along the ditches and through neighbouring fields while I scanned the distance in the hopes I would see Kona. Later, we drove around to the neighbours' to ask if anyone had seen him. No one had. I knew he wouldn't be returning home.

And I also knew he had probably died tragically. He would never have approached anyone and always kept his distance from anything that frightened him. He was microchipped, so if he'd been injured or captured a simple scan would have yielded my information. No, Kona had left on one of his sabbaticals and something had happened to him.

I miss you, Kona. You were loved and you had a home here. I hope you know I did everything I could. I'm sorry.

9

Hitting the Road

I T WAS EARLY summer when Princeton and I started travelling, finally getting to use Poseidon as originally intended. The van hadn't been used since the nights we slept in it following Princeton's amputation. I had put the van in the hay shed and hadn't paid much attention to it since, and although I was confident that Poscidon would be reliable and safe, it hadn't been road-tested except for the short trip to the vet clinic. If we were going to use it for the trips we had planned, it needed a shakedown run. I decided that an overnight journey allowing us to put a good thousand kilometres on it would be a good first trip. If anything went wrong with it, or Princeton had trouble travelling, we would be relatively close to home and could make it back with little difficulty. If all went well and our first journey was successful, we would then venture farther in a trip involving a few nights and a few more kilometres.

Drumheller is a little town located in the badlands of central Alberta. I had been there a few times in the past, the last being about twenty years ago. The town and surrounding area is probably most famous for its deposits of fossils, including dinosaur bones. Because of this, the town refers to itself as the "Dinosaur Capital of the World" and is home to the world-renowned Royal Tyrrell Museum, a paleontological research centre. The last time I visited,

I remembered being fascinated by the surrounding landscapes, especially the hoodoos, rock formations that have existed for thousands of years. It's somewhere I had always wanted to visit again, and since it was about 450 kilometres from home, I thought it would be the perfect place for an overnight trip.

I spent a couple of days before the trip to Drumheller getting Poseidon out of storage and checking it over. In addition to changing the oil and checking the fluids, I wanted to ensure that the repairs and modifications I had performed earlier were still satisfactory. I then placed Princeton inside and headed for the car wash. He loved riding in the van and didn't seem to associate it with the unpleasantness of almost a year earlier; he was content to sit behind me and look out the window. Once the van was nice and clean, it was time to fill it with gasoline. This was an alarming experience. Poseidon has two fuel tanks, and they were both close to empty. I couldn't believe any vehicle could hold that much fuel. Even more alarming, as I would later discover, was the rate at which Poseidon consumed that fuel. After the van's tanks were filled with the remains of what we would soon be visiting in Drumheller, we went home to pack.

As usual, I went way overboard. Packing for Princeton was easy: food, dish, water, bed, medication. Everything he needed, nothing he didn't. The same couldn't be said for me. For our overnight journey I packed too much food, too much bedding, too much junk. Especially tools and spare parts. It's always a good idea to bring tools and spare parts when travelling any great distance by vehicle, but I always end up bringing way too many of them. This is what I brought along for our first trip: two socket sets, a full assortment of wrenches, about six pliers, twelve screwdrivers, hammers, punches, a cordless drill, booster cables, portable battery booster, and a bunch of other crap I didn't need. I should have stopped there, but I didn't. I also brought along some spare parts: an extra battery, a new starter, a new alternator, both in-tank fuel pumps, numerous spare fuel filters, upper and lower radiator hoses, a spare thermostat, three serpentine drive belts, a spare distributor, fuel regulator, an ignition module, a spare throttle body, an oxygen sensor, a new ignition coil, new plugs and wires, a new pickup coil, the switchover canister and module between the two fuel tanks, electrical relay, and spare engine sensors. Do you have any idea how much this shit weighs? Or the room it takes up? Well, it weighs a lot and takes up a lot of room. Regardless of how terrible Poseidon's fuel economy was, I'm sure I made it much worse with all the extra stuff I always insisted on bringing along.

I planned to leave early the following morning but didn't get away until about 2:00 p.m. because I convinced myself I had to check over the van and sort through my collection of tools and parts again. Once that nonsense was completed, I placed Princeton in the van and we were off. I was excited but still concerned about how he would like travelling for extended distances. It turns out I was worried about nothing. For the first hour he sat behind me, looking out the window at all the new scenery. Eventually, he got bored, lay down, and went to sleep. About an hour and a half later, he awakened and began pacing from one end of the van to the other. I took this as a sign that either he was restless or he had to go pee. Probably both. I found a secluded gravel road, drove down it a kilometre, and then stopped. When I opened the sliding door, Princeton jumped out, hopped around, and found something suitable to pee on. He continued to explore his new surroundings, sniffing the ground and hopping farther down the road.

It was important to me that wherever we travelled Princeton could experience new things, so I let him do as he wanted. I stood and watched him as he bounced happily down a quiet country road, stopping only to sniff at something or to look back and make sure I was still there. Watching him, I couldn't help but feel a sense of pride in my old boy. He had recovered from a debilitating surgery and weathered six rounds of chemotherapy. He had lived another year, reaching the average time dogs receiving similar treatments

Catching up to Princeton as he explored a deserted country road.
—Photograph by author

live, and the cancer had yet to reappear. And although a senior citizen in doggy years, he had the enthusiasm of a dog half his age. Soon he was nothing more than a speck in the distance, and I decided I had better retrieve him. I climbed into the van and slowly drove toward him, my little black dot bouncing in the late-afternoon sun.

The van also hummed along without any problems. Except for its alarming fuel consumption, there weren't any issues. It could have been disastrous if we experienced a mechanical failure. If I had been travelling alone, I wouldn't have worried so much, but if something went wrong it would be Princeton who suffered the consequences. If we became stranded and were without cellular coverage, I couldn't possibly leave Princeton alone while I went for help. The van needed to prove itself and perform flawlessly, as we would be travelling for extended periods, often to locations where assistance might not be readily available. Poseidon was responsible not only for getting us to our destinations, but also for providing Princeton and me with security and protection. At times it would be our home, and it needed to offer the type of security only a home can offer. The van must have known this, as it performed admirably. I've repaired and restored enough vehicles to know what to listen to and what to feel for when a vehicle is back on the road for the first time, and Poseidon was happy to be doing what it was intended to do.

After stopping for fuel and finding another secluded spot for Princeton to have a pee, we soon arrived in Drumheller. I couldn't recall much of the town from the last time I was there, so much of it was unfamiliar. The surrounding badlands, however, were just as spectacular as I remembered them. Some people claim that visiting the badlands is like visiting a distant planet, given the coulees that suddenly appear as you drive into the valley. I found the hoodoos the most interesting part of the landscape, marvelling at the thousands of years required to form their unique features. Afterwards we drove up to the Tyrrell Museum to check it out but didn't go inside, as it would have meant leaving Princeton behind in the van. Then it was time to find a campground for the night.

Choosing a campground sounds like an easy task, but we took our time deciding which one we liked best. We drove through several to see what each of them offered. Most importantly, was it one Princeton would enjoy? This would be a new experience for him, and I wanted him to have fun. After visiting three local campgrounds, I picked a private one a little out of town, not far from the Tyrrell Museum. The camping stalls weren't too close together, and there were several open areas I thought Princeton might enjoy. After paying the camping fee, we were directed to our stall, an attractive little spot close to the entrance. When I opened the side door of the van, Princeton immediately jumped down and hopped off to explore the new surroundings. He didn't get very far because this was a campground, and campgrounds have rules. And almost always one of the rules is that dogs are to be kept leashed. This would be another new experience for Princeton. He hadn't been on a leash since I first brought him home. He never had use for one at the farm, and when he visited his veterinarians, I led him along by holding on to his collar. When I attached him to his new leash, he looked up at me, smiled, and started running, dragging me behind him. For the next few years, we would both run a lot.

After a quick jaunt around the campground, where Princeton took the opportunity to introduce himself to as many of his fellow campers as he could, it was time for dinner. And what better dinner than the camper's favourite staple: hot dogs. Three for me and three for him. I was sure they wouldn't be as good as the ones Des cooked, but that didn't stop Princeton from drooling as he sat beside me, watching his dinner hovering over our campfire. An open fire was also something new for Princeton, and he would come to understand that whenever I built a fire dinner couldn't be far away. When we'd finished cooking and eating the hot dogs, it was time to introduce him to another campsite favourite: the marshmallow. Again,

Princeton sat and stared as I toasted a marshmallow over the fire. After it cooled I offered it to him. He swallowed it, looked at me with disgust, and then looked away. He never ate another marshmallow again.

Before we go further, I feel it's necessary to mention Princeton's eating habits, as I'm sure many of you have concerns over his diet. Throughout his lifetime Princeton always ate a good-quality dry dog food, including during our road trips, but always gobbled up things that may have not been ideal for him. In addition to hot dogs and Timbits, he ate table scraps almost daily. He ate ice cream regularly. The ice cream started when I took him to Dairy Queen for a soft cone following his second chemotherapy treatment for being such a good boy, and this continued for each subsequent treatment. It also continued after his treatments were over because, well, he liked ice cream. I never considered these things really all that bad for him and certainly didn't consider them any worse than the dead chickens he'd find in the manure. Where he really indulged was when we travelled, often eating things I would never feed him at home.

During our road trips Princeton wasn't alone in eating stuff that wasn't all that healthy. I did too. At his age I thought he deserved to eat what he wanted (within reason), and our road trips were the perfect excuse to indulge in foods neither one of us ate at home. In addition to the hot dogs we often cooked, Princeton sometimes ate the same hamburgers, french fries, and other fast foods I treated myself to. I'm actually very particular about what I eat and how it's prepared, but I figured a little cheating on the road isn't a bad thing. Would I condone a dog eating this way regularly? Of course not. But Princeton deserved to be spoiled occasionally, and whatever unhealthy stuff he ate never seemed to bother him—not even the bag of jalapeno nacho chips he stole one evening, but we did have to sleep with Poseidon's door open that night.

Princeton also ate a lot of elegantly prepared foods while travelling. He dined on pan-fried salmon numerous times. He also enjoyed grilled chicken and bison fairly regularly. Usually he had sautéed vegetables with either roasted potatoes or steamed rice when he ate his meat dishes. Many restaurant and hotel chefs were eager to prepare something special for him when asked, and Princeton certainly appreciated their efforts. Once a restaurant in Banff presented a meal of broiled chicken, rice, and steamed vegetables to Princeton on a fine china plate placed upon a cloth napkin as he lay outside their front door. Many of the foods we ate were often representative of the places we visited, and it was always important to me that both Princeton and I sampled the local cuisine, whether this was a hamburger from a well-known roadside drive-in or a chicken breast from a luxury hotel.

During our first stay in a campground, I made three discoveries that would influence where we camped and how we interacted with our fellow campers during future trips. The first was how adults reacted to Princeton—or more precisely, a three-legged dog. Princeton had interacted with several people over the last year, but mostly veterinarians and Des's customers. I had come to accept Princeton's missing leg and the odd way he walked as "normal," but during our first night in the campground it became evident that most people considered him anything but.

After our dinner was over, Princeton insisted on pulling me around the entire campground on his leash, wanting to meet as many of his fellow campers and see as many things as he could. Many other campers were out for an evening stroll, sometimes walking their own dogs, and Princeton dragged me over to anyone he saw walking toward us. Almost everyone we met wanted to know why he had only three legs, so I'd tell them Princeton's story, starting with the original diagnosis, followed by the surgery, the chemotherapy, and the alternative treatments. These queries were different from those of Des's customers because I had to answer numerous questions from groups of people at a time, as opposed to questions from a lone individual. Most people thought it was wonderful that

Princeton had managed to come so far and wished him the best of luck as they walked away. We wouldn't get very far before a family or another group of campers came upon us and asked about him. I never minded telling people Princeton's story, as it always made me proud to talk about him. Princeton liked it as well, as he always received plenty of attention from everyone. The few times we were walking without anyone stopping us, I would often hear people in campsites remark in whispered tones, "That dog has only three legs!" as if saying it too loudly would cause Princeton to discover that he really did have a missing leg. He, of course, already knew this—he just didn't care.

The second discovery was the reaction of children toward Princeton. Not only was he a handsome dog, but he was also cute. The older he got, the cuter he became. People often remarked that he looked like a shaggy black teddy bear. Most kids wanted to run up to him and pet him. But the occasional child seemed unsure of Princeton. I soon discovered that it wasn't because they were afraid of him because he was a dog but because he was a dog who was different. As children, we're taught that things around us are constructed in a particular way. Human beings look a certain way. We know that dogs look a specific way and most have, among other things, fur, a tail, and four legs. When something looks weird and you aren't old enough to understand that there are exceptions to nearly everything, you're going to be apprehensive when seeing it for the first time. Over time I learned that if a child was a little shy when first meeting Princeton but obviously interested in touching or petting him, I needed to make them feel comfortable around him by carefully explaining that he was still a dog. He may have been different, but being different is good too.

What I never really got used to, however, were some of the questions kids asked. Children often ask very direct questions, much different from those asked by adults. At first they wanted to know the same thing adults did—what had happened to Princeton's leg. After I had answered, their queries often became more direct: "How does he walk?" "Does he know it's missing?" "Does it hurt?" Or my personal favourite, asked a surprising number of times: "Do you still have the leg?" Sounds as if a simple answer would suffice, doesn't it? It didn't. There were always follow-up questions. Having never had children and not really knowing how to respond in a way they understood, I would give an overly complex answer, usually including medical terminology I had trouble understanding myself. This usually led to confused faces and more questions.

I quickly learned I had to keep my answers as simple and comforting as I could. If a child asked why Princeton had lost his leg, I would explain that he got sick and the leg had to be removed to make him feel better. And no, it didn't hurt at all. Dogs are actually born with three legs and one spare, I'd say, so Princeton has no trouble walking and is just as fast as any other dog. And no, I didn't have the leg because I didn't want to keep it. If I kept my answers simple and short, most kids were satisfied. They'd gather around Princeton and pet him, he obviously lapping up all the attention. After they were finished some would continue on their way while others went running back to their camping spots, and I often overheard them telling their parents about the cool three-legged dog they had just met.

The third discovery during our first camping trip was that Poseidon's sliding side door is really loud when you close it. After Princeton had finished dragging me around the campground that first day, I decided it was time for bed. This was the first night we would be sleeping in the van since his surgery a year before. After one last walk around the campground so Princeton could pee, we were off to spend the night in our van. It had been a long day and soon we were off to sleep. Sometime later I awoke and saw Princeton sitting up and looking at the door. I looked at my watch and saw it was a little after 1:00 a.m., and judging by his behaviour, I figured he probably wanted to go outside and pee. I got dressed and, after attaching his leash, let him outside.

Princeton didn't have to pee. Instead he spent about ten minutes pulling me around the campground, probably looking for someone to visit with. Satisfied there weren't any campers awake to make new friends with, he trotted back to the van. After lifting him up I climbed in after him and closed the sliding door. Poseidon hadn't been manufactured with the traditional "barn-style" doors but instead with a single five-foot-wide sliding door, running from top to bottom. I'm sure it weighed at least two hundred pounds, and closing it from the inside involved gripping both handles, sliding it forward, and pulling it inward just before it made contact with the door striker. When it closed it always made a very loud *whump* sound. In a crowded campground in the middle of the night, the sound was especially obvious, probably even more so for the tent dweller a few feet away from us.

At around 2:30 a.m., I was awakened by Princeton placing his head next to mine and breathing into my face. When he was convinced I was awake, he turned himself around and stared at the door as he had done a little more than an hour before. This time I was sure he needed to pee. I got dressed and let him outside. He didn't pee, choosing instead to drag me around the campground again. After telling him I wasn't pleased with him, I lifted him back into the van and winced as the *whump* of the van door reverberated throughout the campground. A few seconds later a light came on from inside the tent next to us. If Princeton really did have to pee, he'd have to wait until morning.

Princeton's morning came a couple of hours later when I was awakened by his panting heavily and staring at the door. Again I got dressed and let him outside, hoping he truly needed to go pee. He hopped around for a few minutes before finally having a pee. Back in the van I silently muttered an apology to the people next to us as I slammed Poseidon's door closed.

From then on we always tried to get a camping spot as far as we could from other campers. Although sometimes Princeton was content to spend the entire night in the van, other times he insisted on going outside every few hours. This seemed dependent on what sort of day he had experienced. If he had met a lot of people and done a lot of things, he was usually too excited to sleep through the night and wanted to go outside every so often to see if there was anything else to do. I didn't want to bother our fellow campers with Princeton's nighttime idiosyncrasies, and we were usually fortunate enough to get a stall some distance from everyone else.

That summer Princeton was scheduled for another round of X-rays and blood work at Park Veterinary Centre. He didn't seem to be suffering from anything, but routine testing was the only way to determine if the cancer had returned and whether or not it had metastasized. His X-rays came back clear, and the blood work was mostly unremarkable. The only abnormality in the blood work was his alkaline phosphatase, or ALP, which was slightly elevated. ALP, a protein enzyme, is commonly produced by liver cells, and an elevated level can sometimes indicate liver problems. However, it's often found in canine lab work, especially in older dogs, and numerous drugs and several non-liver-related diseases can also lead to increased levels of the enzyme. Because an elevated ALP is not considered a precise indicator of liver disease, and since Princeton wasn't exhibiting any symptoms of liver failure, Dr. Kwantes recommended a wait-and-see approach. If Princeton's ALP levels continued to increase over time and an upward trend could be established, then additional testing would be required. The only thing Dr. Kwantes was concerned about was Princeton's teeth. They weren't decayed but did display noticeable plaque in several areas. Dr. Kwantes recommended leaving them alone, because since Princeton was thirteen and had suffered osteosarcoma, how much time did he really have left? Years later Dr. Kwantes would admit that if he'd known how much time Princeton really did have left, a little pre-emptive dental care would have been a good idea.

It was also time to see Dr. Marshall at the holistic vet clinic.

Princeton was still taking his Chinese remedies and receiving his acupuncture treatments and tolerating both extremely well. I had noticed he had a little stiffness in his legs some days, but each time he had some acupuncture he always felt better. After another thorough examination, Dr. Marshall declared Princeton remarkably healthy, especially considering his age and cancer diagnosis. He had the vigour and strength of a much younger dog, and just as importantly, was happy and upbeat. Dr. Marshall had treated numerous older dogs before and felt Princeton was doing better than any of them. He was doing so well, it was time to fuel up Poseidon and head back out on the road.

10

People and Places

T HE SECOND TRIP was a little longer than the first one, lasting three nights. I still wanted to stay close to home and decided we would go somewhere to do a little fishing. I hadn't been fishing in years, and the closest Princeton had been to a fish was the salmon or tuna I fed him sometimes. I chose to go to a lake at Lac La Biche in northern Alberta. I had been there several years earlier and remembered it as a picturesque lake with plenty of locations to fish from the shore.

I packed Poseidon again with what we needed and a bunch of other stuff we didn't. We secured a nice little spot relatively close to the lake and spent a wonderful few days hiking and doing a little fishing from the shore. Princeton, as expected, was ecstatic to be somewhere new where he could explore and make new friends. As in Drumheller, everyone wanted to know all about him and what he had been through. One incident in particular I remember as very touching. An older lady cautiously approached us as we stopped to rest in front of her and her husband's campsite. We had walked by their site several times since arriving, but neither had expressed an interest in Princeton. This time, however, the woman came from around her campfire and asked if she could meet my dog. She told me she had lost her dog of twelve years a few months before and,

For whatever reason, Princeton never enjoyed fishing.
—Photograph by unknown

because she was still grieving, had been unable to interact with most other dogs. But watching Princeton as he bounced around the campground, she decided he was one dog she wanted to meet. By this time her husband had come out from behind the campfire, and the two of us struck up a quiet conversation about his new truck parked in front of their trailer. We spoke softly as we both watched Princeton and his new friend get acquainted. I asked if she would like to take him for a walk out to the main road. She accepted, and they walked away together.

When I managed to do some fishing, I was disappointed the times I tried to involve Princeton. I don't keep the fish I catch, preferring to use barbless hooks so I can easily release them, but each time I held one up to him before I released it he'd turn away in disgust. I suppose a jackfish is an ugly fish to begin with, but I thought he'd have at least some interest in what I was doing. He didn't. Clearly, he wasn't an angler and preferred his fish to come from either a skillet or a can. He had no problem, however, mucking around in the lake. I think he did this intentionally whenever I was trying to cast out onto the lake. He probably couldn't swim with his missing leg, but that didn't stop him from wandering into the water and submerging himself. Once his long fur was completely wet, he weighed much more than he did dry and often had trouble supporting himself as he walked over the slimy rocks beneath the water. I would then have to put my fishing rod down and go into the water to rescue him. Clearly, each of us had different opinions about what a lake was for.

A friend of mine provided our next excuse for a trip. I'd met Wolfgang several years earlier. He is originally from Germany and immigrated to Canada to work in Alberta's booming oil industry. We met at a local bike night one evening, each of us noticing the other because of the type of motorcycles we were riding. We both ride adventure tourers, a type of long-distance motorcycle suited to both on- and off-road surfaces. We'd kept in touch throughout the years, and as Wolfgang became settled in Canada, he continued his tradition of hosting a yearly motorcycle rally for fans of these types of motorcycles as he'd done in Germany. The attendees are often riders from other countries and always have wonderful stories of all the places they have visited. Unfortunately, my barns have usually been in production the times the rally is held so I've been unable to attend. But during the summer of 2012, I was without birds, as I had leased out my production for an entire cycle so I could spend time with Princeton. The rally, known as MRT, or Motorbike Rally for Travellers, is traditionally held at Toad Rock Motorcycle Campground, located in the Kootenay Rockies, British Columbia. This this would be the perfect opportunity to attend one of Wolfgang's rallies. Princeton, of course, would be attending with me.

Although taking a bike to a motorcycle rally is arguably the proper thing to do, I didn't think Princeton would enjoy being lashed to a luggage rack for an extended ride to the Kootenay Rockies. It would be Poseidon that would take us there; the old van had been resting comfortably in the shed since our last trip. Princeton waited eagerly by the sliding door while I installed the batteries and checked the fluids. It roared into life on the first crank, settling down into a healthy rumble as it warmed up. I slid open the side door and Princeton jumped inside, probably hoping we were leaving immediately. He'd have to wait, as we had much to do before we left. Over the next couple of days, I filled the van with food, clothes, bedding, and other supplies, including all the spare parts, tools, and batteries we had taken the previous trips. As I continued preparing, Princeton would spend the day either inside the van if I was working on it or lying alongside it if I was in the house. Finally, the morning arrived when we would be leaving. After I'd packed Princeton's bed, food, medication, and bowls, he jumped into the van, looking forward to wherever we were off to next.

This trip would be longer than previous ones. I decided we would travel south until we reached Crowsnest Pass (along Highway 3, the Crowsnest Highway), before heading west and into the southern part of British Columbia. We'd continue travelling along the Crows-nest, eventually turning north onto Highway 6, and make our way up to Kootenay Bay and Toad Rock Motorcycle Campground. Several weeks earlier I had phoned the proprietor of Toad Rock, a very friend-ly woman named Mary, and informed her that I would be attending Wolfgang's rally this year, not by motorcycle but with a camper van carrying an elderly three-legged dog. I asked if she could assign me a campsite large enough to accommodate Poseidon yet close enough to the amenities so I wouldn't have to leave Princeton alone for too long if I had to use them. Mary was very understanding and assured me a proper campsite would be waiting for me and Princeton when we arrived.

The first day out was uneventful. The van ran perfectly, and Princeton was excited to be travelling again. As before, I would find a secluded road every so often so he could stretch his legs and have a pee. Each time Princeton was outside, it was an adventure for him. He'd hop around enthusiastically and explore as much as he could. Princeton would hop off into the distance, looking back occasionally to make sure I was still there. If he thought I was too far away, he'd sit down and wait for me to drive up in the van before continuing on his way. When he decided he'd had enough excitement, he wouldn't go any farther and instead would wait for me to open up the sliding door and place him back inside the van. I'd turn around and head back to the highway, and soon we would be on our way once more.

Princeton was usually tired after these little excursions, and after drinking some water, he'd have a nap as I continued driving. We finally made it to a campground in southern Alberta where we would stop for the night. We were lucky, as we got the last campsite available. It was a pleasant site, and more importantly, relatively secluded from the other campers.

When we arrived it was pouring rain—so much so that Princeton wouldn't leave the van, preferring to watch me through the open door as I rolled out Poseidon's overhead awning and set up our small portable cookstove beneath it. Once again we dined on the camper's perennial favourite: hot dogs. After dinner the rain let up somewhat, and Princeton ventured out from the van. As we made our way around the campground, we heard the hushed tones of our fellow campers remarking that Princeton had only three legs. Because the rain had saturated the campground, few people were walking around, but several got up from underneath their tarps and awnings and walked out to us, asking what Princeton's name was and what had happened to him. Soon the rain returned, this time harder than before, so it was time to return to the warmth and safety of Poseidon. The sound of the rain as it fell upon the fibreglass roof was comforting as I lay snuggled in my sleeping bag, Princeton on the floor beside me. Although it had been a long day and I was very tired, I lay awake for some time, wanting the day to last just a little while longer.

The next morning we were up early and looking forward to a day on the road. The rain had stopped during the night, and the morning was clear and bright. Maybe it was because of the rain or his being overly tired, but not once had Princeton wanted to leave the van during the night. We'd both had a restful night's sleep. After rolling up the awning and allowing Princeton one more romp through the campground to say goodbye to our neighbours, we were off in search of breakfast. We found a McDonald's in a nearby town and each enjoyed a nutritious Egg McMuffin. After filling both of Poseidon's fuel tanks, we continued our journey toward the rally.

Heading into southern British Columbia, I discovered I had to adjust my driving style to compensate for the steep hills we were encountering. Although Poseidon was performing without any problems, it became evident the vehicle was ... somewhat under-powered. For such a large van basically built on a bus chassis, it had unfortunately been ordered with the smallest V8 engine available, and in 1991 (when Poseidon was manufactured) horsepower ratings, regardless of engine size, were horrendously anemic to begin with. Our configuration was perfectly fine for travelling on open, flat surfaces with small inclines, but not so good for hilly terrain or mountain passes. Poseidon weighed close to eight thousand pounds fully loaded, probably much of the weight from all the tools, spare parts, and useless crap I insisted on bringing along. I liked to cruise at about a hundred km/h, but our speed would quickly drop on steep inclines. And if that incline was especially lengthy, I would find myself roaring along in second gear and trying to make it over the next crest. On one lengthy incline we were passed by a Volkswagen van (or more accurately, a bus) that had pulled out from behind us. Do you have any idea how embarrassing it is to be passed by a late-sixties Volkswagen bus as you struggle to make it up a hill? I do. The driver pulled up alongside us, smiled, and accelerated, his little air-cooled four cylinder with approximately sixty horsepower leaving me and Princeton behind.

To compensate for this unfortunate situation, I devised an arguably questionable driving technique to ensure that we could make it up a steep hill with only moderate effort. If we were going down a relatively straight hill with little traffic, I would try to get as much speed as I could if I knew an incline was ahead. The van's speedometer only went up to 140 km/h, and a few times we were travelling well past that. Once at the bottom of the hill, I'd try to maintain my speed as we started up the incline, hopefully carrying enough momentum to get us to the top of the hill. This didn't always work, but usually we could make it without too much trouble. If the incline was especially steep and lengthy, I just had to keep Poseidon in second gear and let it trundle up the hill at its own pace, usually pissing off everyone unfortunate enough to be travelling behind us.

Princeton loved the vehicular roller coaster. He'd stick his nose out of the sliding door window during the downhill runs, enjoying the wonderful smells only mountain ranges can provide as they were rammed into his nostrils. When we started uphill and the van slowed noticeably while roaring in second gear, he would pull his face away from the window, move behind me, and watch me as I spoke to Poseidon, encouraging it to make it over the crest. Overall, this worked out well except for Poseidon's fuel consumption. Its fuel gauge still didn't work, but each time I fuelled up it took much more gasoline than expected.

The mountains were something new and thrilling for Princeton. There were no more desolate country roads for him to explore, only small turnouts and rest stops alongside the highway, usually on a mountainside with steep drop-offs. I could no longer let him be off leash when he was outside the van because of the proximity to the highway, but he was perfectly fine dragging me around as he walked from one end of the rest stop to the other, always taking time to peer over a guardrail to see what lay at the bottom.

No, Princeton. If you fall down there, you're on your own. No amount of rope is going to save you this time.

Toward the late afternoon, we made it to Toad Rock Motorcycle Campground. I pulled up to the office, got out, and started looking for Wolfgang. I learned that he and most of the other attendees had gone on a ride somewhere. I let Princeton out of the van, and we went looking for Mary. We soon found her, and she looked exactly as I'd imagined—like everyone's favourite grandmother. She showed us to our campsite and it was perfect—large and located close to the main office and shower facilities. Once I had parked the van in our site, Princeton and I took a walk around the place while waiting for Wolfgang and the others to return.

I've done a lot of camping throughout the years and have had the opportunity to stay in plenty of campgrounds. Many were wonderful—others not so much. Some were memorable only for how terrible they were. Toad Rock was a terrific campground and memorable for all the right reasons. When I first learned it was a motorcycle campground, I didn't really know what to expect. As someone who has ridden a bike for much of my life, I've witnessed plenty of changes and fads throughout the years, from manufacturers influencing a particular riding culture to newbies hopping on a bandwagon, desperately trying to convey a particular image. Most of this I've found annoying, and I couldn't help but wonder if Toad Rock would be the type of place that catered to whatever riding style was fashionable.

I needn't have worried. I soon discovered that it's a campground for riders—riders who subscribe to the belief that a motorcyclist is defined not by their choice of bike or riding style but by a sincere love of travelling by motorcycle. During my stays at Toad Rock, I have been impressed by the atmosphere it openly promotes. Almost everyone there is a rider, regardless of motorcycle type or level of experience. The times I have stayed there, adventure bikes were most popular because of Wolfgang's rally, but I saw plenty of other motorcycle types as well. Everyone gets along with everyone else, and although most are in a celebratory mood, no one is ever obnoxious or unwelcoming to anyone else. People are content to eat, drink, and share stories of the trips they have taken and the places they have experienced.

People from all walks of life and levels of rider ability seem to embrace Toad Rock. Many of the sites are small and obviously geared to the motorcyclist, but sites are available for larger vehicles as well. Some campsites have vehicles in them, including an old school bus and a Volkswagen bus (which in its day was probably quicker than Poseidon), allowing campers to sleep in them if they don't have a tent. Also available are small cabins with multiple bunks that allow groups to remain together. There is even a place to do maintenance on your bike and a small auditorium available to organizers such as Wolfgang to make presentations and provide seminars. The coolest part of the campground, however, is the "social pavilion," the outdoor bar and recreational area. It's basically an open-sided cabin with a pool table, a kitchen area, and a bar. The showers are clean and hot, and most of the toiletries, which are

Princeton at Toad Rock Campground, British Columbia.
—Photograph by author

sometimes forgotten by motorcyclists, are included free of charge. Mary is a wonderful person, genuinely friendly and caring toward her guests. More than once I saw her give clean linen and blankets to a motorcyclist who arrived without his own. All in all, a wonderful place to stay whether you're a rider or not.

Princeton loved Toad Rock. I mean, he absolutely went nuts for it. He instantly realized that this was a place he could run around in and do what he wanted and no one would be upset with him. These were his kind of people. I put him on his leash, but Mary advised just letting him go. No one would care, and everyone would look out for him. She had also recently adopted a new puppy and thought it would be great if he got to know a dog like Princeton. Somewhat reluctantly, I removed his leash and told him to do what he wanted. Initially, he chose to remain with me but later struck out on his own. Mary was certainly right about her other guests—every one of them accommodated Princeton and looked out for him. At first I would worry if he didn't return after a few minutes, but I relaxed when he'd periodically come back to check up on me. After confirming I was around, he'd hop off to see what else he could find or who else he could meet. When Princeton and I first arrived, an outdoor wedding was taking place, and he quickly introduced himself to the newlywed couple and their guests, happily accommodating anyone who wanted to pose for a photograph with him.

Wolfgang returned late that afternoon with the rally's attendees. A few of them I knew and others I was meeting for the first time. Wolfgang had notified everyone that a particular black dog would be attending this year, and Princeton soon introduced himself to everyone. The rally was hosting a barbecue that evening, and everyone made their way down to the pavilion. As the bratwurst went on the grill, Princeton continued to wander through the crowd. When the brats were cooked, he jumped the queue to make sure he was first in line to receive one. Some excellent salads had been placed in the pavilion, we thought to accompany our bratwurst. Unfortunately, they weren't intended for the guests of the motorcycle rally but had been brought by the wedding guests. In the end no one cared, and the rally attendees and wedding guests were soon sharing food and celebrating together. Princeton really liked the bean salad and, after enjoying it and a second bratwurst, decided it was time to relax, so he sat beside me and watched everyone celebrate late into the evening.

The next day Princeton and I remained at the campground while most of Wolfgang's other guests went for an off-road ride on several local trails. A few other attendees had chosen to rest up at the campground. One was a motorcyclist from Germany named Anja. I had met her the night before and found her to be a fascinating person. One day, back in Germany, she decided she wanted to ride her adventure motorcycle across Canada. And that's exactly what she did. Starting out on the East Coast, she rode her motorcycle westward, eventually planning to end up in Vancouver and return home with her bike. She had been travelling for several weeks, taking her time to slowly traverse the country and see and experience as much of Canada as she could.

Anja, Princeton, and I spent the afternoon together. We spoke about various things including her travels, both in Canada and Europe, the places I had visited before travelling with Princeton, and the places I hoped we would visit now that we were travelling together. She was very fond of Princeton and loved hearing how he had so far overcome a disease most people thought would rob him of his life. Princeton really liked her too, perhaps understanding he had met another traveller with an undecided future. Anja's journey was one of self-discovery, while Princeton's was one of recovery from an unwanted burden placed upon him.

Anja asked me if Princeton had a website or blog she could follow to keep up with his recovery and travels. It was at that moment I first thought maybe I should write about him — that maybe this wonderful dog had something to share with others besides me.

Although I didn't start writing about Princeton until several weeks after his death, the seed had been planted there, at a motorcycle rally in 2012. By a woman I had only met a few hours before.

That evening there was another dinner, as well as a seminar on motorcycle safety and riding gear. After the seminar was over and the rest of the attendees went to the pavilion to socialize, Anja, Princeton, and I went back to Poseidon and continued the conversation we had started earlier. We talked until nearly sunrise, Princeton sitting across from us and staring at us as we spoke, our words becoming increasingly intimate as the hours passed, both of us sharing personal details—details you can only share with someone you immediately feel comfortable with but know you will probably never see again. Finally, we said our goodbyes, as Anja would be continuing on her journey in the morning. When I awoke a couple of hours later, I found a note underneath Poseidon's windshield wiper. Anja had placed it there before she left the campground, thanking me for the wonderful conversation and the opportunity to meet Princeton. She hoped that Princeton would continue to recover and he and I would experience many more things together. I read the note to Princeton as we sat beside each other, emphasizing the passages where Anja wished him well and said that he was a remarkable and special dog. I think he understood, like me, that the opportunity to meet Anja was one of the best parts of our trip.

Later that afternoon it was time for us to leave the rally and slowly head home. I was happy knowing he had really enjoyed himself. Everyone at the rally loved him and his company. He made many new friends, several of whom he would see the following year at Wolfgang's next rally. For nearly three days he had the run of the entire campground, doing what he wanted and spending time with people he liked. As we were leaving, Mary presented us with a Toad Rock motorcycle patch, which I affixed to Poseidon's rear window. It remains there today. We were in no rush to return home and, over the next few days, drove throughout the southern and central parts of British Columbia. When he did finally return home, Princeton was refreshed and invigorated, with a little more bounce in his step.

The story didn't end there, however. Several months later I received a call from Wolfgang. He informed me that a German motorcycle magazine had published a picture I would want to see. I eventually received a few copies of the magazine a friend of his had sent from Germany. Leafing through the publication, I found the picture Wolfgang was referring to. The photograph showed most of the attendees gathered together on the second-last day of the rally. There, in front of everyone else, Anja and I were seated on the ground. Between us was Princeton, his head cocked slightly to one side, looking directly at the photographer. Princeton, it seemed, had gained international exposure.

11

Missing

P RINCETON CONTINUED TO do very well throughout the remainder of the summer and into the fall. Our days consisted of work around the farm, trips to Tim Hortons for Timbits, and rides in the Peterbilt to pick up loads of poultry feed. He was still as active as he had ever been, although clearly he was beginning to feel the early aches and pains of arthritis. At his age it was entirely expected, but the ongoing acupuncture treatments given to him by Dr. Marshall alleviated most of his discomfort.

Princeton and Barnie continued their allegiance to each other, often spending parts of their day following me around as I went on with my work. The tenuous agreement between the goat and Princeton continued, each of them staying out of each other's path. If Princeton felt the goat wasn't abiding by their agreement, he wasn't afraid to exercise his authority to keep her in line. He may have been old and disabled, but he was still much too fast for a goat who was becoming increasingly disinterested in anything except eating. Princeton was still lean and muscular; she had become fat and lazy.

There were two incidents, one in late summer, the other in early fall, where I thought something terrible had happened to Princeton. He had always considered it his duty to chase coyotes off the property, and although now a senior, he never missed an opportunity.

He hadn't launched himself off the embankment again, but that was probably only because a coyote hadn't jumped over first. I think it was Princeton's insistence on chasing away anything he considered a threat that caused him to go missing on these two occasions.

The first time I noticed he was missing was when I came out of one of the barns early one evening and Princeton wasn't occupying his usual spot by the door. I called for him for several minutes before deciding that he had discovered something intriguing (probably with Barnie) and was choosing to ignore me. It wouldn't have been the first time. I went into the second barn, and when I came out about forty-five minutes later there was still no Princeton—only Barnie. This was immediate cause for concern. If either Princeton or Barnie discovered something fascinating, the other was never far away. Barnie present and Princeton still not responding to my calls meant he was off alone somewhere.

I abandoned my chores and walked around the property looking for Princeton. He was nowhere to be found. My next thought was that he was probably at the bottom of the embankment again, waiting for me to rescue him. Before he got bored of waiting and decided to find a way up as he had done before, I used the rope to lower myself to where I had seen him the previous times he'd gone for a tumble. He wasn't there. Once back at the top, I continued to walk the property while calling out his name. An hour passed before I got into my truck and drove around in the hopes I would find him. I didn't see him anywhere and, as before when he had disappeared, became concerned that something bad might have happened to him. After stopping at several neighbours' to ask if anyone had seen him yielded nothing, I returned to the farm. I phoned my parents to see if they could walk around their property and call out for him. By now it was completely dark, and still no sign of Princeton. It had been several hours since I had last seen him, and I didn't know what else to do.

For the next few hours, I, along with my parents, continued

looking for Princeton. I descended the embankment again in the hopes he would be there waiting for me, but still no sign of him. Once more I drove around the area, this time with a high-powered flashlight, to scan the ditches and fields. No Princeton. I even looked for him where he'd managed to crawl up from the river's edge the second time he fell down the embankment. Still nothing. When I returned home, I hoped I would see him standing in the yard, wondering what all the fuss was about. Again, nothing. Princeton was nowhere to be found. He wasn't on the property or at the neighbours'. By then I was preparing myself for the worst, thinking he had either slipped into the river or had been drawn away and attacked by coyotes. If either had happened, I knew I would never see him again.

It was now about 3:00 a.m., and I went into my house to retrieve another flashlight. I was prepared to spend the rest of the night looking for him, starting with once again lowering myself down the embankment and following the river to where he had managed to climb up from it before. Just before leaving, I happened to notice a light on my home telephone blinking, alerting me to a recorded message. When I had been in my house a few hours before, there weren't any messages, and I thought it odd that someone had left one so late in the evening. Princeton was wearing his collar with all the tags attached, including the one with all my contact information. Could someone have found him? I went to the phone and listened to the message. It was county bylaw services. They had Princeton, and could I please contact them to confirm he was mine.

I called the number, not expecting an actual person to answer because it was so late (or early). Surprisingly, a bylaw officer answered, and I explained who I was and described the message I'd received. The officer remarked that they had two dogs in the compound and asked if I could describe Princeton.

"He has three legs," I said.

"Yes, one of the dogs here has three legs," the officer replied.

"Jesus, that's Princeton! I'll be down in a few minutes to get him."

"You can't pick him up until morning after he's been processed and any fines assessed have been paid."

"Can I at least come see him? He's old and needs his medication."

This, I'm ashamed to say, was a lie. Not his being old, but except for his Chinese herbs and extracts, Princeton wasn't on any medication.

The officer relented and said that it was okay for me to come see him. He told me where to enter at the back of the county bylaw services building, and that he would be there waiting for me. Ten minutes later I was walking into the back of the building to see my dog. And there he was, a little scruffy but overjoyed to see me. The officer opened Princeton's cage, and I dropped to my knees and hugged him. The officer explained that earlier in the evening a bylaw enforcement officer had been driving around the area a couple of kilometres from my farm and observed a black dog with three legs enthusiastically hopping down the middle of the road, heading south. I wondered if Princeton had chased another coyote off the embankment, fallen to the bottom, and realizing he couldn't get back up, decided to do what he had done before: walk along the river heading north to where it was easy for him to crawl back up and then head south back toward the farm, this time choosing to use the road. Or perhaps he had chased a coyote onto the neighbouring fields and gotten himself nabbed by the county as he was returning home. Either way, he had been picked up and was now in doggy lockup.

The officer thought Princeton was pretty cool and wanted to know how he had lost his leg and how old he was. I told him Princeton's story — what he had overcome, and how his tremendous spirit inspired everyone who came in contact with him. After listening to Princeton's experiences over the last couple of years, the officer told me just to take him, get him home. After all, he'd had a tough night. I didn't have to wait until morning, and there wouldn't be a fine. After thanking the officer profusely, I hoisted Princeton in my arms and carried him to the truck.

Although I was exhausted and upset with him, it felt wonderful to feel him beside me as I drove home. As he lay beside me, I could tell he was very tired and probably even feeling a little sheepish over his escapades. I explained to him that it wasn't anything to dwell on, but *not* to do it again. Everyone does an overnighter or two, even dads. No big deal. But we learn not to do it again. Princeton seemed satisfied with my words and drifted off to sleep for the last couple of minutes of our drive. When we turned in the driveway, the sun was up and a new day had begun. Princeton jumped from the truck, walked around a bit before going to pee, bounded up the stairs to the deck, and lay down on his outdoor bed. I gave him some food and water and watched him hungrily consume both. I told him that it was time to go to work; we had to go into the barns and do chores. Princeton looked at me for a moment, plopped his head down, and quickly went to sleep. I walked to my barns alone.

Following Princeton's latest indiscretion, which had resulted in a run-in with the authorities, I was careful to make sure he rarely left my sight. He didn't leave the farm on his own that much as he got older, but his immense dislike of coyotes always caused him to toss out the window any good judgment he possessed. Even if I was with him, he'd pursue any coyote he saw on the property, barking loudly as he chased it away. As he did this I would be chasing after him, yelling for him to knock it off and return to me, something he would do only once he was satisfied the coyote was far enough away. There were times I wished I had a dog who acted like he was fourteen—a dog content to lie around and not get overly excited over anything. Princeton had always taken his farm duties seriously, however, and as he aged his devotion never waned. He was never what you would consider aggressive, but he was protective of what he considered his. To keep a closer eye on him, I would come out of the barns often, tell him to continue to stay by the door, and go back in to resume my work. If I was away from the farm without Princeton or was finished for the night, I kept him locked up on the deck. Even with all the extra effort, he disappeared again one evening when I left him unsupervised for just a few moments.

I was forced to go looking for him, and as before, he was nowhere to be found. Knowing where he had ended up the last time, I phoned the county to inquire if he had been picked up and was doing more time in doggy jail. Nope, Princeton hadn't been incarcerated. I drove around the area, scanning the ditches and fields. I drove to where he had come up from the river before and waited for him, expecting to see him as he pulled himself to the top. After nearly an hour he failed to arrive, and I decided to go home and wait for him there, reasonably confident he'd show up sometime. Before arriving back at the farm, I stopped by a neighbour's to ask if they had seen him. They had. A dog matching Princeton's description had been walking along the road several kilometres south of the farm. Not north as I'd expected, considering his route home after falling down the embankment the second time he had gone missing, and later, when he was picked up by the county officer. I got back in the truck, drove past the farm, and continued heading south. It was now completely dark and I didn't know if I would be able to see him. After a couple of kilometres, I reached a set of crossroads, turned left, and slammed the brakes hard. There, in the middle of the road, barely visible on the black asphalt, lay Princeton.

I jumped from the truck and, expecting the worst, ran toward him. He appeared to be fine but out of breath. Clearly, he'd been on his way home and decided to lie down and take a rest. A black dog, lying on black asphalt, in total darkness. He was lucky that I, or anybody else for that matter, hadn't run him over. I carefully lifted him up, placed him in the cab of the truck, and drove him home.

I had no doubt he had seen another coyote, this time opposite the embankment, and chased after it. He likely continued chasing it as it left the property, went onto the road, and headed south. Princeton was surprisingly fast for a dog with three legs and would have continued chasing it until he was satisfied it was no longer a threat, especially if I wasn't around to call him back. I have no idea how far he chased it, but judging by how long he had been missing, probably several kilometres. After Princeton had decided the coyote was far enough away, he turned around and headed home and, tired after all the excitement, decided that the middle of a road was as good a place as any to lie down and take a breather. Although I was relieved to have found him, I was also very angry with him. Not only had he left the property again, but he had also put himself in a dangerous situation; he could have easily been killed. It was obvious Princeton wasn't prepared to act like a disabled senior battling a deadly form of cancer. I admired his resilience and drive, but clearly I had to do something to ensure he wouldn't do this again.

As Princeton was mostly always with me, there was little I could do short of keeping him chained up continually — something neither of us would enjoy. What I needed instead was a way for him to be constantly supervised, a way to keep track of his movements during the rare times he was out of my sight. I started to investigate a tracking system to monitor his whereabouts. After a week of researching various options, I discovered a GPS system Princeton could wear on his collar. It was a small device, about the size of a C battery and weatherproof, that I would permanently attach to his collar. I'd need to purchase an airtime package in addition to the device itself, but I would then be able to track his movements and know his exact location by monitoring him on my cellphone or computer. I was a little skeptical about how well it would work but ordered it online and hoped it arrived before another one of Princeton's disappearances.

When the tracking device arrived a few days later, I attached it to Princeton's collar, purchased the necessary airtime, and voila, instant doggy monitoring. It worked perfectly. Unless Princeton was hiding under the deck or somewhere the satellite had trouble locating, I could find his exact location within a minute. Most importantly, it worked reasonably well in forested areas. It might take a few attempts to locate him if he was underneath a tree, but I could eventually find him. I found myself playing with it even when I knew where Princeton was, such as in a veterinary clinic or sitting beside me in the truck. It was a marvellous little device.

It also turned out to be a complete waste of money. Whether Princeton had decided leaving the property wasn't worth the effort or he understood how upset I was with him the last time, he never left the property on his own again. Ever. He'd still chase coyotes and other intruders but would stop at the edge of the embankment or the other limits of the property, turn around, and trot back to wherever he was before. In time I removed the GPS device and cancelled the airtime subscription. I suppose things like this happen.

12

Nothing Amiss

I N THE FALL Princeton went in for another round of X-rays and more blood work. I was always worried each time I took him for these tests but understood the importance of frequent monitoring to determine if the cancer had returned or metastasized. If either were to happen, any further treatments would have a greater chance of success the earlier they were administered. Everyone knew that Princeton was now past the expected lifespan of a dog battling osteosarcoma, and I don't think anyone except me would have been surprised if the osteosarcoma had returned. It was always difficult, however, sitting alone in the reception area of Park Veterinary Centre, waiting for the preliminary X-ray results. The wait was usually only about half an hour, but I still found it agonizing. As difficult as these times were, I remained unwavering in my belief that if any dog could beat the odds, it would be Princeton.

Princeton, as usual, was behind the counter, visiting with Laura and Amanda when Dr. Kwantes came out to the reception area to discuss his test results. He informed me that, as with all the previous X-rays, he'd seen nothing to worry about on initial assessment. The blood work results would again take a few days, but he didn't expect any changes. Although no one was prepared to consider him cured of one of the most aggressive canine cancers known, Princeton had become an anomaly, surpassing a time limit bestowed upon him by veterinary medicine.

As I drove home, watching Princeton as he sat beside me happily looking out at the world around him, I was once again reminded of what a truly remarkable dog he was. I had known this for a long time, well before his osteosarcoma diagnosis, surgery, and chemo-therapy treatments, but now I felt especially proud of him. It had been sixteen months since his diagnosis. For the cancer not to have metastasized to his lungs or appeared anywhere else was incred-ible. Not only that, but except for the plaque on his teeth, he was in remarkable condition, especially considering his age. He still walked several kilometres a day, jumped in and out of pickup trucks, sat proudly in big trucks, and possessed an enthusiasm and vigour that impressed everyone. More than ever before, I felt confident that, ex-cept for Princeton's missing leg, osteosarcoma would soon become a distant memory for us both.

As I continued to drive back, I also thought of what lay ahead for Princeton and me. I knew I had been given a gift, an opportun-ity to share whatever time my best friend had left. In addition to overcoming the deadly disease, at over fourteen years of age he had also surpassed the natural lifespan of a dog his size. Although the treatments of Dr. Kwantes and Dr. Marshall, and eventually others, would contribute to Princeton's longevity and well-being, it was Princeton's spirit and determination that allowed him to continue living. It was my responsibility to honour these qualities in him the best way I knew how. I knew Princeton loved two things: being with me and travelling.

When we arrived home I took Princeton's head in my hands, looked into his soulful brown eyes, and told him how proud I was of him, and that we would do more of the things he loved. If I had to take a step back from the farm and other commitments for us to experience more together, I was prepared to do that. I also told him that if things ever became too difficult for him, he must take what he needed from me. Together we would always share and overcome. I realize now that those words didn't need to be said. Princeton and I had been doing that for thirteen years. And we were just getting started.

The winter was mostly uneventful. Princeton continued to defend his territory, chasing coyotes whenever he saw them, but he no longer left the property. I had received the blood chemistry results from Princeton's last checkup in October, and except for the ALP trending a little higher, everything looked excellent. The two of us continued raising chickens, but I always made sure we took time to do the things Princeton enjoyed. Unable to go camping during the winters, we often went on day trips to places where he could roam and explore. And Princeton still adored his daily Timbits and Saturday afternoon hot dogs.

Poultry farming during the winter, especially the coldest months, is always a tremendous amount of work. In addition to the constant monitoring and equipment repairs, it's very important to closely watch and adjust environmental conditions inside the barns. Much of this involves the movement of air—controlling how much of it enters the barn, heating it to a precise temperature, and exhausting it outside. This is critical during the winter months, as barn conditions can deteriorate rapidly if you ignore heating and ventilation requirements or don't follow the correct procedures. Air quality inside poultry barns is very important for maintaining the health of the chickens and making sure they remain comfortable. If you don't allow enough air to enter the barns, it usually means you're not exhausting enough of it. This air will become stagnant and often saturated with moisture, leading to wet conditions that make the chickens uncomfortable and increase their risk of disease. But if you exhaust the air too quickly, you subject the heating systems to greater stresses and the chickens will often be too cool, again increasing the risk of disease. It's a very delicate balance, and it's not uncommon to find a conscientious poultry farmer spending much of their day constantly making adjustments to provide ideal living conditions for their flock.

Because of the need to monitor these conditions, I find myself in the barns every three hours during the coldest months. And every time I ventured to the barns in these freezing temperatures I was accompanied by my ever-faithful companion, Princeton. As old as he was, he was still an outdoor dog, sleeping in his heated doghouse even if it was bitterly cold. But regardless of how cozy he was in his little house or how cold it was outside, he'd always accompany me on my barn checks. I'd often try to make him stay where he was, but he considered it his duty to follow me to the barns no matter how lousy the weather was. If I closed the gate to the deck, he'd sit outside his doghouse, barking until I relented and returned for him. Even in the middle of the night, the snow almost up to my knees, he'd still insist on accompanying me, trying to follow my steps in the deep snow. It was often hard for him, trying to navigate through the snow with only three legs, but eventually he'd make his way to the barn entrance. Once there he preferred to stay outside, often refusing to enter the warm furnace rooms. When I reached the entrance, Princeton would turn around and lie down, his eyes continually scanning ahead, prepared to defend what he considered his. Often I would be in each barn for well over an hour making adjustments because of the extreme cold, and when I opened the exterior door, Princeton was always there, his shaggy black fur covered with snow. I have never experienced any creature so loyal and determined.

In February it was again time for Princeton to see Dr. Kwantes for a checkup, including X-rays and blood work, followed by an additional assessment and acupuncture by Dr. Marshall. This time I felt much more at ease than I had during Princeton's previous checkups. I really believed that the worst was over and he'd beaten the cancer. As before, once Dr. Kwantes performed the X-rays and took the blood, I returned to the reception area to wait while Princeton visited with Laura behind the reception desk. Princeton had become one of those special patients who was allowed to do pretty much what he wanted, the staff aware of what he had endured and of his excellent progress so far. In the years that followed, if Princeton had an appointment with Dr. Kwantes, I would often leave him on his own outside the clinic while I went inside and checked him in. He'd hop around, sniffing at all the scents left behind by the other patients before he bounced up to the front door of the clinic, plopped his ass on the concrete, and stared through the glass doors. This would naturally be followed by lots of "Aaaaaawwww"s and someone going to the door to let him inside. He would wait for me to carry him either to an examination room or behind the front desk so he could visit his girlfriends.

Dr. Kwantes eventually came out to discuss his initial impressions of the X-rays. They were, as expected, nothing to be concerned over. He mentioned that Princeton's heart appeared slightly enlarged but didn't feel it was anything to worry about. The lungs and surrounding tissues were clear, and nothing indicated that the osteosarcoma had returned. A day or two later, the results of the blood work arrived, and although the ALP was still elevated, the remaining values were unchanged. Princeton continued to be the model of good health.

Dr. Marshall's assessment was just as positive. In addition to a physical examination, she gave him some acupuncture, the ongoing treatments really helping with his arthritis. It was also the first time she referred to Princeton as "tough as nails," and she continued to describe him this way until his death. Dr. Marshall also changed his supplements from those thought to slow down the progression of osteosarcoma to ones that would instead provide general support for his immune system. Although not yet concerned about Princeton's ALP levels, she also recommended the use of milk thistle to see if it would reduce them.

For now, both she and Dr. Kwantes were cautiously optimistic about Princeton's survival but realized that we were in uncharted territory. Living almost two years post-osteosarcoma is almost unheard of, especially with no sign of the disease. Both wanted to continue to evaluate Princeton every three months, and although a return of the disease wouldn't be entirely unexpected, it would still be surprising considering his progress so far. Everyone seemed content to focus their efforts on the positives and not give too much consideration to the negatives that unfortunately take many other dogs in Princeton's position.

Both doctors, however, suggested that a complete ultrasound be performed on Princeton in case the X-rays had overlooked something. The ultrasound could be used to check for abnormalities not only in Princeton's lungs, but also in his entire abdomen. Again, I don't think either of his veterinarians expected to find anything beyond age-related changes, but both wanted to confirm the cancer wasn't hiding somewhere they weren't looking.

Ultrasound imaging uses sound waves transmitted into the body to create an image. These sound waves are reflected off structures in the body and recorded. They are then translated into computerized images that are later analyzed. The biggest advantage of an ultrasound over an X-ray is that the images are recorded in real time and allow for a complete view of a particular region. It is also non-invasive with few or no side effects. For a complete view of Princeton's abdomen, a complete ultrasound would be much better than regular X-rays. Depending on what the ultrasound yielded, standard X-rays performed later would be sufficient to monitor any changes. So in early March, Princeton went in for an ultrasound.

The only negative was that Princeton would need to be sedated. To achieve the most accurate images, the patient needs to be completely still. Princeton didn't like to lie still and was best described as squirmy when forced to remain in one position. On the day of his ultrasound, he was sedated and his belly shaved. I was allowed to be present during the procedure and thought he looked pretty ridiculous lying on his back with his legs apart, his belly and chest shaved and his tongue hanging out the side of his mouth. After lots of lubricating goo was applied to his bare skin, the procedure started. Although the veterinarian was trying to be as thorough as she could, she was still very accommodating in response to my questions, took the time to describe what she was doing, and detailed her findings as the examination continued. After about twenty or so minutes, she concluded the procedure and announced that she could find nothing wrong with Princeton. The results would need to be sent to a specialist for further assessment, but nothing appeared out of the ordinary to her. Nor were there any of the age-related issues you would expect to find. With no indication the osteosarcoma was metastasizing, Princeton appeared to be refusing to accept that he was an old dog supposedly past the end of his natural lifespan.

Before I exited the theatre, I asked if someone could deal with the only thing anyone could find wrong with Princeton during his frequent checkups over the last twenty months: the plaque on his teeth. I hoped that while he was still sedated someone could give his teeth a good once-over. Princeton's favourite tech, Jodi, agreed and scraped a good amount of plaque off his teeth. That done, except for the missing leg, Princeton was almost as good as new.

As spring arrived everything continued to go well with Princeton. I was really looking forward to getting out on the road with him again, as it was something we both loved. The only thing I could see that was troubling him was his arthritis. He was still very active, but he favoured his remaining rear leg at times. Acupuncture continued to help him greatly, but later that spring he was also prescribed the painkiller Rimadyl for his arthritis. Rimadyl is a non-steroidal anti-inflammatory, or NSAID, often prescribed to reduce inflammation and subsequent pain in dogs. It was a drug Princeton would be on for the rest of his life, usually at a low dosage. He would need to have his kidneys checked regularly to make sure that the medication wasn't harming them, but since he was having blood work performed every three months and kidney values were included in the results, this was never a problem.

A month after starting the Rimadyl, Princeton was back in for another round of X-rays and blood work. The tests came back as expected: unremarkable. His kidney values were fine, and he wasn't experiencing any of the side effects sometimes associated with Rimadyl. Princeton's ALP was still elevated, but as before, the value wasn't clinically significant. The X-rays were clear, and nothing seemed amiss. Princeton continued to do remarkably well, so it was time for a road trip.

13

Two Strong Spirits

THE TRIP WE would take that spring would be short, no more than a few days, but it remains one of the most memorable because of what happened between Princeton and one particular little girl.

Cancer is a terrible disease. Any person, regardless of sex, age, or ethnicity, can develop cancer. Although lifestyle and genetics are arguably factors in determining who's at risk, it's not a disease that discriminates. The same applies to animals. Princeton was always healthy, and although neither Labs nor border collies typically develop osteosarcoma, he developed it nonetheless. After his diagnosis, Princeton had fought back valiantly. I was aware of what he had experienced and endured for close to two years, but it would be foolish, even selfish, of me to say that I understood what it's like to have the disease. I don't think anyone can unless they've suffered from it themselves. It would be during this trip that Princeton would meet someone who understood the terrible disease he had triumphed over so far.

The story began when I learned of a particular car for sale in Saskatchewan that interested me. I had some time off and decided I would go and look at it. Even if I didn't buy it, it was an opportunity for another road trip with Princeton. After contacting the seller and setting up a time to view the car, I loaded up the van with enough supplies for a few days and we hit the road. The last time I had been in Saskatchewan was several years earlier to bring back another car I had gone to look at and purchased. Unfortunately, Princeton wasn't with me at the time, so this would be his first experience travelling to the province.

After nearly a day on the road, but still about an hour from our destination, I stopped for the night at a nice little campground a few kilometres off the highway. I don't remember the name of the place, but do recall it was located along a pleasant little river. After checking in, I chose a spot and Princeton and I settled down for the night.

The next day, shortly after lunch, I met with the individual selling the car. After an inspection and test-drive, followed by a complete mechanical inspection at a nearby dealership, the seller and I began negotiations. This went on for much longer than I expected, and we couldn't agree upon a sale price. We decided that each of us would take the evening to think about what we'd discussed during our haggling, and maybe one of us would reconsider, allowing us to come to a deal.

Tired and frustrated, I returned to the campground we had stayed at the night before. After we ate our dinner, Princeton and I took a stroll around the campground so I could think more about the day's negotiations. We soon came across a group of children playing at the campsite's playground, and they immediately abandoned what they were doing to come and see Princeton. As always, I did my best to answer the questions about the old three-legged teddy bear they were fawning over, trying not to mention cancer specifically. This group of children, however, and especially one little boy, wanted much more detail. Simply stating that Princeton had gotten "sick" and "he was all better now" weren't adequate responses. I finally relented and explained that Princeton had gotten sick because of an aggressive bone cancer and his leg was removed as part of his treatment. The little boy asked if Princeton had received chemotherapy, and although a little taken aback by his question, I said that he had. I explained that Princeton was fine now, and hopefully the cancer wouldn't appear again. The little boy smiled and told me that was good.

He then pointed to a little girl, younger than he was and standing apart from the others surrounding and petting Princeton, and said, "She had cancer."

Silence. I remember not being able to say anything. I mean, what could I possibly say? All I knew at that moment was that I was looking at a little girl who couldn't have been any more than ten but had already experienced hardships no one should ever have to endure. After a few moments I said to her the only thing I could think of: "Would you like to pet him?"

She looked at me, then Princeton, smiled, and replied, "Yes."

She went up to Princeton, got on her knees, and hugged him. It was, and still remains, one of the most heartwarming things I have ever seen—one of those rare and special moments that refuses to fade regardless of how much time passes. Princeton pressed his face against hers as the little girl continued to embrace him. She stood up and stroked his black fur as all the other children stood back from both of them. Still smiling, she ran back to the playground with her friends running after her.

I never bought the car. I didn't want it anymore. As short as the trip was—we returned home the following day—I'm glad Princeton and I went because I had the opportunity to see two strong spirits share something only they could. Princeton and his new friend each understood what the other had experienced, and I know it made both of them stronger.

Princeton had proven himself to be a survivor. Wherever that little girl is today, I'd like to think she's still a survivor too.

14

The Travelling Itch

L ATER THAT SUMMER, Princeton and I were once again off to
attend Wolfgang's Motorbike Rally for Travellers at Toad
Rock Motorcycle Campground. Princeton had had such a
wonderful time there the year before, and I was sure he'd enjoy seeing
many of his friends. We took a few days getting out to the rally, this
time taking a slightly different route that would require a ferry ride
across Kootenay Lake before we reached the campground.

We spent a relaxing few days at the rally, Princeton happy as
hell to be allowed the run of the campground again. He had met
several of the guests before, but a few from overseas he was meeting
for the first time. And this time there was someone special Princeton
would meet: another three-legged dog. This dog had lost a front leg
due to injury and, like Princeton, had no problem getting around.
Unlike Princeton, he bounced on his remaining front leg instead of
the rear. It was a little weird seeing them together, each missing a
limb, bouncing around, and neither conceding status to the other.
But Princeton soon established his dominance, and they, along with
Mary's black Lab, spent much of their time bouncing through the
campground.

When the rally was over, Princeton and I headed toward Vancouver. It would take us a couple of days to get there, and although

I wasn't planning to travel directly into the city, I did want to show him something I've always felt an attachment to: the Pacific Ocean. I was aware of a small beach outside of Vancouver where people can take their pets and let them walk along the sand and play in the ocean.

When we arrived at the beach, I was surprised to discover that Princeton was unenthusiastic about being there. As I led him out to the water, he looked at me, turned around, and started heading back to the van. I spun him around and, tugging on his leash, led him into the water. He still looked bored but decided that since he was in the water, he might as well have a drink. Before I could stop him, he took a big gulp of seawater.

"What the fuck?" the look on his face said.

"Well, I never said you were supposed to drink it. You're supposed to play around in it instead."

Princeton, thinking that perhaps he had misjudged the taste of the water, took another gulp.

Two minutes later we were back at the van, Princeton concluding this was all bullshit and I was pretty much an asshole. Water wasn't supposed to taste so bad, especially when there was so much of it. When I gave him a bowl of fresh water, he gave me a long, accusatory look and refused to drink it. I hadn't warned him about the seawater, so he suspected what I had just given him would be the same. After I spent about a minute coaxing him to take a drink, he was reasonably satisfied I wasn't trying to kill him or make him sick for my personal amusement, and he drank all the water from the bowl.

Confident he wouldn't be the butt of some cruel joke, Princeton let me take him onto the beach again. For the next half hour or so, we walked along the water's edge, Princeton being careful not to walk into the ocean. Compared to how he was when we first arrived, he seemed to be having fun. It did become boring after a while, however, because the area where dogs were allowed was very small, taking us only a few minutes to walk from end to end. Nonetheless, I could tell Princeton was becoming increasingly interested in the ocean as the afternoon went on, but he probably would have liked it even more if he were allowed to run on his own.

After the beach visit I was still feeling bad about the seawater incident and decided to take Princeton for a late lunch at a nearby bistro to make up for it. After he'd eaten the corned beef sandwich and ice cream, the salty seawater was a distant memory for him.

We spent about a week getting home, taking our time travelling through much of southern and central British Columbia. It had been a good trip, with Princeton meeting several people and having the opportunity to visit lots of places. Poseidon continued to run well, but I wasn't convinced we could leave some of our spare parts at home the next time we travelled. Princeton would still have to share the floor of the van with spare batteries and a big tool box. As we continued our drive home, I figured out where we would be travelling to the following summer: Vancouver Island.

Princeton continued to do well after we returned from our trip. The farm was in full production until the end of the year, so we were unable to travel anywhere else. In late fall he went in for routine X-rays and blood work, and as expected, everything was fine. His ALP was still elevated but not rising quickly enough for Dr. Kwantes and Dr. Marshall to be overly concerned about it. It was nearing two and a half years since the osteosarcoma diagnosis, and the cancer still hadn't reappeared. The only thing bothering Princeton was his arthritis, but with medication and acupuncture, he still remained active.

Princeton's biggest health concern that winter came from something he ate (big surprise). I had left him alone in the truck while I ran into Costco briefly after we had been grocery shopping. When I returned I discovered he had decided to dine on half a litre of eggnog (to Princeton's credit, he had only consumed the low-fat kind), about a half cup of almonds, several white mushrooms, and a handful of popping corn. *Gee, thanks, Princeton. It's bad enough you're battling cancer, but now you've decided to toss a little pancreatitis into the mix.* I immediately phoned the vet clinic, they in turn finding the entire scenario amusing. The veterinarian on duty said that knowing Princeton, the worst that would happen to him was a tummy ache. She recommended keeping an eye on him and suggested I congratulate him on knowing the difference between regular and low-fat eggnog.

After ending the phone call, I turned to Princeton and said, "You're an idiot."

He looked at me, replying with a woofy burp.

By January of 2014 we both had the travelling itch. Whenever we walked in the shed, Princeton would run up to Poseidon and lie alongside its sliding door. If I opened the door, he'd hop in, lie down, and wait for me to get in the driver's seat so we could begin another journey. We didn't have chickens at the moment, but the unfortunate part was that it was a traditional January in Alberta—traditional meaning about eight hours of sunlight, –30°C temperatures, and lots and lots of snow. It wasn't the best time to be running around the countryside in an old camper van with an old dog and looking for things to do. We did have the time, however, so perhaps we could sneak away somewhere for a week. The problem was where to go and where to stay when we got there. We'd have to drive somewhere but wouldn't be able to take Poseidon. We wouldn't be camping but staying in pet-friendly hotels.

I decided we should travel to southern British Columbia. The winters there are very mild, often above freezing, and I thought Princeton would enjoy running around someplace where there wasn't any snow and ice. It had been a lousy winter, and he was having difficulty navigating through the deep snow. Because we would be driving through mountain passes in treacherous conditions, both Poseidon and the old F-150 were out of the question. I had recently purchased a four-wheel drive crew cab F-150 and thought it would be a better vehicle for our trip. The next day I had the new truck outfitted with dedicated winter tires and made a little bed for Princeton in the extended portion of the cab.

A day later we were heading west on the Trans-Canada Highway, not knowing how far we would get or where we would be staying. Unfortunately, we had left on one of the worst days possible; it was snowing heavily and the temperatures were dropping rapidly. An hour into our journey, we started to come across several vehicles in the ditch, including some that were overturned and abandoned. Soon after, all vehicles were detoured onto country roads for several kilometres, as a multiple-vehicle collision had blocked the highway. Eventually, everyone was rerouted back onto the highway, but the road conditions were so poor, none of us could travel faster than half the posted speed limit. After nearly eight hours we finally made it into the small town of Jasper, usually no more than a four-hour drive from the farm if highway conditions were good. It was dark, and Princeton and I were both hungry and tired. That was as far as we were going that day, so I began looking for a place for us to stay.

Jasper is a municipality within Jasper National Park, which is located in the stunningly majestic Canadian Rockies. It attracts a tremendous number of tourists during the summer months, including many from overseas wanting to experience its spectacular beauty and wildlife. In the winter it's a favourite for skiers and those wanting to participate in other outdoor activities. I had been to Jasper numerous times, but never with Princeton. Although we would pass through it several times during the next few years, sometimes staying at campgrounds in the area, the night we arrived there together for the first time will always remain the most memorable time for me.

Our first priority was finding accommodation. Several hotels and motels are available in Jasper, but not every one is pet friendly, and those that are don't always provide any stimulating things for a dog to do. When Princeton and I first started travelling together, I decided that wherever we ended up would be a place where he'd have fun. A dog like him wouldn't be happy sitting in a hotel room with nothing to do other than look at a television. As I drove around trying to find somewhere suitable, I remembered a place I had stayed with a girlfriend a few years before: the Jasper Park Lodge. It was fairly secluded, situated just outside of town, and located next to a lake—the perfect place for Princeton to romp around and enjoy himself.

Jasper Park Lodge is a Fairmont property. Its occupies about seven hundred acres along the shores of Lac Beauvert. In addition to the lake, there is also a golf course, spa, and shopping. As we drove along the resort's driveway to the main entrance, the grounds looked beautiful all lit up on a cold winter's night. It also looked frighteningly expensive. Princeton watched out of his window as he sat behind me, fascinated with everything he saw. At the main entrance we were immediately greeted by the doorman, who asked if we were checking in as he came out and opened the truck's door for me.

"Not entirely sure yet," I replied as I exited and opened the rear door to let out Princeton.

I was beginning to think maybe the lodge was a little too elaborate and posh for a couple of weary travellers only looking for a night's accommodation. Princeton, on the other hand, was completely engrossed in everything that was happening.

"C'mon, Princeton, let's check it out," I said as I followed him into the lobby. The front desk is located directly by the entrance, and Princeton knew where to go. He hopped up to the woman behind the reception desk and plopped himself on his ass. This, he had decided, was where we'd be staying for the night.

"Good evening, sir. Checking in for the evening?" the clerk asked, her eyes dropping to the dog staring up at her intently from the other side of the desk.

"Do you take pets?" I asked.

"Of course! So you don't have a reservation, then?"

I replied that I didn't. Throughout our conversation the reception clerk looked down and smiled at Princeton, who continued sitting where he was, not doing anything except looking and smiling back at her.

It was then I knew Princeton had her hooked. I asked how much it was for the night. After she quoted me a price, I asked if she could possibly give us a better rate because, after all, Princeton really wanted to stay here, and I didn't want to disappoint him. After a little negotiation we agreed on a rate, expensive but reasonable, and we were set for our first night in a hotel together. As the doorman held the door for Princeton so we could return to the truck and I could retrieve our things, I had the feeling that if we stayed in another hotel, Princeton would probably expect similar treatment.

Our room was located in the chalet on the second floor, giving Princeton the chance to ride in an elevator for the first time. We declined the offer of a doggy bed and bowls, as Princeton had brought his own. After I unpacked we went down to the main floor to get something to eat. Princeton wasn't allowed into the restaurant (probably a good thing), but our food was brought out to us as we relaxed by the fireplace in the lounge. I don't remember what I ate, but the chef on duty prepared a delicious dinner of chicken breast, rice, and vegetables for Princeton. After our meal we walked around the grounds before bedtime. We must have walked for at least two kilometres, Princeton dragging me along as he insisted on looking at nearly everything. I knew his arthritis had been bothering him before we left, but for the next hour or so, he convinced himself not to let it bother him. It was I, obviously more tired than he was, who insisted it was time to return to the lodge. Once back in our room, I placed his little bed on the floor beside mine, and we were off to sleep within minutes.

Surprisingly, Princeton didn't wake me up to take him outside during the night. This was to be the norm whenever we slept in hotels, he being content to remain on his bed until morning. There would still be times we camped in Poseidon, however, when he

Stopping for a break while travelling to Banff, Alberta.
—Photograph by author

would insist on leaving the van every few hours even if he didn't need to pee. Why the difference? I don't know. Whatever it was, it was nice not having to take him outside every few hours.

By morning it had stopped snowing, and I hoped our travelling would be a little easier. Princeton went out for a pee, which turned into another hour-long walk around the grounds. When we checked out I let the staff know how much I appreciated the special allowances made for Princeton. They told me that the lodge is very pet friendly and they have a rescue dog who greets the guests when they enter the lodge. Unfortunately, he wasn't there when we checked out, having gone home with the manager the night before and not yet returned. I left Princeton by himself at the front desk as I went to get the truck. When I pulled up to the entrance, the doorman opened the lodge's door for Princeton, who hopped outside. The doorman then opened the rear door of the truck, and I lifted Princeton inside. He was becoming accustomed to such lavish attention.

During a breakfast of coffee and pastry at a bakery in Jasper, I decided we would head to Banff National Park, approximately four hundred kilometres south of Jasper. From there we would travel into British Columbia. Travelling through the Canadian Rockies has always been one of my favourite things to do, especially by motorcycle. The mountain ranges, streams, and wildlife are all breathtakingly beautiful. Although it was now winter, and the coldest month of the year, the Rocky Mountains looked as majestic as they always had. I spoke to Princeton as I drove, pointing out to him all the wonderful things I wanted him to see. He sat up in the back of the cab, looking at whatever I pointed at and listening intently as I explained to him what I knew about it. It was a wonderful experience having him share in all the things I've always enjoyed but until then had experienced without him.

Our drive to Banff was much more relaxing than the previous night's drive. The snow had stopped, the sun was shining brightly, and it was a comfortable –10°C. We stopped every so often to stretch our legs and marvel at the scenery. Princeton was feeling great, completely rested from the day before, and loved exploring wherever we stopped to take a break. I was surprised he was doing so well, considering how much running around he'd done the night before. Eventually, we came upon the Columbia Icefield, the largest icefield in the Rocky Mountains. A visitor area stands on one side of the highway and the Athabasca Glacier on the other. Apparently, the glacier is always moving downward, travelling up to a few centimetres a day. Sadly, due to increasingly warm temperatures, the glacier has also lost much of its volume. I first saw it when I was around ten years old, and forty years later, it was not nearly as imposing. Nonetheless, I decided it was something Princeton should see.

Snow had been piled at both the entrance and the exit of the visitor centre, making it clear it was closed for the season. On the other side of the highway, the entrance to the glacier was blocked by a large gate, but it was obvious several vehicles had driven around it. Thinking Princeton probably needed to pee, and wanting him to see at least a little of the glacier, I drove around the gate too, stopping about forty feet past the entrance.

And another vehicle followed behind me.

Shit. My first thought was that I had probably been followed by a park official wanting to know what the hell I was doing. When I exited the truck, I was a little surprised to see that a minivan had pulled in behind us. And the people inside weren't that official looking. All five of them got out of the van, smiled, and cautiously walked toward me. One of the group introduced himself, saying he was a translator for the others, a group of tourists from China. They too wanted to see the glacier and, thinking I knew where I was going, had followed me around the gate.

So here we all were, the uninformed following the stupid. I explained to the translator that the glacier was likely closed for the winter and we probably shouldn't be where we were. After he translated what I had said, the tourists looked a little disappointed but started taking pictures of the glacier. The translator asked what I knew about it, and after I told him what little I knew, he translated the details back to his group. Everyone appeared satisfied with my limited knowledge and appreciative of my help, nodding at me as they continued taking photographs of the glacier. I returned to the truck and let out Princeton, who bounced up to the group, eager to introduce himself.

For about ten minutes the tourists directed questions about Princeton to their translator, he relaying them back to me in English. Of course the first thing they wanted to know was why he was missing a leg, and upon learning why, they asked about his chemotherapy sessions and other treatments. Finally, they wanted to know how old he was; everyone was visibly surprised when I told them. After that it became a photography session. Princeton by himself. Princeton and me together. Princeton with each of them. Princeton with them as a group. Princeton, me, and each of them. Lastly, I had the translator take a picture of me and Princeton with the glacier behind us. As we were all saying our goodbyes, one of the group went up to Princeton, placed a hand on his head, and performed some sort of blessing. After all of us shook hands, we returned to our vehicles and exited the way we'd come in.

I wouldn't be surprised if there's a magazine somewhere in China with a picture of Princeton inside it.

As we continued to Banff, I still hadn't figured out where we would be stopping for the night. I thought maybe we'd continue through the park a little longer and, just before reaching Lake Louise, a small hamlet, turn west and drive to the town of Golden. After stopping for the night, we would continue to Kelowna, where it would be relatively warm and, most importantly, without snow. However, I decided to drive to Lake Louise and continue on to another Fairmont property, the Chateau Lake Louise, for dinner. Afterwards we would backtrack slightly and drive to Golden.

15

A Pampered Pooch

HE CHATEAU LAKE LOUISE is a stately old hotel, surrounded by mountains and the Victoria Glacier. It also overlooks a stunning lake and is one of the most beautiful places I have ever seen. Whenever I am near Banff, I always make a point to stop by and visit, and this time I wanted to share the experience with Princeton.

I had never been to the chateau during the winter months, but as with Jasper Park Lodge, the snow and lights made it as lovely in the winter as I remembered it being during the summer. As I drove the winding road from Lake Louise up to the chateau, I told Princeton that we would not be staying there. We were only there for dinner and for a short walk around the property. When we arrived and parked, I attached him to his leash and let him out of the truck. First he wanted to visit the grounds beside the lake. Plenty of people were there, which meant an opportunity for plenty of introductions and friendly pats on the head. I was surprised by how busy it was, everyone enjoying ice skating, walking, or horse-drawn sleigh rides. A recently completed ice castle sat on the lake, and several ice sculptures dotted the shoreline. The entire thing reminded me of a picturesque winter wonderland, something you'd see on a Christmas card. Princeton was wildly excited, first dragging

Me and Princeton at Chateau Lake Louise, Alberta.
—Photograph by unknown

me to look at the ice sculptures before heading toward the lake. He dragged me down onto the ice, which naturally meant he ended up on his ass. Several skaters stopped and surrounded him, asking him if he was all right. Being smart, Princeton made it look as if he was having difficulty getting back up, as he obviously loved the attention everyone was lavishing upon him. Growing tired of watching him take advantage of everyone's good nature, I told him to get off his ass. It was time we went inside the hotel to get something to eat.

If Princeton loved the hotel grounds, he was completely euphoric about the interior. He entered before me, hopping through the front doors and making his way to the centre of the foyer. With its high ceilings, impressive architecture, and majestic chandelier overhead, the hotel was something special, and Princeton knew it. After making a few more friends, he continued to drag me along, going from one end of the hotel to the other. Thankfully, he didn't have much interest in exploring any floors other than the main one. He did, however, have an interest in the people dining in one of the restaurants. The main restaurant is situated across from several boutiques and shops and surrounded by a short barrier. Princeton insisted on walking the entire length of this barrier, stopping every few feet to sit down and stare at people enjoying their dinner. I'd apologize to the people Princeton was expecting to feed him and pull on his leash, only to have him sit down after a few feet and stare at someone else. After realizing no one was going to feed him, he decided to visit every shop and boutique on the main floor. He'd bounce to the entrance of each one and, understanding he wasn't allowed to enter, would stare intently at everyone inside before moving on to the next.

And then he saw the stairs.

Still in sensory overload, Princeton pulled me toward the stairs and promptly began to descend them. The stairs were marble, and he did quite well until he slipped on the last step and landed on the hard floor with a pronounced *oof*. This was followed by the horrified gasps of several guests who had watched the three-legged dog bounce down the stairs. Princeton quickly righted himself, looked around at the onlookers, and headed toward the pub located directly across from the stairs, where he was greeted and immediately pampered by two hostesses. I decided I'd had enough of Princeton's escapades. I was tired of being dragged around and apologizing for him. The pub was where we would get our dinner. And I wanted a drink. I asked the hostesses if Princeton could sit by the entrance while I went in and ordered us some takeout and had a drink at the bar. They agreed, and Princeton sat dutifully at the entrance and greeted the patrons. He had only been inside the hotel for about half an hour, but I'm sure nearly everyone staying or working there was now aware of him.

After our food was prepared, I thought it best that we eat it outside, away from all the distractions that were making Princeton so excited. We went back outside the hotel, found a bench, and ate our sandwiches.

"Well, I'm glad you had a good time, but it's time to get back on the road," I said as he finished his meal. "I know you'd love to stay here, but it's pretty expensive." Feeling a little guilty, I asked, "Wouldn't you rather we go somewhere warm? Where there's some grass? Where you can run without tumbling over?"

Princeton seemed to understand that we had to leave but was a little sad as I lifted him into the truck. As we pulled away from the hotel, I glanced behind me and saw him do something I had never seen before. Princeton, the dog who loved to travel and was always looking through the windshield or out the sides of the truck or van and wondering where we were off to next, was looking out the back window, watching the hotel disappear. As we drove down the road and toward the main highway, he continued looking at where we had come from.

As we headed to Golden, Princeton was noticeably quiet. I'm sure much of it was from being tired from all the adventures at

Chateau Lake Louise, but I also knew he was disappointed. Truthfully, I was a little disappointed too. Princeton was thrilled by the hotel, and I felt guilty for depriving him of it. When we reached Golden it had been dark for several hours and I didn't really feel like going any farther. After gassing up the truck, I turned to Princeton and said, "Fuck it." A few moments later we were back on the highway, headed to Lake Louise.

"Okay, Princeton, your job is to look cute. Same as yesterday. Be nice and don't bark. If anyone leans over the desk and smiles at you, smile back," I said as we pulled up in front of the Chateau Lake Louise for the second time that day.

We got out of the truck, and Princeton, much happier now, strode into the lobby and followed me up to the front desk. I asked if any rooms were available and what the rates were. I was prepared for expensive, but not *that* expensive. I mentioned that Princeton and I had stayed at Jasper Park Lodge the night before, and I wondered if the chateau could match their rate. The front desk clerk replied that it wasn't possible but countered with a somewhat better rate. Finally, after some good-hearted negotiation, and my admission that Princeton really wanted to stay at their hotel, we agreed to a price. Admittedly, I had already conceded we would be staying regardless of the rates; Princeton had seen to that. The clerk asked how many nights we planned on staying. When I looked down at Princeton, the look on his face told me we wouldn't be going any farther this trip; he had chosen where he would be spending his winter holiday. Looking up at the clerk I said, "At least three. Maybe more."

Our room was small but beautifully appointed and more than enough for me and Princeton. As with Jasper Park Lodge, they offered a sanitized doggy bed and bowls, both of which Princeton politely declined. After unpacking, we were off to find somewhere to grab a quick bite. It was now very late and the hotel restaurants were closed, but a delicatessen on the main floor was open twenty-four hours. It offered some tasty sandwiches and fresh pastries.

Princeton, realizing he wasn't allowed to enter any of the shops or restaurants, sat at the entrance while I chose some sandwiches for us. Before retiring to our room, we went outside for a quick walk so Princeton could look around a little more and have a pee.

We'd had a long day, and both of us fell asleep quickly after we ate our sandwiches and were in our beds. I had no idea what we would be doing tomorrow but was glad knowing we were some-place Princeton clearly wanted to be.

The next morning, after breakfast, he continued his inspection of the chateau. He dragged me toward and introduced himself to anyone who smiled at him, which was practically everyone. As always, there were plenty of inquiries about how old he was and how he'd lost his leg. Several other guests had dogs as well, but Princeton was clearly the outlier of the bunch. He was the rough-and-tumble farm dog, surrounded by perfectly groomed purebreds and tiny lapdogs who had probably never experienced a muddy paw. Princeton quickly grew tired of dogs like these. He was in-itially friendly with them and their owners but assumed a look of boredom if any of these dogs tried to socialize with him for any length of time. And if ever they became a little too friendly or yapped too much, Princeton would warn them with a snarl. He liked to be around dogs like himself, a little disobedient and rough around the edges.

After another visit to the lake, I decided we would drive into Banff to look around and get some lunch. Banff is a little resort town located within Banff National Park, about half an hour's drive from Lake Louise. I didn't know exactly what we would do there, but I was sure we could find something to entertain ourselves with. Soon Princeton and I were walking down the main street of Banff.

I was amazed at how busy the town was, especially considering it was the dead of winter. Most people were probably there for the skiing, but as I learned later, Banff offers numerous other winter activities. As Princeton and I walked down the sidewalk of the main street, people would give us a wide berth, wanting to give the three-legged, bouncing old dog as much room as they could so he could pass easily. Sometimes we would stop, allowing people the chance to give Princeton lots of friendly rubs and head scratches.

If I came across a particular shop or gallery I wanted to visit, I'd leave Princeton by the entrance before I went inside and asked if he was welcome. Although a few proprietors preferred he remain where he was, most had no problem with his coming inside. If the shop or gallery was crowded or had very expensive items, I'd have him remain just inside the doorway, but usually he followed me as I looked around.

One of the places we stopped and visited was an art gallery that promoted local artists. A number of prints and photographs were on display, many of them depicting local wildlife and locations within the park. I asked the manager if he knew where to do a little hiking and photography and was told to check out Tunnel Mountain, just outside town. I thought this would be a good place to spend the afternoon, and after ordering some grilled chicken and salad to go from a local bistro, Princeton and I were back in the truck to look for Tunnel Mountain.

The gallery manager had told me that the trail up the mountain was relatively easy, especially if we took the shortest route, starting in a parking area along Tunnel Mountain Drive. Apparently, at the summit you can see the entire town of Banff and much of the surrounding area. This would be an excellent way to spend the afternoon. As I parked the truck, I turned to Princeton and asked, "Ready for this? Ready for a hike up a mountain?" I'm not sure whether he knew what I was asking, but he was certainly aware we would be doing something.

After packing our lunch, water, and camera, we were off. Although the trail itself is only moderately difficult, we stopped often, as Princeton was having some difficulty walking toward the summit. I knew he must have been sore from all the exercise he'd had over

Princeton on Tunnel Mountain, Alberta.
—Photograph by author

the last few days, and the snow on the trail was making things even more difficult. His enthusiasm wasn't enough to overcome his physical limitations. It hadn't been that long ago that he was pulling himself up river embankments and hopping down country roads, but it was clear he no longer had the strength he'd had when he first lost his leg. I could tell he wanted to keep walking up the trail, pushing himself forward, but it was becoming increasingly difficult the farther he went. As I stood beside him while he looked longingly up the hill, I realized that as determined and tough as Princeton was, some things he could no longer do unless I helped him. Although a fire still burned brightly within him, nothing could change the fact that he was an old dog with a physical disability that made him work much harder than an able-bodied dog. It was truly a wonder he could still move around the way he could. I took Princeton's head in my hands, looked into his eyes, and asked him, "Had enough? It's fine if you have. I understand." He looked away from me and at the trail going up the mountain. I placed the knapsack around my neck, lifted Princeton in my arms, and started carrying him toward the summit.

And this was how it went. Sometimes I carried Princeton while he rested; other times he walked up the trail on his own. Carrying him made me that much more aware of how much harder Princeton had to work because of a missing leg. Soon we stopped to eat our lunch and take in the view. When it was time to continue, I tugged at Princeton's leash but he refused to move. I thought perhaps he wanted me to carry him, but when I lifted him up to my chest, he made it clear he wanted to remain on the ground. Concerned, I placed him where he'd been and asked him what was wrong. Princeton ignored me, his eyes locked on something off the trail and down the side of the mountain.

I don't know much about moose, but I could tell this little guy was just a baby. He slowly walked toward us, stopping about forty feet from Princeton, studied him briefly, and began grazing. After thinking he was incredibly cute (for a moose), I wondered where the hell Mama Moose was. I was confident Mom wouldn't want Baby so close to a dog and a person. Princeton didn't seem concerned at all and continued to look at the little fella. Eventually, Mom appeared about a hundred feet away and, after eyeing us suspiciously, started grazing too. After a few minutes the little guy moved to less than twenty feet from us, obviously interested in Princeton. Princeton remained relaxed, understanding this was an animal he wasn't to bark at or chase. The mountain was his home, and we were his guests.

For nearly twenty minutes Princeton and the baby moose remained a few feet from each other. Baby eventually came within fifteen feet of him, but neither he nor his mom appeared concerned about the woolly black dog. I sat down about fifteen feet behind Princeton, ready to scoop him up if Mom wandered over to us. Finally, Princeton decided it was time to say goodbye to his new friend so he and I could continue our journey up the mountain. He slowly raised himself on his three legs, looked at his new friend one last time, turned around, and began hopping up the trail.

I'll always remember when Princeton met his little friend on Tunnel Mountain. Had it been just me on that trail that afternoon, I never would have had the opportunity to see something so wonderful. It was because of Princeton that the little moose felt comfortable getting as close to us as he did.

Tired and sore, we made it as far as the trail would go. For us it was an accomplishment, our Everest moment. We had made it to the summit, an out-of-shape middle-aged man and a three-legged old dog battling cancer. As Princeton sat beside me, I stroked his head and told him how proud I was of him—not only for the climb to the summit, but also for everything he'd overcome the last few years.

Our walk had taken longer than I'd planned, and with little sunlight left, it was becoming quite chilly. It was time for us to get our asses off the mountain and back to the warmth and comfort of the chateau. Princeton had no trouble going downhill, quickly discovering that downhill momentum is a three-legged dog's best friend. A few times I went for a tumble as I held on to his leash as he ran down the hill. He'd turn to look at me each time as I got up and brushed myself off, wondering what the hell the problem was. He stopped where his moose friend had been, and after waiting to see if he would return, Princeton realized he had gone on his way. He continued hopping downhill to where we had parked. It was dark and I was exhausted, but Princeton had gotten his second wind and probably would have run all the way to Banff if I'd let him. Instead he had to be satisfied with a gulp of water before I placed him inside the truck for our drive back to Lake Louise.

When we arrived back at the chateau, we were ravenous. We went up to our room, and I ordered some grilled salmon, rice, and vegetables for both of us. After the day we'd had, I wanted nothing more than to have a good dinner and watch a little TV before bed. This was not to be. After Princeton ate his dinner, he was clearly up for more adventure. He was in a luxury hotel with *people*. He could *run around* on *carpet*. He had places and things to *see*. It was his winter vacation, and he wanted to do everything *now*. I wasn't even close to finishing my dinner and he was already sitting a few feet from the door of our suite, waiting for me to let him out. For a moment I thought about opening the door and letting him run around unaccompanied on our floor until he became someone else's problem. Quickly realizing this wasn't a good idea and would probably end our hotel stay prematurely, I ate the rest of my dinner and attached Princeton to his leash.

As late as it was, the chateau was still very busy. People were returning from skiing and other winter activities. Princeton thought it was his responsibility to greet these returning guests as they walked through the main entrance. I had no interest in this and, since no one seemed bothered by him, sat in one of the lobby's comfortable chairs and watched him as he sat on his behind a few feet from the door. People would walk through the doors, see him there, approach him, and ask him things like "What's your name?" or "Who do you belong to?" I heard the occasional "I saw you yesterday!"

Princeton would have been content to spend the entire night greeting his fellow guests, but I grew bored and wanted to find other things to do. Unfortunately, this meant his dragging me from one end of the hotel to the other, stopping only if someone wanted to approach him or he found something interesting. Most of the shops and boutiques were now closed, but he nonetheless found plenty of things to interest him: other dogs, children, skis, hotel staff, furniture, guest luggage, and anything that smelled intriguing. Basically the same things that had interested him yesterday and probably would tomorrow. By now I was exhausted and wanted only to go back to the room and watch TV, so I suggested to Princeton that maybe we should save some excitement for tomorrow. After I took him outside for a pee and a quick jaunt down to the lake to see the ice sculptures, we were back in our room.

The next couple of days we stayed around the chateau, eating a variety of foods and finding plenty of things to do. Princeton, quite disturbingly, was becoming accustomed to being pampered at a luxury hotel. Each day, he dined on fresh meats and vegetables, was welcomed almost anywhere inside the hotel, and thought it his duty to meet everyone as they walked through the lobby doors. Several people, including some staff, were calling him by name whenever they saw him. As happy as he was, all his recent walking was beginning to compound his arthritis. Not wanting him to get more sore, I decided it was time to get back to the farm.

One of the last conversations I had at the hotel was with a young couple who approached me and, after learning why Princeton had lost his leg, asked if I would I put him through the same experience again. They had seen him dragging me throughout the hotel the last couple of days but hadn't had a chance to speak to us. They went on to explain that they had a dog waiting for them at home and were agonizing over whether or not to have his leg amputated as their veterinarian had suggested. It wasn't due to cancer but a previous injury that hadn't healed correctly and was now causing chronic pain. Their veterinarian had explained that their dog might experience some unwanted side effects and require rehabilitation therapy but would soon adapt to being a three-legged dog.

As Princeton sat beside me, I carefully explained his experiences post-surgery and what they could expect. Did I have any regrets? Absolutely not. Princeton was my best friend and deserved everything I could offer him, and considering how well he moved around with three legs, I knew he didn't have any regrets either. The couple thanked me for our time, the woman bending down and giving Princeton a kiss on his head. As they walked away I felt confident their dog would have the surgery and live the remainder of his life without any pain. I'd like to think Princeton was responsible for that.

Princeton and me at Sign Post Forest. Poseidon's hubcap is affixed to the post behind, several feet above our heads.

—Photograph by unknown

While visiting Tunnel Mountain, Princeton's new friend,
a baby moose, calmly grazes a few feet away from him.
—Photograph by author

This photograph was taken at Horsethief Canyon, a few kilometres
from Drumheller, Alberta. It was the first photograph taken
of our travels together. The years that followed would lead
to many other destinations and many more photographs.
—Photograph by author

Princeton was always very protective of his friend Barnie. Here he carefully
watches the goat to make sure she doesn't do her any harm.
—Photograph by author

Princeton was always very happy when we travelled together.
He's seen here on the dock in Ucluelet, Vancouver Island.
Behind him is the Ucluelet Aquarium.
—Photograph by author

As Princeton aged and faced mobility issues, he still fought to remain
active and fulfill his farm responsibilities. There were times he had
to ride in his John Deere Gator, but would proudly
sit up straight and survey all that was his.
—Photograph by author

Many times during our adventures, Princeton and I passed through Jasper, Alberta. We would always take the time to walk through town, he being the focus of all the tourists.
—Photograph by unknown

This photograph was taken at a motorcycle rally at Toad Rock Campground, British Columbia, and later appeared in a German magazine. Princeton sits between me and our new friend Anja, who at the time was riding her bike across Canada.
—Photograph by Tim Yip

The Chateau Lake Louise was Princeton's favourite winter destination. Pampered each time he visited, he also spent hours exploring both inside and outside the hotel. During the winter the lake freezes over, allowing visitors and guests to walk on its frozen surface.
—Photograph by author

This is the last photo taken of Poseidon and Princeton together.
It was taken on the last day of our last trip.
—Photograph by author

I don't think anything needs to be said about this photograph.
—Photograph by Cam Shaw

The afternoon sun on our backs and the Pacific Ocean at our feet.
—Photograph by Cam Shaw

16

The Prize

THE FIRST TIME Princeton and I met Dr. Fowler was in the spring of 2014. Dr. Fowler is a well-respected surgeon who was the proprietor of Guardian Veterinary Centre for emergency and specialty care. Outside of emergency care, animals admitted to Guardian must be referred by another veterinarian for advanced diagnostic services and specialized treatments. Princeton was referred by Dr. Marshall, who during a routine examination found a lump on his left thigh. Finding a lump on any pet is always a worry, but finding one on an animal who has recently overcome a deadly form of cancer is especially worrisome. Because the lump was rather soft and appeared unconnected to bone, Dr. Marshall didn't think it had anything to do with Princeton's osteosarcoma, but she wanted Dr. Fowler to examine the mass and remove it if necessary.

I'll always remember the first words Dr. Fowler said to Princeton as he entered the examination room: "Princeton! You win a prize!" Although I thought I already knew what the prize was, I still asked Dr. Fowler what he meant. He explained that it was extremely rare to see a dog nearly three years post-osteosarcoma. And one who hadn't experienced any metastasis was nearly unheard of. Dr. Fowler had a wonderful manner toward Princeton, calling him "sweetheart" as he gently examined him and palpated the area where the lump was. Princeton, enjoying Dr. Fowler's gentle touches and soothing words, liked him immediately.

The doctor gave Princeton a full physical examination and recommended a biopsy be performed immediately. This would be done by fine needle aspiration. A very fine needle would be inserted into the lump, a sample collected, and its contents placed on a slide and sent away for analysis. Although Princeton was the one with a lump and was having a biopsy performed, I was the one feeling panicked. Once again he had an unexplained lump, and the experiences of his osteosarcoma and subsequent treatments were still very much with me. Princeton had certainly beaten the odds and proven himself a survivor, but I knew that cancer plays by its own rules, often reappearing suddenly and more aggressively than before. Preparing for the worst but hoping for the best, I watched Dr. Fowler insert the needle into the mass, obtain a sample, and transfer its contents onto several slides. Smiling, he said that there was nothing to worry about.

Fat. Your basic, run-of-the-mill body fat. Or more precisely, adipose tissue. Or if you prefer the more traditional medical terminology, a benign lipoma. Dr. Fowler was sure that's what it was once he had finished the slides. Princeton, meanwhile, lay on the floor of the examination room, looking at me and probably assuming there was nothing to worry about. He was, after all, Princeton—a dog capable of overcoming anything.

Dr. Fowler again remarked on how tremendous it was to see a dog overcome a typically life-ending disease. He escorted us out of the examination room and to the reception area, telling the receptionist there wouldn't be any charge for the visit. I now found myself liking him as much as Princeton had. As Princeton walked out the door, I'm sure he was wondering what had happened to the prize Dr. Fowler had told him he'd won.

Once we were in the truck, I explained to Princeton that he had already received his prize. Many times over. I don't know if he was satisfied with my explanation, but the two hot dogs he had at Des's cart after his appointment more than made up for any disappointment he may have felt earlier.

17

Tranquil Tofino

THE SUMMER OF 2014 would be our trip out to Vancouver Island. Once there we'd tour around for a few days before driving to Tofino, a small district on the west coast of the island. I had leased out my farm production for a cycle, allowing us to travel for most of the summer. So on a June afternoon we started out, making it as far as Jasper the first night. I'm not sure if Princeton was expecting to be staying at the Jasper Park Lodge again, especially since we'd taken a drive up to the hotel once we reached Jasper, but he seemed content to spend the night in Poseidon in a campground a few kilometres from town. For much of this trip, Princeton would be wearing a specialty harness except when sleeping in the van. His arthritis was progressing, and although he didn't seem to be in much pain, the harness allowed me to hold up his hindquarters if he needed a little help.

We travelled into British Columbia from Alberta the next morning, taking a route I had travelled by motorcycle a number of years earlier and really enjoyed. We would continue travelling on Highway 16, heading toward Prince George. From there we would travel on Highway 97, passing through Quesnel and Williams Lake, eventually taking Highway 99 toward Whistler and then Vancouver. It wasn't the most direct route to Vancouver Island, but since we had several weeks, Princeton and I weren't in a hurry to get anywhere.

Although I had taken this trip before, travelling with Princeton in the van made it feel like a new experience. As usual, if I saw something I knew he'd appreciate seeing, I would tell him about it and point it out to him. He'd raise himself from his bed and peer out the window as we drove by. Sometimes we'd stop and I'd attach his leash, and Princeton would bound from the van to investigate whatever I had drawn his attention to. By now he was completely used to travelling, and I would let him take as long as he wanted when he wanted to check something out. Sometimes he'd return to the van within a few minutes, while other times he wouldn't want to go back to it for half an hour or so. Princeton understood that Poseidon was a second home, but if we weren't in a campground and it was still daylight, he knew there would be more things to see and experience.

The first day we were in British Columbia there had been plenty of things for Princeton to stop and see; we'd travelled only a few hundred kilometres before evening came and we had to find a place to camp. The following day was much the same, with frequent stops so Princeton could explore to his heart's content. That night we made it to the town of Whistler, about two hours away from Vancouver and the ferry I had chosen to take us to Vancouver Island. Whistler is recognized for its skiing and snowboarding facilities, and was a venue of the 2010 Vancouver Winter Olympics. What I remember most about Whistler, however, was that it cost nearly a hundred dollars just to camp for the night. It is known as an expensive place to visit, but I was still surprised that a little plot of gravel to park Poseidon for the night would cost so much.

The next morning after Princeton did his usual meet-the-neighbours routine, we were off to the ferry terminal. The ferry ride from Horseshoe Bay to Nanaimo on Vancouver Island is just over an hour and a half, and I hoped to arrive sometime in the early afternoon. Except for a couple of river crossings, this was Princeton's first time on a large ferry. I was aware that I wouldn't be able to take him to any of the observation decks but was curious how he'd behave on a large ship. Shortly after parking on one of the ferry's many decks, I heard the ship's whistle blow and we began our journey across the strait. A few minutes later I locked Princeton inside the van and headed toward a restaurant on one of the observation decks to get us some lunch.

Once there I asked a steward if there was any place I could take my dog on the ferry. He said it was okay to take him, on leash, to any of the lower decks where the vehicles were parked. I picked up a couple of cheeseburgers for our lunch before heading back down to the van to let Princeton know that he wouldn't have to remain in the van for the entire crossing.

If you've ever been on a large commercial ferry, I'm sure you're aware of the constant vibrations reverberating through the ship. When I placed Princeton on the steel floor of the deck, I could tell he was a little unsure. It's not that he was frightened, but he was obviously puzzled by the constant vibration. With some hesitation, he started moving among the parked vehicles, making his way toward the front of the ship. We could only go so far, as there was a barrier about thirty feet from the bow. Still, Princeton had a clear view of the ocean in front of him.

He was in awe of what he saw. Of what he smelled. Of the ocean breeze as it passed over him. Once he made it to the barrier, he didn't want to go anywhere else. He sat down and stared intently ahead. The look on his face was one of wonderment. I let go of his leash and sat down beside him, the two of us staring out over the ocean and eventually the land coming toward us. Except when they quickly acknowledged a few fellow passengers walking by us and saying hello, Princeton's eyes rarely deviated from what lay in front of him. For the rest of the trip he continued staring out over the water, even when I left him alone as I got up to stretch my legs. Only when the ship's whistle blew and the announcement was made for all passengers to return to their vehicles did Princeton move from his spot. Realizing how much he enjoyed the ferry ride to the island, I promised him I would find a way to take him for another boat ride when we were in Tofino.

I had made arrangements to meet an old university buddy on Vancouver Island. It had been several years since I had last seen Gerrit, who had moved to the island several years before. He and his wife had purchased a home in Victoria, a large city on the southernmost tip of Vancouver Island, and they invited me and Princeton to stay with them for a few days. But Princeton and I would travel to Tofino before taking Gerrit up on his offer. I had been to Tofino a few years before and hoped Princeton would like its sandy beaches and spectacular scenery. I knew he hadn't entirely loved his last visit to the ocean, but I hoped Tofino would be much more enjoyable. It was mid-afternoon when the ferry arrived in Nanaimo, a city and ferry port on the eastern side of Vancouver Island, and I thought it best that we find a campground to stay at for the night and drive to Tofino the next morning.

The drive to Tofino from Nanaimo isn't really all that far, only about two hundred kilometres, and I've always thought the most scenic attraction along the route is a place called Cathedral Grove, located within MacMillan Provincial Park and known for its giant Douglas firs and ancient western red cedars. Cathedral Grove consists of trails on each side of the highway where visitors can experience either the giant Douglas firs on the south side of the highway or the ancient western red cedars on the north side. Some of the fir trees are up to eight hundred years old and more than nine metres in circumference.

Princeton loved it. As I opened the van door and attached his leash, he clearly thought this was something he shouldn't miss. Cathedral Grove has a scent like no other, and I think it's what interested him most of all. It's an earthy, foresty smell that I suppose appeals to dogs. Princeton jumped onto the ground, sniffed his way around the van, and headed for the trail entrance. We had parked on the north side of the highway, so we would be visiting the huge western red cedars. The trail is one big loop and probably takes a half hour or so to complete. This is, of course, without a dog who insists on stopping every few feet to smell something or stare intently at a bug or some sort of vegetation he considers mesmerizing. Half an hour later, instead of having completed the trail, we could still see Poseidon. Princeton would bounce down the trail, dragging me along as I held on to his leash, stop suddenly to sniff at something, move a few feet to smell something else, turn around and go back to where he was earlier to make a comparison, turn around again, and continue down the trail. After an hour we were only about halfway through, and I was becoming bored. I then made the mistake of doing something that would add about another half hour to our walk.

Throughout the trail several trees, for whatever reason, have been cut down. The stumps left behind are usually several feet high and across. On one of these stumps I decided to place Princeton to get a picture of him. He looked very regal sitting on his stump, and I was sure some of the pictures would turn out well. Just before I was about to lift him down from the stump, a group of tourists came up and started snapping pictures of him. So I wasn't the only one who thought Princeton sitting on a stump four feet off the ground, surrounded by ancient red cedars, made for a terrific picture. Soon other people arrived and started taking pictures. A few of them asked the usual questions about his age and missing leg. So for the next half hour or so, I told the story of Princeton several times over and answered questions about him while he was being photographed. Several people climbed onto the stump with him to have their picture taken. Others gathered around him to talk to him and stroke his fur. Thinking back on it now, I realize it must have looked a little weird—an old dog sitting on an immense tree stump surrounded by people. Those who left and continued along the trail were replaced by others. Princeton was savouring all the attention.

Princeton on his stump at Cathedral Grove, Vancouver Island.
—Photograph by author

For all I knew, he thought of himself as a doggy deity surrounded by his adoring subjects. Finally, there came a moment when I could lift Princeton the supermodel down from his stump and we could continue on our way.

The last half of the trail was much like the first, with Princeton dragging me as he continued smelling and looking at everything. Another half hour had passed since the tree stump episode, and we finally made it back to where we had started. Apparently, this wasn't good enough, as Princeton turned around and headed back in the direction we had just come from, intent on walking the trail again. And of course I let him. This time we moved a little quicker, probably because I wouldn't let him investigate every damn thing he came across. When we came to the stump where he had begun his modelling career, I made sure we kept moving. Eventually, we made it back to the entrance, and I quickly led him back to the van. After I placed him inside and filled his water bowl, I told him that we would *not* be doing that again.

It was late afternoon when we finally made it to Tofino. I was tired from both the drive and Princeton's romp around Cathedral Grove and started looking for a campground. There is a provincial campground a few kilometres from Tofino, Green Point Campground, but it was full. I learned from the attendant at the gatehouse that it fills up months in advance from reservations. She mentioned that there were a couple of private campgrounds in the area, but they usually filled up quickly, especially this late in the day. I looked behind me and told Princeton that it was all his fault. If we had arrived in Tofino a little sooner, maybe we would have a place to camp. If he was feeling remorseful, he didn't show it. I was tired, hungry, and dealing with a dog still in sensory overload from his Cathedral Grove adventure. I decided to travel into Tofino in the hope we would luck into something.

The district of Tofino is truly a gorgeous place. Fewer than two thousand people live there full time, but the number of tourists who visit the area each year is phenomenal. The beaches are probably the best in Canada, with plenty of opportunities for sightseeing and hiking. Often these visitors have difficulty finding camping spaces or other accommodations. And because Tofino doesn't allow franchises of any sort, you can't park an RV for a few hours in the parking lot of a Tim Hortons, McDonald's, or that mainstay of the urban RVer, Walmart. In fact, signs all over the place indicate that overnight parking of any kind is prohibited except in authorized areas. Princeton and I were in arguably one of the most beautiful places in North America, but we didn't have a place to camp.

Deflated, we left Tofino, hoping to find a campground near Ucluelet, a municipality about forty kilometres away. I stopped at Green Point Campground again to ask the attendant I had spoken with earlier if she could recommend something in or near Ucluelet. As I drove up to the window, she said with a friendly smile, "We just had a cancellation! Do ya want it?"

"Absolutely," I replied.

As she assigned a camping spot, I inquired how often cancellations occur. She told me that although they happen infrequently, they aren't unheard of. She also mentioned that although people make reservations online, travellers who arrive in person can take them if they become available. Princeton and I were lucky enough to be there when a cancellation occurred. I turned to him and apologized for telling him earlier that because of him we wouldn't have a place to stay, but he didn't seem to care one way or the other.

Before we left to find our camping stall, the attendant also let me in on a little tip: if I wanted to stay for any additional nights, I should show up at the gatehouse when it opened in the morning and ask if there were any no-shows from the night before, as sometimes people who make reservations don't show up. Most often, they fail to cancel their reservations or even try to get their deposits back. If the party who made the reservation hasn't shown up for two consecutive nights and hasn't cancelled the reservation, any remaining days can be assigned to someone else before they're placed back into the reservation pool. Since reservations at Green Point are usually made for multiple nights, someone else often has a chance to get the spot for at least a night. Even though it was paid for by the person who made the reservation, it still has to be paid for again if assigned to someone else. A small price to pay.

So I followed her advice. Each morning I'd be at the gatehouse when it opened. I'd ask if anyone who had made a multiple-night reservation hadn't shown up the last couple of nights. There was always someone who'd failed to show, and I'd be assigned whatever was left of their reservation. Most times this was only for a night, but it was never a worry because there would be someone else who hadn't shown up when I asked the next morning. As long as I was there, first in line, with my nose pressed against the glass of the gatehouse when the attendant arrived, Princeton and I always had a place to stay. We also got a change of scenery almost every night as we moved from one stall to another. A couple of times we managed to get one of the prime spots, the ones overlooking the ocean. Listening to the ocean crash against the rocks while you're curled up in your sleeping bag with your dog sleeping beside you after a wonderful day on the beach is too perfect to describe.

Green Point Campground is one of the best campgrounds I have ever stayed in. Most of the camping spots are surrounded by very tall trees, offering lots of shade and privacy. After we had set up camp that first night and eaten dinner, Princeton, still a little wound up from his visit to Cathedral Grove, insisted on dragging me around to visit our neighbours. After that he felt it necessary to inspect the recycling and washroom facilities. Satisfied that both our neighbours and the amenities were to his liking, he let me take him back to the van. He may not have been tired, but I was exhausted and wanted to turn in. Lying in my sleeping bag with Princeton sleeping beside me, I thought about what we would do the next day. It turned out we would do a lot.

Princeton's first time at Incinerator Rock, Vancouver Island.
—Photograph by author

The next morning we began the short drive into Tofino but never quite made it. Instead we ended up at Incinerator Rock, a beach located on the northern end of Long Beach. Incinerator Rock may have an odd name, but how it got its name is actually quite pedestrian: at one time an actual incinerator was there. During World War II the Canadian Army and Royal Canadian Air Force had a base nearby, and all the trash from the airbase and nearby camps was burned at the beach. Nothing remains of the incinerator now, but that part of Long Beach has been known as Incinerator Rock ever since. It's a favourite of surfers and swimmers, as well as those simply wanting to walk along the beach and look at the beautiful scenery.

It was there that Princeton discovered how intoxicating the ocean could be. Unlike the first ocean beach he had been on, just outside Vancouver a year earlier, Incinerator Rock interested him. After parking in a small lot adjacent to the beach, I attached his leash and carried him onto the sand. He looked at the ocean, sniffing the air as the water rushed toward us. He got up and started walking toward the waves. We walked into the water and stopped, Princeton looking down as the waves came up to him and then receded. We walked farther into the water, stopping when another wave rushed toward us and surrounded us. We did this several more times until the waves were nearly up to Princeton's chest. Deciding this was maybe a little too far, he turned around and hopped back a few feet until the waves just reached his paws. Princeton looked down the beach for a few moments and started to run along the water's edge. Pulling on his leash, he ran beside the waves, seeming to understand that the sand was a little harder there and easier for him to run on. After a couple hundred yards, we stopped, not because he wanted to but because I was having trouble keeping up with him. I then did something I knew wasn't allowed but seemed appropriate at the time. I removed his leash and said, "Run."

Princeton, now by himself, ran along the water's edge for another couple hundred yards before coming to a stop. He plopped himself on his ass, turned to face me, and waited for me to catch up. Just before I reached him, he lifted himself up and started running again. He ignored the swimmers and surfers coming out of the water. He ran past people walking along the beach. He ran around other dogs (all attached to their leashes). He was no longer a sixteen-year-old dog with three legs but a young dog again, oblivious to old age and its diseases and aches and pains.

I only caught up to him when he stopped to look at something out in the ocean. As I sat beside him I asked, "Had enough yet?" Princeton ignored me and continued looking at the water. He had the same look of contentment he'd had when we sat at the bow of the ferry coming over to the island. Princeton, ever the intelligent and thoughtful dog, probably wondered what lay beyond.

During the two trips we spent on the beaches of Tofino, Princeton never wore a leash again. It's marked all along Long Beach that all dogs must be on a leash, but no one ever complained about his not having one. Even the people assigned to patrol the beaches never said anything about it. I don't know if it was because people felt sorry for him, an elderly three-legged dog hopping along by the waves, or because they were smitten with his enthusiasm for being on the beach. He never bothered anyone, even when I left him behind on the shore and went into the water without him. As always, lots of people would come up to him and give him a friendly pat, but he'd always remain in the same place if I wanted to swim in the ocean. As long as he could see me, he was content.

We spent the entire day at Incinerator Rock. We'd either walk or run beside the ocean or sit down on the sand and watch the waves. When the day began to draw to a close, we sat against a large log that had washed up onto the beach and watched the sky dim around us. We must have walked (or run) several kilometres that day, but surprisingly neither one of us felt tired. It was close to 9:00

p.m. when we said goodbye to the few remaining surfers on the beach and headed back to the campground.

The next morning, after another stop at Incinerator Rock for a few hours, Princeton and I made our way into Tofino. Although Tofino's economy depends largely on tourists, it still manages to have a laid-back vibe to it. Most of the businesses support each other, using products and items that are locally produced. As mentioned earlier, you won't see anything like a Starbucks or McDonald's. Nor will you find big box stores like Home Depot or car dealerships. Instead you will find privately owned businesses independent of the franchises often seen elsewhere. These businesses depend on the large influx of tourists, and most aren't under the control or influence of a large corporate entity.

One such place is Chocolate Tofino, located on the outskirts of town. Chocolate Tofino offers outstanding homemade chocolates and gelato, and it was the first place Princeton and I visited in town. It's also where I first met Kim, and later on her husband, Cam, the proprietors. It was one of those rare moments when you meet someone and immediately like them and a friendship quickly follows. My friendship with Kim and Cam continues to this day, and both were instrumental in creating some of the wonderful memories I have of first visiting Tofino with Princeton.

I met Kim when I went into her store to order two gelatos—one for me and one for Princeton. I don't remember how I ended up speaking to her about wanting to take Princeton on a boat ride, but she recommended a small charter that would probably take us for a tour of the area. I hadn't forgotten my promise to Princeton of taking him on a boat ride once we arrived in Tofino, and I hoped to find someone open to giving us a private tour. Kim recommended Clayoquot Connections Tours and thought the owner, Dennis, could probably set us up with something.

I found Clayoquot Connections easily enough, but there was no Dennis. I assumed he was probably out on a tour. I managed to get

As promised, Princeton had a personal tour of the
waters around Tofino, Vancouver Island.
—Photograph by author

his cellular number from a business located next to his and gave him a call.

"Hi," I said. "I understand you give boat tours around the area."

"Yes, I do," replied Dennis.

"I'm looking for someone to take me and my dog around the area. Show us the sights. A private tour if possible."

"Just you and your dog?"

Sensing there was a problem, I repeated it was for me and my dog.

"I need to take a minimum number of people out each time. Taking out one person and a dog at one time doesn't generate enough revenue," he replied.

Although I had yet to actually meet Dennis and our conversation had been brief, I felt comfortable with him. I asked him the minimum number of people required to make it worth his while.

After he told me, I asked, "How about if instead of paying for just me and my dog, I pay whatever you want to make the trip worthwhile for you? And a little extra so we can have a personalized tour. I have a dog who finds lots of things interesting."

Dennis thought about this for a few moments, laughed, and agreed. He would take us out that evening, after his last tour was completed.

When we met later that day, Dennis was just as I was expecting —a kind-hearted, weathered old sailor type. He even lived on a sailboat in the marina where he kept his charter vessels. Best of all, he loved Princeton. Dennis had recently lost his own dog, and it was obvious that Princeton helped fill, if briefly, the void left behind. For the next two hours, Dennis steered his boat through the waters around Tofino, often with one hand on the wheel and the other on Princeton's head, the two of them together at the stern. Throughout the tour Princeton moved from one side of the boat to the other, thoughtfully looking at whatever Dennis pointed out to us.

Dennis showed us many of the small islands and told of their remarkable histories, including their significance to the many

Indigenous peoples who have occupied the area for generations. He pointed out specific water passages and how the currents behaved within them. We talked about his boat and his travels to Asia during the off season. Princeton enjoyed the tour, often sniffing the ocean air and staring at the seabirds circling us. Dennis really went out of his way to make sure we had a good time. When we finally arrived back at the marina, I think he felt a little disappointed the tour was over. Once we were all on the dock, he showed us the houseboat where Cam and Kim lived, their little dog Moku waiting impatiently by the gate for their return from work. Dennis then offered the use of the marina to park the van if we ever returned to Tofino and needed a place to camp.

As Princeton and I walked to the van, I thought, and still think today, that maybe Tofino wasn't a place I'd plan to visit regularly. Instead, someday I'd live there.

Once back at the campground, Princeton insisted on his usual meet-and-greet with our fellow campers. If he was lucky, people would offer him a hot dog or some other tasty treat. Princeton, not wanting to be rude, always accepted whatever was offered him — except for marshmallows. Those were still gross. After walking nearly the entire loop of the campground, we ended up at the entrance. That was where we first met Troy.

Troy is best described as the quintessential surfer dude. Single and with a young son, he does maintenance work at one of the local resorts during the day and sells firewood and snacks during the evening at a little store located just inside the campground. When he isn't working he's either hanging out with his son or surfing. Princeton not only liked Troy, but also took it upon himself to be the guardian of the firewood. Whenever a camper needed firewood, they first paid Troy and then had to step over Princeton to get their bundle of wood. Most people would walk up to him, pat him on the head, and ask, "Who do you belong to?" I don't know if Princeton was really guarding the woodpile or he thought it was the best place to receive some attention. Whatever his reason, that was where we spent most of our evenings—he lying in front of the woodpile, greeting everyone, and I talking with Troy.

The following morning we were back at, well … I'm sure you know by now. The longer we hung around Incinerator Rock, the more we seemed associated with the surfer crowd. The parking lot of the beach was usually full of an odd assortment of vans, little pickup trucks, and SUVs with numerous decals affixed to them proclaiming where the owners had travelled and their preferred surfing gear. Some of the same vehicles were parked there day after day. As Princeton and I pulled into the parking lot and found a spot, someone yelled in our direction.

"Dude!" a passenger in a van a few stalls over yelled out. "Way to rep it hard!"

I'm being serious. This is exactly what he said.

Huh? I thought as I got out of the van and looked around. I had no idea who he was talking to or what he was talking about.

"Way to rep it hard!" he said again. "The van!"

Realizing I had no idea what was going on, he got out of the van with another passenger, walked over to me, and explained that he was only admiring my van. He and his friends had seen it the previous couple of days parked at the beach, and everyone was impressed with how nice it was. He explained further that vans were something most everyone surfing or hanging around the beaches took an interest in. As Cam said, they were "the perfect Tofino starter home." Old camper vans were especially admired, and Poseidon definitely stood out. It was old, almost twenty-five years then, but cherry. Since Princeton and I had started travelling in Poseidon, it had always received numerous looks and compliments, but in Tofino it was especially admired. As much as it stood out against the usual Volkswagen Westfalias and the rest of the camper vans, some of the attraction surely had to do with the three-legged old dog who lived in it. Whatever the reason, Poseidon was quickly becoming part of the Incinerator Rock landscape.

My new friends spent several minutes checking out Poseidon. Princeton, anxious to hit the beach, jumped down from the van and hopped from the parking lot onto the beach. After waiting patiently for me for a few minutes and realizing I probably wasn't coming soon, he made his way down to the water and started to run along the shoreline.

During the days that followed, Princeton and I were always welcomed by the surfers and swimmers who pulled their rigs into the Incinerator Rock parking lot when the gates opened each morning. Princeton was, of course, popular with everyone. He'd made several new friends, and each of them would spend a little time with him. He'd often sit for a few minutes watching people as they either swam or rode the waves. Other times we'd walk along the shoreline for hours, stopping only for Princeton to rest. Although I was always concerned he was being too active, the long walks didn't seem to bother him. Sometimes we went back to the van to rest, but after Princeton slept for an hour or so, he'd sit up and stare at the door, wanting to be let out so he could get back on the beach. Wanting to remember as much of this as I could was how I came to know Cam.

Having spoken to Kim several times while getting gelato (Princeton had decided he liked it and I was now treating him to it daily), I phoned her and asked if she could recommend any professional photographers in the area. I wanted someone to follow me and Princeton for an hour or two while we walked along Long Beach. Someone who would capture forever the special moments Princeton and I shared. Kim, as helpful as ever, got back to me within the hour with some recommendations. There were three photographers she thought would do a good job, but when I contacted each of them, none of them were available. Kim phoned me later to ask how it had worked out, and I had to explain that two of the people she recommended were out of town and the third was unable. After listening she said, "I think Cam could do it."

Cam and Kim had first visited Tofino several years earlier, and as many people do, they fell in love with it. At the time they lived in Saskatchewan, comfortable in their chosen careers. After visiting Tofino, however, they realized they would be happiest if they could both live and work there. Chocolate Tofino was an existing business and had come up for sale. Possessing the gumption most others lack, they decided to take a chance and buy the business. They lived in their Volkswagen Westfalia for nine weeks before moving onto their houseboat. And they've never looked back. After suggesting that maybe Cam could be our photographer, Kim mentioned that he had been a graphic designer. And he had some really cool camera equipment.

After Kim and I spoke, she gave Cam a call (it was his day off, and he was surfing at Incinerator Rock) and explained what I was looking for. He agreed to help me, and after we spoke briefly on his cellphone he went back home to change and retrieve his camera and equipment. The plan was that I would meet him later at Incinerator Rock, and he would follow me and Princeton around for a couple of hours and take pictures of us.

It was early evening when I arrived at the Incinerator Rock parking lot to meet Cam.

"Are you Cam?" I asked as I walked toward someone matching the description Kim had given me.

"Yep," he replied. "And you must be Terry. And this handsome boy must be Princeton."

We shook hands, and after thanking him once more for agreeing to act as our photographer, I asked what he wanted me and Princeton to do.

"Just do whatever you've been doing," Cam replied. "Walk along the beach, in the water, rest ... it doesn't matter. I'll either be close by or off in the distance. Try to forget I'm even here."

Me, Cam, and Princeton at Incinerator Rock, Vancouver Island.
—Photograph by unknown

So that's what we did. For nearly two hours Princeton and I walked along Long Beach. Sometimes we'd walk along the waves; other times we'd stop and rest. Sometimes I'd walk alone, as Princeton would be off on his own, but for the most part we were together, doing the things that had made us so very happy the last few days. It was difficult at first, trying to ignore that we were being constantly photographed, especially when we could hear the click of Cam's shutter amid the sounds of the waves and people's shouts. But we soon learned to be ourselves.

On one occasion Cam wanted us in a particular location: atop a small bluff, about fifteen yards above the shoreline. He thought Princeton and me sitting together and looking out at the ocean would make a wonderful picture. I had to carry Princeton up the bluff, where we sat together as Cam took several photographs. Afterwards, while I carried Princeton back down to the beach, Cam took a picture that will always remain one of my favourites: a silhouette of me and Princeton as I carried him down the hill, the sun behind us and far in the west, getting ready to set over the ocean. Cam didn't plan for this shot; on a whim he placed his camera by his feet, aiming it and snapping the shutter. I've always felt that particular photograph represented the love Princeton and I had for each other and the bond we shared, especially at that point in our lives. Princeton, now needing help from time to time, trusted me to give it to him, and there was nothing I wouldn't do for him. But as strong as that bond was, the day would come when the sun would no longer shine down on us together. I knew, however, there was still enough sunlight in the sky for us to be together a little while longer.

Cam took over three hundred photographs that day. He wanted to go through each of them and choose which ones were the best. We agreed to meet the next afternoon at Chocolate Tofino, where Cam would give me a disc that contained all the photographs he had taken.

Both Princeton and I were tired when we headed back to the

campground, but I was really pleased I had found someone to take photographs of us together. I was even more pleased knowing that Cam understood the relationship Princeton and I shared, and that the pictures he'd taken captured our feelings toward each other. Overall it had been a great day. It wouldn't be a great evening.

After we had our dinner, I decided to bring some bottles to the recycling bin located in another part of the campground. After that I planned to walk up to the store and visit with Troy for a while. Princeton was feeling bushed, and I thought he would like nothing better than to rest on his bed for the evening. Before closing the van door, I kissed him on the head and told him to be a *good dog* while I was away. He wasn't.

When I returned about an hour later and slid open the door to the van, I expected Princeton to be dozing away on his bed. Instead he was sitting up with a satisfied grin. He also looked … different. He looked … brown. Not all brown, but there was a definite brown tinge on his muzzle and patches of brown on his bed. He also looked extremely pleased with himself, a definite look of "Look what I did!" on his face. My eyes fell to the mangled little white packets scattered on the floor of the van. I picked one up to study it and, realizing what it was, said the first thing that came to mind: "So this is how it ends, huh, Princeton? All those battles, all that money, only to be done in by this."

While I was away Princeton had decided to see what I had hidden away in the cupboards. One of the things I had packed (and forgotten about) was a box of hot chocolate mix. Thinking this was probably good stuff (why else would Dad lock it away in the cabinet?), he had decided to chew away at the little packets to get at the yummy stuff inside. All eight of them. Seeing them scattered around the van and the satisfied look on Princeton's face, I was more pissed off than concerned. But then I became concerned, remembering that dogs aren't supposed to eat chocolate. And then I panicked, remembering that dogs sometimes die from eating chocolate.

Princeton had yet to be concerned, his expression telling me he had no regrets about what he had just done.

As beautiful a place as Tofino is, its cellular service sucks. It can best be described as spotty, sometimes working in town or various places on the beach. One of the places it definitely didn't work was in Green Point Campground. I already knew this as I ran around the campground, holding my phone to the sky and hoping for an elusive "bar." Of course none appeared. The only option was to leave the campsite and drive to somewhere I knew would have at least some cellular service. A few minutes later we were roaring past the gatehouse and onto the highway. A few minutes after that, I pulled into a spot where I knew my phone had worked before. It was late in the evening, and I was unable to get a hold of any of Princeton's regular veterinarians. I phoned the emergency clinic in Edmonton, knowing it was open twenty-four hours, but was placed on hold. I told the receptionist that I would phone back in a few minutes. Wondering what to do next, I googled "chocolate and dogs."

I discovered that (big surprise) dogs shouldn't eat chocolate. I also discovered that the level of toxicity is dependent on the amount of chocolate ingested and the size of the dog. The type of chocolate also makes a difference. In large dogs, lots of chocolate needs to be consumed to be fatal, and dark chocolate is much worse than milk chocolate. I read the list of ingredients on one of the little packets Princeton had gotten into, but there wasn't a lot of actual chocolate in it. Lots of milk products, sugars, chemicals, and artificial flavours, but chocolate was near the bottom of the list. I was still concerned that Princeton had eaten the contents of all the packets, but I was beginning to feel confident he was going to be fine. He had burped a few times as he sat behind me, but he didn't seem to be suffering any ill effects.

I phoned the emergency clinic once more, and although they felt that I should be concerned, they confirmed what I had read online. Deciding that there wasn't much else to do, I drove back to the campground, parked in our spot, and spent the entire night watching Princeton as he slept. Once in a while I would push him with my foot to see if he was still alive (and to piss him off if he was). He made it through the night without a problem.

I'm glad one of us got some sleep.

The next morning Princeton was alive and well—and completely rested. He jumped from the van, hopped away, and had a pee. He came back and waited for me to feed him. While he ate I went through all the cupboards to see what else he might try to eat. Unless he knew how to use a can opener, there wasn't much else Princeton could get into. Satisfied I had nothing to worry about, I attached one end of a twenty-foot cable I had brought from home to his collar and the other to Poseidon's rear bumper. Cam and I had agreed to meet after lunch at Chocolate Tofino, and I hoped to get a little sleep before then. I looked at Princeton and told him to be a *good dog* while I slept for a few hours. He was.

The pictures were incredible, better than I'd ever expected. Cam, Kim, Princeton, and I sat together outside of Chocolate Tofino looking at all the photographs Cam had loaded onto his laptop. Cam told me he and Kim had spent much of the night looking at the over three hundred photographs and deciding which ones were the best. Kim said she became quite emotional at times, clutching little Moku as they itemized the photographs and put them to disc. They had been strangers until a few days ago, and what they did, taking the effort to preserve special moments for me and Princeton, meant a great deal to me. A year later Princeton and I made a return trip to Tofino, and while having dinner with Cam and Kim, I asked Cam why he'd agreed to take the photographs in the first place and why he and his wife had tried to make our stay in Tofino as enjoyable as possible. Looking at me, he replied, "It was the right thing to do. Anyone who watched you and Princeton together would know that."

That night Cam, Kim, and I had dinner at one of Tofino's fine restaurants. It was one of those three-hour dinners that went by far too quickly. Throughout the years Princeton and I had the good fortune to meet many great people while travelling together, Cam and Kim being the most special. I still talk regularly with both of them, and I know they were very sad when Princeton passed. A picture of Princeton, lying on the sand as the waves roll into Incinerator Rock, this time taken by me, hangs in their store.

For nearly another week Princeton and I continued to stay at Green Point Campground, visiting Tofino and the surrounding area. We would spend several hours at the beach but also took the opportunity to explore other places. Several times we went into Ucluelet, a fishing village. Although Ucluelet has become touristy, it still has a working-class vibe to it; it's probably how Tofino was three or four decades ago. One place I loved in Ucluelet was the aquarium. It isn't that large, but its exhibits are an impressive display of animal and plant marine life native to the area. An interesting feature is that most everything is released back into the ocean after being on display for a few months. New specimens are then brought in, and they too are later released and replaced. I enjoyed the aquarium so much, I visited it three times while Princeton and I were in Ucluelet.

Wickaninnish Beach, about halfway between Tofino and Ucluelet, became another favourite of ours. Troy, who ran the store at the campground, recommended it. Often less crowded than Incinerator Rock, it still offered a great beach and spectacular views of the ocean. Princeton and I often spent our late afternoons there, enjoying the peacefulness and solitude. The Kwisitis Visitor Centre, overlooking Wickaninnish Beach, is another wonderful attraction. It focuses on the area's history, including that of the First Nations people. Numerous displays showcase fauna native to the area. All in all, a great way to spend an afternoon.

Shorepine Bog Trail, not far from Wickaninnish Beach, is another place we visited. Surprisingly, it receives few visitors. I have no idea why this is, as I found the trail fascinating. It consists of a wooden boardwalk about a kilometre long and allows visitors to experience vegetation and trees grown in highly acidic soil. Shorepine Bog Trail is the complete opposite of Cathedral Grove; there are no giant cedars or pines, only stunted, gnarled trees. Several other types of vegetation grow in the bog, such as mosses, and they too differ in appearance from anything else that grows in other areas of Pacific Rim National Park. Much of the park can be considered rainforest, but the bog offers a glimpse of plants able to grow in an isolated, harsh environment.

Princeton, somewhat surprisingly, liked his visit to the bog. Judging by the way he behaved at Cathedral Grove, I thought little trees and stunted plants wouldn't interest him, but he hopped along the entire length of boardwalk, stopping every so often to sniff at things. He understood that he shouldn't jump off the little wooden trail, which was a relief because I didn't feel like chasing him through a bog. We walked through together, looking at all the plants that have adapted to what are generally accepted as lousy growing conditions. We spent nearly two hours walking the trail, and as much as we enjoyed it, I was glad Princeton didn't insist on turning around and walking the entire route again as he had at Cathedral Grove.

Tofino and the surrounding areas were wonderful places for Princeton and me to visit. All of our previous trips had been special, with plenty of things for us to see and do, but Tofino was different. It offered us a tranquility we hadn't experienced anywhere else. The longer we spent there, the more it felt as if we belonged there. I think we could have spent the entire summer there, but the time had come to leave and meet Gerrit and Carol in Victoria. On our last day we went for a walk along the beach and headed into town to stroll the main street before saying our goodbyes to Cam and Kim. As we drove out of town and headed for Victoria, Princeton, for the second time in our travels, stared out the back window when he realized we were leaving. I promised him we would return the following year. And we did.

18

Victoria

I HAD FIRST met Gerrit in university, over three decades before. Although we don't see each other often, we've always kept in touch throughout the years. Several years ago Gerrit had moved from Edmonton to Vancouver, and then to Victoria, meeting Carol and marrying her. I had yet to meet her, and I was excited to spend a few days with them both. Gerrit had offered the use of their driveway to park Poseidon while we were in Victoria, but I knew that Princeton would be more comfortable in a campground where he would be free to roam around. When we arrived in Victoria, I managed to find a campground a few kilometres from Gerrit and Carol's place, and I agreed to meet them later that evening for dinner.

After dinner Princeton and I returned to the campground. Fortunately, the owner of the campground took an instant liking to Princeton and let him wander around without a leash. Princeton continued his tradition of introducing himself to his fellow campers and let it be known he wasn't averse to anything yummy offered to him. Although he had been feeling a little sad since leaving Tofino, his mood improved once he visited our neighbours. Gerrit had agreed to meet up with us the following morning and take us for a personal tour around Victoria, so I decided an early night was in order. It had been a long day, and we were quickly asleep after I slid Poseidon's door closed for the night.

I had been to Victoria a few times, and like most visitors, limited myself to the well-known attractions. Gerrit had been living there for several years and promised to take us to a few places that were a little off the beaten track. Our first destination was Fisherman's Wharf. The last time I had been there was over a decade earlier, and boy, had it changed. The three of us walked up and down the wharf, admiring all the brightly coloured houseboats before having a lunch of fish and chips. Even the fish and chips place had changed; it was now a bustling outdoor restaurant instead of the old shack with a few picnic tables it had been years before. I felt a bit sad that the place had evolved into what it was now, but the food was still great. Princeton thought so too, and he bounced from table to table looking up at the other patrons, his brown eyes asking if they could share. Naturally, I got up from our table and apologized to anyone he was bothering. Nonetheless, Princeton managed to guilt a few people into sharing their meals. I should mention that this was after he'd had his own piece of fish, which I ordered specifically for him. After that little mealtime fiasco, it was time for us to pile into Gerrit's car and see what else Victoria had to offer.

Gerrit started the tour with a drive down by the water. After we'd driven a few kilometres, I had him stop, as there was a crowd of people with their dogs wandering around some display booths.

"Let's check it out," I said. "It looks like some sort of dog event."

"No problem," replied Gerrit.

Soon we were out of Gerrit's car and mingling with everyone else. Whatever the event was, it was winding down, but a fair number of people and their dogs were still present. Some of the dogs were wearing brightly coloured costumes. Many of the owners were same-sex couples and openly affectionate toward each other. And one of the display booths was celebrating—I'm not sure of the correct way of describing this — an alternative lifestyle. A couple of media people were also there, one of them enamoured with Princeton.

"Uh, Gerrit," I said quietly. "I think we're taking part in some gay dog thing."

Gerrit said something that still makes me laugh to this day whenever I think about it: "That's bullshit. How would anyone know if your dog is gay?" As soon as he said this, he realized I wasn't talking about the dogs.

As I found out later, Gerrit, Princeton, and I had unknowingly wandered into the Big Gay Dog Walk, an annual event in Victoria.

We didn't really know how we should proceed. Neither of us cared about anyone's sexual preferences, but it still felt uncomfortable walking into something we weren't expecting. After a few minutes, however, we realized it wasn't anything to be concerned about. We stayed for some time, talking with some really cool people and meeting their dogs. Princeton had fun too, getting lots of love and attention from everyone. Eventually, we left, Gerrit and I joking about how he would explain himself to Carol if he showed up on the evening news.

For the remainder of the day, we drove the Scenic Marine Route, Gerrit giving me a short history lesson about the places he was familiar with. It's always great to have someone who lives in a place you're visiting to act as a guide. You see and experience much more of the area than you would just visiting the traditional tourist spots. Princeton sat in the back of Gerrit's car, looking through the open window. Each time we stopped to look at something more closely, I'd let him out of the car and he'd bounce off to explore. If we happened to stop beside a beach, that was even better, as Princeton would head straight for the water and splash around. His fur all wet and paws full of sand, he was lucky Gerrit always allowed him back into the car.

For the next few days, Princeton and I visited much of Victoria,

On our last day in Victoria, Princeton and I went for a horse-drawn carriage ride through the Inner Harbour and James Bay.
—Photograph by author

Gerrit taking us to places he thought we would enjoy when his work schedule permitted. The last day we spent in Victoria, I decided to do something special for Princeton. Down by the waterfront a couple of businesses offered horse-drawn carriage rides. We had seen the carriages around the Inner Harbour a few times, and he had been completely engrossed in the impressive-looking horses that pulled the carriages. As they passed he would sit on the sidewalk, staring at them, often offering a subdued woof if any of the horses turned toward him. The carriage rides were obviously geared toward couples or families, but I thought Princeton would love going for a ride in one of them.

I approached one and asked if they would consider taking Princeton and me for an extended ride around Victoria. Somewhat surprisingly, they agreed. I lifted Princeton onto the seat directly behind the driver and took the seat at the rear of the carriage.

Before we set out I said to the driver, "Princeton is a very special dog. He's very smart and likes to be involved with everything. If you can, show us things he might enjoy. Speak to him, not me, and point to what you want him to see. He'll understand."

Our driver, a pleasant young lady, said that it wouldn't be a problem. For the next hour or so, she took us to places she thought we would enjoy, speaking to Princeton as he sat up in the seat behind her. She would talk to him, explaining the history and significance of what we were looking at. Sometimes she'd point to something and say, "Princeton! Look!" She'd turn in her seat to scratch his head while explaining in detail something she wanted him to see. Whether he was looking at the house that Canadian artist Emily Carr once lived in or something of note in Beacon Hill Park, Princeton listened carefully. I was pleased our driver took the time to involve Princeton in everything, and I knew he appreciated it too. I was also aware of all the people looking and pointing at us as we went along, obviously not used to seeing a dog as the primary passenger in a horse-drawn carriage and having a personal tour. Princeton was thrilled by his tour, and I felt it was a fitting end to our Victoria visit.

The next day Princeton and I said our goodbyes to Gerrit and Carol. Both were wonderful hosts, and I really appreciated the effort Gerrit had made to ensure that we had a good time. We had now been away from home for nearly three weeks, and it was time to slowly make our way back. Princeton had another checkup coming up, and although he continued to do well—some of his physical strength returning while we were away—it was something I didn't want him to miss. His arthritis, bothering him when we had left home, seemed much less pronounced while we were on the road. The only problem Princeton had while we were away was running out of dog food. He was on a specialty diet formulated for aging dogs with joint problems, and because he had been so active on the trip, he'd consumed much more of it than I had expected. In Victoria I had managed to find a veterinary clinic that sold the same formula and purchased enough of it to get us home.

19

Another Hurdle

ALMOST A WEEK later we pulled into the driveway of our farm. We had been gone for nearly four weeks. Although we were both glad to be home, I was already thinking of where we would be going next. But first Princeton needed to have a complete examination by his veterinarians. As I watched him bounce over my desperately-needed-to-be-mowed lawn, making sure everything was as we had left it, I wondered how much longer he could maintain his energetic lifestyle and good health. He was now well past his best-before date, and really far past the expected one-year survival of a dog diagnosed with osteosarcoma, but he was as happy and active as ever. As I leaned against Poseidon's bug-splattered hood, watching him as he ran off to find the goat and brag to her of our latest adventure, I wondered how much longer the best friend I had ever known would be with me. As it turned out, it would be some time yet, but first we had to deal with another health scare—one that would cause me a few sleepless nights and see Princeton undergo yet another major surgery.

As in people, the liver is a very important organ in dogs. Not only does it detoxify the blood, but it also aids in digestion and produces the proteins required for blood clotting. Liver disease in dogs is somewhat common, and although some forms of the disease can be successfully treated, others can lead to premature death. When dogs experience liver failure, many exhibit symptoms such as jaundice (yellowing of the skin tissue), decreased appetite, weight loss, vomiting, and increased thirst. Some dogs also experience neurological issues such as seizures and disorientation. And then there are dogs like Princeton who don't display any symptoms at all, but the results of their blood work include elevated liver enzymes, such as alanine transaminase (ALT), alkaline phosphatase (ALP), and aspartate transaminase (AST). Sometimes albumin and bilirubin are also elevated. Often these increased enzymes are non-specific, indicating only that the liver is stressed, and further testing and analysis are required to determine why they are elevated.

Princeton's blood work had mostly been great. Over the last several checkups the only abnormalities were the elevated liver enzymes, mainly his ALP. We'd never been overly concerned, as the values weren't considered too high, but they were definitely something to keep an eye on. Princeton went in for a complete checkup when we returned from Tofino, and everything was normal except for ALP, elevated as usual. The value still wasn't that bad, but it had increased substantially since his last checkup. Keep in mind that results are not linear, so if a value is twice as high as it was previously, this doesn't mean the liver is twice as stressed as it was before. It does, however, indicate a trend. And a trend is more indicative of a problem than an actual value. Princeton's blood work had shown a steady rise in liver enzymes over the last couple of years, the last two examinations clearly demonstrating an upward trend. Dr. Marshall had prescribed milk thistle for general liver support, but it had failed to halt the ever-increasing enzyme values. Throughout all this Princeton was exhibiting none of the traditional liver failure symptoms. He continued to be happy and energetic, amazing everyone, but clearly something was causing his liver enzymes to steadily increase.

In early December of 2014, Princeton went in for a complete abdominal ultrasound to determine why his liver enzymes were increasing. The findings were both good and bad. Good because most of Princeton's organs were normal. None of the age-related abnormalities you would expect to see were present. Bad because a large lesion, approximately six centimetres in diameter, was found in Princeton's left dorsal liver. The mass was possibly a primary hepatocellular tumour, meaning it had most likely originated in the liver. Although the vet felt that the liver tumour had nothing to do with Princeton's previous osteosarcoma, it was cause for concern. If the tumour turned out to be malignant, the rate of metastasis could be as high as 60 percent. Left untreated, the prognosis wasn't good, about three to four months' survival time even if the cancer didn't spread. Fortunately, up to 75 percent of the liver can be successfully removed if required. Princeton, once again, was facing a disease with the potential to end his life.

Dr. Kwantes recommended surgery to remove the mass and referred Princeton to Dr. Fowler for a second opinion about whether surgery was a viable option. Liver surgery is a very tricky procedure, especially for a dog as old as Princeton, and Dr. Kwantes felt that Dr. Fowler would be more qualified to deal with such an invasive procedure. A few days later, Princeton and I would meet with Dr. Fowler a second time.

Upon examining Princeton and studying the ultrasound and blood work, Dr. Fowler offered a slightly different diagnosis. He felt that the tumour was probably a primary liver adenoma. He agreed it had originated in the liver but thought the tumour probably was benign and wouldn't metastasize. He also felt that if it was a malignant tumour, it was of low grade and metastasis was unlikely. He further explained that, considering Princeton's advanced age, the surgery could be more of a risk than the disease itself. He recommended no surgery and another ultrasound in four to six weeks. If the tumour had increased in size significantly, then he would consider surgery. If it remained relatively static, then ongoing monitoring would be the best option.

In the second week of January, an associate of Dr. Fowler, Dr. Sereda, who specializes in internal medicine, performed another ultrasound on Princeton to determine if the liver tumour had grown. The results weren't as definitive as I would have liked, as some views revealed a four- to five-millimetre increase, while others were consistent with the original ultrasound. Dr. Sereda recommended performing another ultrasound in four or five weeks. Princeton had yet to exhibit any symptoms of liver disease and was doing well around the farm. As always, if he was concerned about anything, he didn't show it.

Although Princeton seemed to think there was nothing to worry about, the same couldn't be said about me. The last ultrasound caused me great concern. If the tumour had increased dramatically in size, surgery would have been the obvious choice. But no one could determine with any certainty whether the mass had grown or remained static. Hell, no one was even sure what type of tumour it was. I accepted that I had to place my faith and confidence in those much more qualified to determine what was best for Princeton, but I was having a difficult time doing nothing except waiting.

I continued to mope around the farm, losing sleep and palpating Princeton's abdomen half a dozen times a day to see if I could feel his tumour (I could not). I'm sure he thought I was being a real pain in the ass. As I watched him trundle through the deep snow, his belly still shaved from the last ultrasound and dragging against the snow, I realized that worrying about Princeton's liver wasn't going to change anything. Whatever happened, we would get through it together as we always had. Until then we had some things to see. I walked up to Princeton, who was lying on his back and barking at the snow as it came down on his bald belly. "Pack your stuff, Princeton. We're going back to Lake Louise."

He knew what I meant.

He'd had such a great time at the Chateau Lake Louise the previous winter, I knew he would love to visit it again. I made a few

calls to the hotel (they remembered us) and reserved the same room
we had stayed in before, and we were on our way. About six hours
later we were at the chateau. I pulled up to the main entrance and
opened the rear of the truck so Princeton could jump down. He
smiled at the doorman, who held the door for him, and confidently
hopped into the lobby. Knowing exactly where he was, he strode up
to the reception desk and waited for me to join him. The look on his
face informed everyone that he was a regular guest and had returned for his winter holiday. When I opened the door to our room,
he walked in and went to the same place he'd slept a year ago and
lay down. Looking up at me, he was pleased to be back. If he could
have talked, I'm sure he would have said, "I'll have the pan-fried
salmon, rice, and steamed vegetables. And get a little something for
yourself too."

Princeton had arrived.

I didn't know it when I reserved the room for us, but the chateau was hosting the annual Lake Louise Ice Magic Festival. The
hotel was nearly filled to capacity and very busy. The International
Ice Carving Competition is the highlight of the festival. Magnificent
ice sculptures are displayed on the grounds facing the lake. The
carvings are stunning and connected by a series of paths, allowing
hotel guests to walk from one sculpture to another. After dinner
(yes, Princeton got what he asked for) we made our way to the outdoor bar for a drink before looking at the carvings. After spending
a few minutes watching me drink my hot chocolate and Baileys,
Princeton became bored and checked out the sculptures on his own.
I wasn't really concerned about this, as the paths were all intercon-
nected, and with the snow piled up on either side of them, it would
be difficult for him to wander off. After I finished my drink, I spot-
ted him on one of the pathways, making friends with a group of
people. I walked over to the carving closest to the bar, and as I
made my way to another, I saw Princeton bouncing toward me. We
passed each other and continued in our different directions.

This is how it went for the next forty-five minutes—each of us passing the other on the maze of pathways as we visited the sculptures. I have no doubt Princeton considered this a game, and each time our paths crossed I'd say to him, "Good day, sir. I hope this evening finds you well." Princeton would hop on by with a grin on his face, looking forward to the next time we met. After I'd seen each sculpture at least twice, it was my turn to become bored, and I headed back to the bar for another hot chocolate and Baileys. Princeton continued bouncing along the pathways for several more minutes before deciding he'd better find me, eventually turning up at the bar. I asked him if he'd had enough and was ready to go back into the warm chateau. He had, and after a quick liqueur, we went back into the hotel.

Except for the one day we visited Banff, we spent all our time at Lake Louise, walking inside and outside the hotel, eating wonderful food, and meeting plenty of people. Several of the staff remembered Princeton from a year earlier and would approach him after calling out his name. As always, we were inundated by hotel guests wanting to know why he had lost his leg. Several were astonished to learn how old he was, especially considering his agility and his youthful attitude. Others asked something I was beginning to hear quite frequently: Does Princeton have a Facebook account? During the last couple of years, several people mentioned that they'd like to be kept informed about how he was doing. I never did set up a Facebook account for Princeton but took the contact information of those interested in his journeys and let them know how he was doing. I guess the fact that so many people wanted to be updated about him reinforced my desire to write his memoir.

After a few days of Princeton being pampered at the chateau, it was time to return home. There was still the matter of his liver. My gut feeling told me that Princeton would probably have to endure another surgery, but as with his amputation, he wouldn't have a problem. I knew the chance of morbidity from surgery increases the older an animal gets, but Princeton was old in years only. He still behaved like a young man. Looking at him as he slept on his bed during our final night at the hotel, I felt confident the old mutt would battle through whatever lay ahead of him.

The decision to have a liver lobectomy performed on Princeton wasn't taken lightly. And as his veterinarians repeatedly said, there wasn't a right or wrong decision in this instance. I carefully considered the recommendations of Drs. Fowler, Kwantes, and Marshall. There were sound arguments for adopting a wait-and-see approach as well as for being proactive and removing the mass. Princeton's veterinarians, each of them with different experiences and specializations, had his best interests in mind. Dr. Kwantes was the most adamant that surgery was warranted, Dr. Marshall was concerned about the use of an anaesthetic in a dog of Princeton's age, and Dr. Fowler felt that we still had more time to see what the tumour would do before having to make a decision. As with his osteosarcoma, Princeton left the decision of what to do to me.

On January 29 Princeton and I made our way to Guardian Veterinary Centre and the waiting scalpel of Dr. Fowler. Later that morning an eight-centimetre mass was removed from Princeton's left lateral liver lobe. I waited in a private room while the surgery took place. After he completed it, Dr. Fowler came into the room and asked me to go with him to the back of the clinic. When I entered I noticed that Princeton had been laid on a mattress on the floor, surrounded by metal gates. Before I managed to speak his name, he looked up from where he was resting and smiled.

"You know who this is, don't you?" Dr. Fowler said to Princeton as he escorted me to see him.

Princeton, always the trouper, was already coming out of the anaesthetic. Dr. Fowler told me that he'd had no troubles during the surgery, the entire experience being rather "uneventful." I think everyone at the clinic was surprised how well Princeton did, the nurses and technicians commenting to me that he was indeed one tough doggy. I stayed with him for a few minutes before leaving him so he could rest. As I walked out to the truck, I knew there was somewhere I had to go. I had to get a hot dog for Princeton.

For the next twenty-four hours, Princeton remained at the clinic for observation. When I took him home after he was discharged, he was content. Other than a shaved belly and a few staples keeping the incision closed, you wouldn't have known he had just undergone a major surgery. He didn't even seem to be in much pain, trying to jump from the truck as I opened the door when we arrived home. When I lifted him from the truck and placed him on the ground, instead of walking to the warm house, he hopped toward the barns, probably wanting to make sure that things were the same as when he'd left a couple of days before. Nevertheless, I wanted him to rest, and I picked him up and brought him into the house and laid him on his little bed. Looking into his calm but inquisitive eyes, I was confident he would make a complete recovery. After all, he was Princeton.

For the most part, his recovery went well. Except for a slight infection a few days after the operation and some soreness, he continued to recover as his incision healed. Probably the most difficult part was waiting for the lab report from the analysis of the tissue samples Dr. Fowler had sent in. It was important to determine what type of tumour had invaded Princeton's liver so we could decide if any further treatments were warranted. In early February Dr. Fowler contacted me with the results.

The cancer in Princeton's liver was identified as a low-grade hepatocellular carcinoma, or an HCC. It was considered primary liver cancer, meaning that the tumour had developed within the liver and not from a cancer elsewhere in his body. Primary liver cancer is very rare, accounting for less than 2 percent of all cancers in dogs. Of these primary liver cancers, hepatocellular carcinoma accounts for approximately 50 percent. The growth pattern of Princeton's carcinoma was massive; it was a large tumour on a single lobe. An HCC can also be nodular, with multiple tumours on several lobes, or diffuse, indicating that the cancer has invaded the entire liver. Dogs who suffer from nodular or diffuse hepatocellular carcinomas usually show metastasis and suffer a poorer prognosis than dogs with massive tumours. It also appeared that the tumour had increased in size since the last ultrasound, so surgical intervention was definitely warranted. Left untreated, the cancer could have caused end-stage liver disease and/or abdominal hemorrhaging. The lab studying Princeton's liver tissues reported no signs of metastasis and determined that the cancer was low grade. That, combined with the complete excision of the tumour with clear margins, meant that Princeton's long-term prognosis was excellent. Blood work scheduled approximately a month after his surgery would show if the surgery had been successful in lowering his liver enzymes.

So Princeton had dodged another bullet. Four years after being diagnosed with osteosarcoma, a disease that should have taken his life in about a year with even the best treatments, he had managed to overcome another form of cancer. And just as importantly, he hadn't suffered any complications while being under the anaesthetic. The only side effect was a noticeable weakening of his rear leg, probably because he had lost abdominal muscle tone from the surgery, but that improved within a couple of months.

Princeton was now getting quite the reputation within the veterinary community. I recall being in Guardian Veterinary Clinic with Princeton a short time after his surgery, both of us sitting on a couch waiting for Dr. Fowler, and being approached by a woman I had never seen before. She came up, sat in the chair opposite us, and asked, "Excuse me, but is that Princeton? The dog who survived bone cancer?"

Somewhat surprised, I answered, "Yep, that's him."

"My vet told me about him," the lady replied. "She told me he's quite the remarkable dog."

She went on to name her veterinarian and the clinic she dealt with, but neither was familiar to me. She and her dog had been referred to Guardian for a matter unrelated to cancer, but after seeing Princeton there too, she assumed he was the dog her veterinarian had told her about. She gave him a pat on the head, said that I was a good dad, and told me to continue taking care of him.

Besides Princeton's regular doctors, other veterinarians would cite Princeton as an example of unusual longevity when talking to the owners of dogs with life-threatening cancers. Although he was an anomaly, he was also proof that animals can sometimes far exceed their expected lifespan when suffering from various forms of cancer. Some animals, when given an opportunity, do much better than expected, surprising both their owners and veterinarians. I know that Princeton was indeed very special, but I also know he gave others hope. And sometimes, it's hope that's needed most.

In mid-March Princeton returned to Park Veterinary Clinic for X-rays and complete blood work. It had been about seven weeks since his liver surgery, and I was excited to see if Princeton's liver enzymes had come down. The X-rays were, as everyone expected them to be, clear—no signs of metastasis anywhere in his body. The results from the blood work were just as encouraging. Princeton's alkaline phosphatase, or ALP, had decreased to about half of what it had been in December. The results were so good, Dr. Kwantes suggested that Princeton might not have to come for another checkup for six months. And when he did return, perhaps I should consider only blood work. When I asked the doctor why not X-rays, his words to me before he walked out of the examination room were "Because we're not going to find what we keep looking for."

Princeton, nearly seventeen years old and having battled cancer twice in his lifetime, was considered completely cured of osteosarcoma. The significance of this cannot be overstated. When first diagnosed in 2011, the prognosis was approximately one year if he was lucky, and only if he had amputation and chemotherapy. Four years later, the veterinarian who had performed both treatments had implied what so many were hesitant to say: cured. I know that the quick actions of Dr. Kwantes and the supportive treatments of Dr. Marshall played a tremendous part in prolonging his life, but I believe that Princeton's will also contributed to his beating the disease. He had an infectious enthusiasm and determination that everyone who met him quickly became aware of. I think he decided that there was no way in hell anyone was going to tell him when it was time to check out. He was often disobedient and refused to listen to anyone, me included, but it was this attitude that helped him overcome the obstacles placed in front of him. He was a dog who relished every waking moment. He loved life and took his duties as a farm dog seriously. Princeton still felt that he had things to do. Things to see. Things to eat. Nothing was going to prevent him from doing what he wanted.

After a few minutes of love from his girlfriends behind the counter, he swaggered from the clinic and back to the truck in a manner that only someone given a clean bill of health can. I opened the door, lifted him inside, and asked, "Wanna go for a hot dog?"

20

Woof

ARCH 2015 WAS special for me because it was when I received my Christmas present from Princeton. I always talked to him as if he could understand much of what I said, and although he might not have understood what I said word for word, I believe that he recognized and reacted to my gestures and tone of voice. Each day I discussed with him the things we needed to do. During our talks he'd sit and look at me, head slightly cocked to one side, his eyes and smile letting me know he was listening. In all the years I spoke directly to him, however, he hardly ever replied with a woof or other sort of acknowledgement. Just before Christmas 2014 was one of the times he did.

I've always been a fan of the Ford Mustang. I've been fortunate enough to have owned a few over the years and have always enjoyed them. For 2015 Ford planned to release an all-new model to celebrate the car's fiftieth anniversary. I had known about the new model for some time but hadn't yet made plans to purchase one.

In December, while sitting in the Tim Hortons drive-thru, I was reading a magazine article about the upcoming new model. I turned to Princeton and showed him a photograph from the article.

"Wanna buy me one for Christmas? It can be your gift to me."

Princeton looked at the magazine, then looked away.

Princeton tries out his custom-built platform in the new Mustang.
—Photograph by author

"If I can have one, say 'Woof.'"

Princeton looked back at me and said, "Woof."

There it was, clear as day. *Woof.*

As much as I tried to convince myself that Princeton's response to my request was nothing but a fluke, a mere coincidence, we found ourselves at the dealership just before Christmas to place our order. I was told the car would arrive sometime in March.

Since Princeton had given me such an amazing gift, I wanted him to be involved with the car as much as possible. Over the next couple of months, we visited the dealership several times to take measurements of the back seat of whatever display Mustang was in the showroom. I wanted to build a platform that covered the rear seat so Princeton could go for rides with me. The dealership was very accommodating, not only allowing me to take the necessary measurements, but also letting me test fit the final product several times so I could make adjustments. During each of the visits, Princeton lay on the floor of the showroom and watched me work.

Eventually, I finished the platform and test fitted it to the rear seat of the display car. It fit perfectly. The sales manager insisted that Princeton enter the car to make sure everything was perfect. So about two weeks before my car was scheduled to arrive, Princeton sat on his custom-made platform in the new Mustang while several people took pictures of him.

Finally, in the third week of March, our car arrived. I placed Princeton's platform inside it and then carefully placed him inside the car. Most of the staff of the dealership came outside to watch and say goodbye to Princeton. A few moments later, with everyone waving, we rumbled out of the dealership parking lot in a retina-searing bright yellow Mustang GT.

Thank you, Princeton. That was the second-best gift I've ever received.

21

Getting Around

O NE OF THE biggest challenges Princeton tackled toward the end of his life was mobility. As dogs age, sore joints, arthritis, and muscle wasting are normal. If you're an old farm dog who's missing a leg and could easily stand to lose a pound or two, you'll probably have even more trouble getting around. By the spring of 2015, Princeton was still very active, probably more so than dogs years younger than he was, but he was having difficulty walking and running from time to time. He was still taking Rimadyl and receiving acupuncture treatments regularly, but he was becoming increasingly dependent on me to maintain his active lifestyle.

Around this time Princeton came under the care of Dr. Webster, a chiropractor who treated people and specialized in animal care. She recommended he receive weekly chiropractic treatments, probably for the rest of his life. He was also fitted with various harnesses by an animal health technologist who specialized in pet mobility issues. I also purchased a John Deere Gator, a small utility vehicle that he could ride around the farm in when he was having difficulty walking on his own.

All of these things helped Princeton a lot, allowing him to keep doing what he enjoyed. There were now times that he was content to lie on the grass and watch me while I went around the farm, but mostly he still insisted on taking an active role when he could. He just needed a little help sometimes.

Although he was still relatively mobile, his veterinarians suggested that Princeton might eventually require one of those dog wheelchairs—something that would support his hindquarters but still allow him to be active on his own. They suggested that although he didn't need one at that time, it would be a good idea to at least get him used to it. Penny, the animal health technologist who had fitted Princeton with his harnesses, gave me one to try. The wheelchair had been used by another dog who had passed away, and the owners graciously gave it to Penny with the understanding that it be given to another dog who could use it. The wheelchair was the proper size for Princeton, and after a few modifications, I eased him into it to see how he would like it.

He didn't. He hated it. I could see it on his face. Princeton refused to move no matter how hard I tried to convince him. Finally, I yanked him forward by his collar, and he collapsed on his front legs, his ass stuck up in the air. I lifted him back up and he just stood there, a look of disgust on his face. I took him out of the cart, and he bounced away on his own, walked from the shop to the house, bounced up the ramp to the deck, and went into his doghouse. He refused to come out for nearly half an hour. It was fair to say that Princeton was *not* going to get used to the wheelchair.

From then on, whenever Princeton needed a little assistance walking, I had to help him by holding on to the handle of his harness. I didn't have a problem with this except for one small detail: Princeton was often more active than I was (or sometimes wanted to be). If we worked around the farm all day and I felt too tired to take our nightly walk, Princeton wouldn't care. Although he was usually strong enough to walk unassisted throughout the day, once the evening arrived it was obvious he was sore—but not sore enough to deter him from his sometimes two-kilometre walk on the road leading to our farm. This meant I had to go for a two-kilometre walk (or run) too. What made this so uncomfortable was my height. At nearly six foot five, I had to stoop over to hold on to Princeton's harness. I'd run with a lopsided gait while bent over him as he pulled me along. It wasn't long before Princeton's chiropractor also became my chiropractor.

By early spring of 2015, Princeton had begun to rely more heavily on his harness and my assisting him. He could no longer jump from the truck, instead depending on me to lift him down and onto the ground. Around the farm he'd walk on his own for about a hundred feet, sit down, and wait for me to catch up. I'd walk to where he was, grab onto his harness to lift his hindquarters, and walk with him until he was able to walk on his own. We'd repeat the process several times until we got to where we were going. Overall he was still very active, but it was clear that he was depending on me more than he had in the past. I didn't mind. He would have done the same for me.

As Princeton needed more help around the farm, I started thinking of the time when I would be without him. Although he was still a remarkable dog, and healthy and enthusiastic, I knew there would be a day when the fire that shone so brightly in his eyes would leave him. And then he would leave me. It terrified me to think of when that time would come, but as his best friend and the one he trusted to make decisions about what was best for him, I told myself that I needed to prepare myself for the eventuality. I hoped we would have at least one more summer left, and if we were lucky, the following year. Nothing indicated that Princeton was close to the end of his life, but I also knew we had been fortunate up until now. He had proven to everyone that he was indeed a wonder dog, but even the most wonderful dogs don't last forever. But summer was now upon us, so it was time for another adventure.

22

Northern Odyssey

T HE SUMMER WOULD consist of two trips, each at least two weeks long. The second trip would be back to Tofino, the place Princeton and I had loved so much the year before and I had promised him we would visit again. But we had to figure out where to travel to first. We would be going west later in the summer, so it didn't make sense to head in that direction. We'd gone both east and south the previous summers but had never really travelled north. When Princeton was younger and I used to take solitary trips with my motorcycle, I had always wanted to travel to the northern part of Canada, into the Yukon and to Dawson City. Maybe beyond. It was remote and increasingly desolate the farther north you travelled, but that always appealed to me. I thought it would appeal to Princeton too. North it was.

It was exciting knowing I'd be driving on roads I'd never been on before and going to places off the beaten track. It was even more special knowing Princeton would be with me, and together we would be seeing things neither of us had ever seen before. Since we would be travelling in remote areas, I took several precautions that hadn't been required during our previous travels together. The first thing was to completely inspect Poseidon stem to stern. Everything had to be in perfect working order. I went through my extensive

Northern Odyssey
—Photograph by author

parts collection, adding spares to the spares I already had. If we experienced a mechanical failure, minor or catastrophic, I needed to be able to perform repairs wherever we were. The second thing I had to do was to pack a few extra things for Princeton. He had to have additional food and medication. I also included a doggy emergency medical kit including hydrogen peroxide to induce vomiting if he decided to eat something he shouldn't. Lastly, I borrowed a satellite phone for emergency use. I wasn't concerned about myself, but I was very much aware that I was travelling with a very old three-legged dog. If there was an accident or the van suffered a mechanical failure I couldn't repair, I would need to contact someone. I would also need to contact Princeton's veterinarians if he suffered a medical emergency.

After a few days of preparations, we were off. We would be travelling westward on Highway 16, passing through Jasper and continuing into central British Columbia. From there we'd travel northward on Highway 37, which would lead us through the northern part of the province and into the Yukon.

"Well, Princeton, let's see what's out there," I said as I lifted him into the van. He had been lying by Poseidon's sliding door for hours the day we left, eagerly waiting for us to leave.

Princeton, smart doggy that he was, was probably thinking we were heading back to Tofino as we drove toward Jasper. We had made the drive to Jasper several times now, and I'm sure much of what he saw when he looked out the window was familiar to him. Whenever we stopped at a rest area we had visited before, he'd wander around looking at the same things he'd seen before, probably wondering if anything had changed. The only thing that was different was that I sometimes had to help him by holding on to the rear part of his harness as he bounced along. After a good walk each time we stopped, he'd hop back to the van and wait for me to lift him inside.

The first place we stopped for the night was somewhere new: a Walmart parking lot. A few times Princeton and I hadn't stayed in regular campgrounds, choosing instead to camp in isolated (and free) areas, such as a cutline or in a field sheltered by trees, but we had never stopped for the night in a Walmart parking lot. I had seen plenty of RVs parked in these lots throughout the years but always thought it was a little weird. Cheap-ass campers, camping on asphalt. Where's the fun in that? But there we were, parked at the far end of the Hinton Walmart parking lot with about a dozen other campers.

Princeton thought it was cool. There may not have been as much to do there as there was at our usual stops, but he found ways to entertain himself—first by introducing himself to all the other travelling cheapskates who had stopped for the night, and second by visiting with Walmart shoppers as they put their purchases into their vehicles. And since I was responsible for holding up his hindquarters with his harness, I too had to meet our fellow campers and Walmart shoppers. After we had made our presence known to everyone, I thought I should probably go into the store and see what, if any, restrictions were in place for staying the night. Princeton immediately made himself a Walmart greeter, parking himself in front of the entrance doors. I no longer tied him to anything if I left him alone for a few minutes, because I had no doubt that if anyone took him they'd soon realize how old he was and that he was missing a wheel and would promptly bring him back. So after telling Princeton to stay, I entered the store and asked a cashier what the deal was. She replied that they only requested I pick up my garbage and, if I needed anything, to purchase it in store. Seemed like a fair deal.

To be honest, I didn't find our concrete campground all that bad, and after a good night's sleep, we were back on the road the next day. Once we passed through Jasper and headed into central British Columbia, Princeton became very much aware that we were travelling a route we hadn't taken before and became fascinated by what was around him. He'd look out one side of the van briefly before turning his attention to the other side. I stopped often so he could explore areas and things that were new to him. It reminded me of the first time we'd travelled, Princeton bouncing around and looking at and smelling everything. Our rest stops were taking up much of our travelling time, but we weren't in a hurry and didn't have anywhere we needed to be. When we made it to Prince George, we decided to stop there for the night.

The next day we continued travelling on Highway 16, stopping for the night shortly before turning onto Highway 37, which would take us into northwest British Columbia. By then there were fewer travellers on the road, and many of their licence plates were from other parts of Canada and the United States. Speaking with several of them, I discovered that most were heading toward Alaska or to Dawson City in the Yukon. A few were planning on going north as far as they could, hoping to reach the Arctic Circle.

At the campground that evening, Princeton and I spent our time visiting with a guy and his dog who had just begun their vacation. They had travelled from Prince Rupert, a port city on British Columbia's northwest coast. Princeton and the other dog spent the evening chasing and tackling one another, each of them trying to establish dominance over the other, while his owner and I talked about his profession: he unloaded container ships. It was fascinating hearing about the procedures involved and the types of goods he often removed from the ships. In the years Princeton and I travelled together, one of the most enjoyable things was meeting new people (and often their pets) whenever we stopped for the evening. I think Princeton had a lot to do with this. People were naturally drawn to him. In a campground, if several of us were with our dogs, it was always Princeton people gravitated to. This had just as much to do with his enthusiasm and friendliness as it did his missing leg. Even people who didn't really like dogs confessed that there was something about him that made them want to come up to him.

One of the many bears we encountered while travelling the Yukon.
—Photograph by author

The next day we headed northward, travelling on Highway 37. As the hours passed we saw even fewer vehicles than we had the day before but much more wildlife. It wasn't uncommon to see a moose or a bear beside the road. Princeton, naturally, found the increase in wildlife fascinating. He'd sit in the van, safely behind the glass, growling or barking whenever I stopped the van to show him an animal much bigger than he was. He was very brave, sitting behind Poseidon's sliding door, as certainly anything he barked or growled at would have felt threatened if only they could have heard him.

That night we found a campground about an hour away from the British Columbia-Yukon border. Unfortunately, I can't remember the name of it, but it was one of the best provincial campgrounds I'd ever been in. Very clean and obviously well managed, it was located next to a lovely lake. Princeton and I managed to get a spot right beside the water, and it was here I discovered that travelling this far north during the summer is different than travelling somewhere else during the summer.

"Tired, Princeton?" I asked him as we completed our dinner. "We'll go to bed once it gets a little darker."

After what felt like an hour, I told him again that we'd go to bed once night came upon us. I went into the van to get a magazine, as it wasn't dark out yet. After reading and watching the campfire for a while, I went into the van to get something to drink. I glanced at my watch as it lay by the sink; it was almost midnight.

I had always heard that much of Northern Canada stays illuminated during the summer months, but it was still surprising to realize how late it was and how much daylight there was. I should have caught on that it was late when Princeton's biological clock told him it was time for bed; he had been snoozing away in front of Poseidon's sliding door for some time now.

"Sorry, fella," I said as I awakened him. "Go for a pee, and then we'll go bed."

He got up and yawned, his expression telling me that he was

More than once we camped at abandoned gas stations
while travelling the Yukon Territory.
—Photograph by author

already in bed and didn't appreciate being awakened in the middle of the night, and hopped away for a pee. He yawned again as I lifted him into the van and was asleep in a few minutes. I, on the other hand, was not. I lay in my sleeping bag for several hours, waiting for the darkness that never really came. At last I managed to get a couple of hours of fitful sleep just as sunlight was slowly creeping into the van.

The thing I remember most about arriving in the Yukon wasn't the extended daylight hours, the wildlife, or the occasional feelings of isolation. It was the bugs. Not only were the mosquitoes huge and ferocious, trying to drain me of my blood at every opportunity, but all the other insects looked disturbingly large and creepy. Especially one furry, frightful-looking winged thing that attached itself to Poseidon's windshield wiper a few minutes after we crossed into the Yukon from BC. I had never seen anything like it before. Though it could obviously fly, for some reason it decided to hitch a ride with me and Princeton. Briefly, I considered turning on the windshield wiper to attempt to dislodge it, but I thought that would only piss it off. And it looked like a bug capable of holding a grudge. I had an uneasy feeling that if I inconvenienced it by turning on the windshield wiper and making it fly away, it would only attach itself to another part of the van I couldn't see. During the night I'd awaken to find it sitting at the edge of my sleeping bag, staring angrily at me as if it had a score to settle. No, best to leave it alone. Let it choose when it wanted to leave. About an hour later it had either decided it had reached its destination or realized it was being driven in the wrong direction; it left on its own. Creepy little bastard.

Something I quickly learned while travelling in remote parts of Northern Canada was to keep your vehicle full of gas. Don't ever trust any roadside sign telling you that fuel is available whatever distance up ahead. More than once I passed a roadside sign promising fuel and other services, only to find the station had closed its doors some time ago. In fact, while travelling in some parts of the

Princeton struck out on his own to explore the
Sign Post Forest, Yukon Territory.
—Photograph by author

Yukon, Princeton and I twice camped beside abandoned old gas stations. It wasn't like that throughout the entire territory, but in some places roadside signs had yet to be removed or altered. I generally stopped and tanked up whenever fuel was available, regardless of how far we had gone from the last station.

Because of this uncertainty, I decided to travel to Watson Lake for fuel. We were driving west on the Alaska Highway, and because Poseidon's fuel gauge still wasn't working, I turned around and headed to Watson Lake for fuel and groceries. While in town, we came across a remarkable attraction called the Sign Post Forest.

The Sign Post Forest is basically what the name implies: a collection of signs nailed to posts. I had never heard of it before but learned it's one of the most famous landmarks along the Alaska Highway. A homesick American GI named Carl Lindley started it in 1942 while working on the Alaska Highway. Apparently, while repairing a signpost one day, he affixed a sign pointing to his hometown of Danville, Illinois. Mr. Lindley didn't know it at the time, but he would be responsible for starting a tradition that continues to this day. Since he first erected his sign, others have followed suit, attaching signs they've brought from their hometowns or made on the spot to posts erected around his original sign. People have brought signs from all over the world, and it's considered tradition for anyone who passes through Watson Lake to post a sign indicating where they're from as they head through the Yukon or continue on to Alaska. Today there are over a hundred thousand signs attached to posts spread over several acres.

The Sign Post Forest is visible from the highway, and although I didn't know what it was at first, it looked like something Princeton and I would like. We spent at least two hours wandering around and looking at all the signs. In addition to the many signs from Canada and the United States were a tremendous number from overseas. I saw signs from Germany, Switzerland, China, Australia, Israel, and England, to name a few. Several were commercial signs that appeared to have been removed from signposts from wherever people were visiting from. It was a fascinating experience, looking at the signs from faraway places and marvelling at the journeys they had taken to be there.

At a reception area on site, people can learn more about the Sign Post Forest and its history. A small area has also been set up where people can make their own signs from wood and paint and attach them with a hammer and nails to the ever-increasing number of posts being erected.

As I visited the reception area, wanting to get more information about the forest, Princeton remained on his own outside the entrance, greeting everyone walking into the building. I thought it was a great idea to leave a sign and said to Princeton as I walked out the door, "Should we leave a sign? You and me? Something that will be a memory for us and will announce to everyone else that we were here?"

I thought wood and paint were okay, but I wanted something more permanent—something that would still be there for decades. A hand-painted small sign nailed to a post wouldn't last as long as I wanted it to. It was the third member of our crew, the van, that solved the problem.

As I pried off Poseidon's right front hubcap, I knew the old van would never get another. Replacing it wouldn't be right. Poseidon had carried Princeton and me in safety and comfort for tens of thousands of kilometres, and except for an obscene amount of gasoline, it had asked for nothing. This was its chance to leave a part of itself behind, proving to others that it too had been a traveller. Sitting on the floor of the van, the hubcap lying on a piece of wood between Princeton's front legs, I spelled out his and my name and where we were from by making a series of small holes with a punch and hammer from my tool collection. I drilled two holes (remember, I had packed a cordless drill as well) so I could screw it to a post.

New posts are being erected all the time in the Sign Post Forest, but I wanted to place our sign among those that had already been there for a long time. All such posts were covered with signs, many of them overlapping one another. Some of the signs completely obscured the others. Princeton and I wandered around the forest for half an hour, trying to find a small area on one of the established posts where we could attach our hubcap and it would remain undisturbed. Eventually, we found the perfect place.

Out of hundreds of posts, we found one that was completely covered with signs except for a tiny area at the very top. Most of the signs attached to it looked several years old, and since the one open space was out of reach, no one could easily cover our sign with one of their own. It was perfect. And being that it was perfect, it was also inaccessible.

When Princeton and I were first walking around the forest, we had come across two young women with a ladder and cordless drill. I had spoken to them, asking them about the forest and what they were doing. They explained that they were performing maintenance, reattaching signs that, over the years, had broken away from where they were attached. It was also their responsibility to reattach signs from posts that had been replaced. Hubcap in hand and Princeton bouncing alongside me, I approached them again and asked if I could use their ladder.

"We're not allowed to do that," one of the women replied. "In fact, we discourage anyone from using anything to stand on to attach their sign."

"Couldn't you make an exception?" I asked, probably sounding a little too whiny.

"Sorry, we just can't," the other repeated. "There are lots of posts toward the back of the forest you can use."

Throughout the conversation Princeton sat beside me, looking adorable as only he could. Naturally, the conversation shifted from borrowing the ladder to him. I explained what he had endured the last few years and spoke of the places we had visited and of those we still hoped to see.

As had happened with so many others, Princeton's specialness and gentle manner melted their hearts. Princeton made everyone smile, often making people want to do things for him, and it was no different this time. He was unlike any other dog, often bringing out the best in people if they were fortunate enough to spend time with him. After the two young women spent several minutes with him and wished us both good luck in the future, one of them asked for Poseidon's hubcap and the screws I was carrying.

If you ever have the opportunity to visit Sign Post Forest, our sign is attached to one of the older posts closest to the highway. It's located near the top, out of reach to anyone: a hubcap from a 1991 Ford Econoline E-350 that carried two travellers throughout much of Western and Northern Canada.

After filling the van's fuel tanks, we were back on the Alaska Highway heading west toward Whitehorse, looking for a place to spend the night.

Whitehorse is the capital of the Yukon Territory. It's named after the historic rapids on the Yukon River that look like the manes of white horses. Originally a First Nations settlement, Whitehorse is a vibrant city, home to about twenty-five thousand people. Steeped in history, starting with the gold rush days, it was a place I'd always wanted to visit but never had the opportunity. It seemed the perfect place for us to spend a couple of days before travelling to Dawson City. We found a great little campground east of Whitehorse and prepared to spend some time just taking it easy.

There are numerous things to do in or around Whitehorse. Princeton and I spent two days in the area, not nearly enough time to visit all of the town's attractions. Although we visited several, the ones I enjoyed the most were the S.S. Klondike National Historic Site, the site of a two-hundred-foot, fully restored sternwheeler used to carry ore, goods, and passengers until 1955; the Yukon Transportation Museum, which displays all modes of transportation, from basic snowshoes to aircraft, used in the area during the last

century; and the MacBride Museum of Yukon History, which show-
cases the natural and cultural history of Whitehorse.

During our third day in Whitehorse, Princeton and I decided
we would head to Dawson City. Dawson City is about five hundred
kilometres north of Whitehorse and is associated with the Klondike gold rush of the late 1800s, when approximately a hundred
thousand prospectors flocked to the area hoping to strike it rich.
Located on the banks of the Yukon River, Dawson City was originally a First Nations camp. At one time about forty thousand people
lived there, but when the gold rush ended a few years later, the number fell dramatically. In 1902, when Dawson was incorporated as
a city, only about five thousand people remained. Today that number
is under two thousand, but the city remains a popular tourist spot
for people from all over the world.

The highway is paved the entire way from Whitehorse to Dawson
City, and although there are plenty of hills, it's nothing like travelling
through the mountains. The scenery and wildlife are spectacular.
Remaining behind Poscidon's steel and glass, Princeton continued
to issue stern warnings to anything bigger than he was. We had left
early in the morning, and we were nearly at Dawson City when
Poseidon began to feel a little different. It didn't have a lot of power
to begin with, but what had been there had definitely taken a sab-
batical. Troubled, I pulled off into a roadside turnout to have a look
under the hood. Not finding anything wrong, I pulled onto the highway and continued driving. A few kilometres later Poseidon was
once again losing power, especially on inclines. It also was leaning
out during brisk acceleration. Once again I stopped, this time inspecting the entire van.

Not finding anything out of the ordinary, I turned my thoughts
to the fuel system. When a vehicle loses power and is experiencing
a lean condition, it often means it's starved for fuel. I had switched
between the van's two tanks while driving when the trouble first
started, thinking an in-tank fuel pump in one of the gasoline tanks

may have been the problem, but the issue persisted. I removed the in-frame fuel filter to see if contaminants were causing the problem.

Clogged. The fuel filter was full of crap (and perhaps water). I replaced the old filter with a new one (See? Spare parts *do* come in handy), and Poseidon fired up after a few cranks. After a few hard acceleration runs, the lean condition failed to reappear and the van was back to its old self. I added some methyl hydrate to both tanks to remove any water that may have been in the fuel. Poseidon was running like new.

I was still concerned, though. I had obviously picked up some bad fuel along the way and was concerned about what might still be in Poseidon's fuel tanks. I had two unused fuel filters left, and spare tank and lift pumps, but I was unsure if Princeton and I should continue heading to Dawson City. If it were just me travelling, I would have had no problem continuing on, but I had to think of Princeton in case of further mechanical problems. In the end, and only about an hour away from Dawson City, I turned around and headed back to Whitehorse. Whitehorse is much larger than Dawson City and would probably have facilities I could rent if I needed to perform more repairs.

It turned out Poseidon had no further problems. I alternated between both fuel tanks every fifty kilometres or so, and the van ran fine. Whatever had been in the fuel tanks had evidently been taken care of by the fuel filter. Nonetheless, I felt we had made the correct decision by turning back.

I loved the trip to Northern Canada. It's not the sort of trip I would recommend to someone interested in lots of commercialized roadside entertainment, but instead to more adventurous souls wanting to explore a region steeped in a history of exploration, gold mining, and highway construction. The area has some of the most attractive scenery I have ever seen, much of it unspoiled by civilization. I loved the isolation that parts of the Yukon also provided, which made me feel more comfortable than being surrounded by scores of people. In some ways, travelling with Princeton on a desolate road, uncluttered with other vehicles, felt as special as the times we had walked together alone on the beaches of Tofino during the late evenings.

One of the most memorable experiences while travelling in Canada's North was the time we stopped for gas one evening at a rundown old service station. We pulled alongside the only pump, an ancient unit tilted to one side. An elderly attendant came out and, after asking how I was doing, asked if he could fill up the van. As he filled the tanks, I noticed that the dollar display on the pump was no longer functioning. Only the volume indicator worked, ticking off the litres as Poseidon greedily gobbled up all that was offered. After the van was full of gasoline, I followed the attendant into the office and watched as he calculated on a piece of paper how much I owed. My eyes then fell on the bulletin board behind him. Thumbtacked to the board were two bags of potato chips, a few chocolate bars, and a roadside map. The attendant told me what I owed, and after paying him I walked out to the van, which I'd parked behind an ancient gas pump and in front of a desolate highway, and behind that, mountains and forests too spectacular to describe.

How cool is that?

This is only one memory of our travels up north, and although it's certainly not representative of much of what we saw, it's how I like to remember our trip. For years I'd planned to travel north but I'd never had the chance. With Princeton I was finally able to make that journey, and I'll always be grateful we experienced something together that neither one of us had done before. In time I'll travel there again, alone, on a motorcycle, and I'll buy fuel at that little station Princeton and I had visited before.

23

Trouble along the Way to Tofino

W E'D HAD SUCH a terrific time in Tofino the year before, I promised Princeton that we would return, and in late summer of 2015, we did. It would be the last trip we would take together, and one that nearly didn't happen.

It started out well enough, the first night spent once again in the Hinton Walmart parking lot. As before, Princeton spent the evening running around introducing himself to our fellow campers and inspecting the purchases of Walmart shoppers as they walked to their cars. Other than some soreness in his hindquarters, he seemed to be his old self. That night he slept soundly, only once wanting to go outside for a pee. In the morning, however, he seemed a little off. He didn't appear to be sore or tired but definitely wasn't his usual happy self. Assuming he might have overdone it the night before, I kept my eye on him as we started to travel toward Kamloops, BC, about five hours away from Jasper. We stopped at several rest areas, most of which Princeton had visited during previous trips, but he didn't seem interested in walking around. When he was in the van, he had little interest in anything. He'd lie on his bed, choosing not to look out the windows like he usually did.

After a few hours he didn't seem to be feeling any better, and I was concerned that something might seriously be wrong with him.

We were an hour away from Kamloops, and I decided to continue on and see how he was feeling when he got there. About fifteen minutes from Kamloops, I stopped at a rest area and took him from the van so he could have a pee.

"How you feeling, old boy?" I asked him as he lay outside the van. "Is there something wrong? Do you want to go home?"

Princeton looked up at me, sadness in his eyes, and put his head between his legs.

Once in Kamloops I made the decision to head home. There was something wrong with Princeton, and I wanted to get him home as quickly as I could. If I drove continually, only stopping for fuel, we could be home in maybe nine hours. As the hours ticked by, Princeton didn't seem to be getting any worse, but he wasn't improving either. He didn't appear to be in any pain, and his temperature and blood circulation seemed fine. I palpated his entire body and couldn't find anything out of the ordinary. Nonetheless, he needed a veterinarian to check him over.

I remember being very concerned as I continued driving home. Princeton was always such a stoic dog, so for him to be behaving this way meant there had to be something wrong. I worried that perhaps the cancer had returned and he was in pain. Maybe I had let him do too much, and maybe he wasn't the indestructible dog I thought he was. An old girlfriend, Terri, who often called me on the road to see how we were doing, phoned me just after we had left Kamloops, and I told her that we had to go home. I then called Kim and told her that we wouldn't be making Tofino this year. Princeton was sick.

Just before the town of Golden, about an hour from the British Columbia-Alberta border, I stopped in a rest area. It had been a couple of hours since we had stopped, and I thought Princeton would have to pee. I lifted him from the van and placed him on the ground, expecting him to just stand there with a sad and uncomfortable expression. Instead he looked up at me, and as a smile appeared on his face, he bounced off on his own toward the woods by the rest area. I ran after him, calling out for him to return.

When I caught up to him, I placed his head in my hands and looked into his face. His eyes were clear and bright. The sadness I had seen a few hours ago was gone. Once again I felt his body and checked his gums. Still nothing out of the ordinary. I took him back to the van and gave him some dog food, which he quickly ate. When he finished he looked up at me, his face saying "More." Princeton, it seemed, had returned to his old self.

Why he had been so lethargic before was puzzling. Not wanting to take a chance, however, I still thought it best that we went home. I loaded Princeton back into the van and continued to drive to Golden. From Golden we would continue on to Banff and then back to Edmonton.

Princeton, now back to normal, resumed his regular task of looking out the windows as I continued to drive. During the next two hours, we stopped twice more, each time Princeton dragging me around as he explored his surroundings. It was now late evening and it had started to rain, but that didn't dampen his enthusiasm. Considering how he was feeling, I started to reconsider taking him home. Maybe he'd had a bout of the flu. I'm sure dogs get the flu just as people do. Maybe he'd had tummy troubles; at one of the rest stops he had a pretty impressive poop.

Whatever it was, it was clear he was glad to be on the road and was looking forward to wherever we were going. The question remained, however, whether to continue our trip or return home.

When we were just outside Princeton's favourite winter retreat, the Chateau Lake Louise, I decided to find a campground for the night. It was late and we had been travelling for most of the day. Only about five hours from home, we'd spend the night in the campground and re-evaluate things in the morning. However, it was a problem finding a campground that had space available. I stopped at two campgrounds, but both were full. Not wanting to go any farther, I decided to drive to the Chateau Lake Louise and get us a room for the night instead. About a kilometre from the hotel, I passed a small turnout that was usually occupied by a dog sled company during the winter months and, instead of continuing to the hotel, thought this would be a good place to stop for the night. When I pulled into the turnout, I noticed that three other RVers had had the same idea. There was room for a fourth.

The next morning Princeton was in fine form, running around and introducing himself to the campers he hadn't had a chance to meet the night before. I decided to take him to the Chateau Lake Louise for breakfast, wanting him to experience the hotel he loved so much when it was warm and green instead of cold and snowy. As usual he romped around the hotel, stopping only when I sat down to phone Dr. Marshall. She agreed with me that although Princeton had experienced some discomfort the day before, there probably wasn't anything to worry about now. Relieved, I took Princeton outside the hotel, where he saw a squirrel beneath a tree and immediately took off after it, leaving me to chase after him as I yelled at him to come back.

Our trip would continue.

I suppose there are worse things than a twelve-hour detour. Princeton didn't seem to mind. He felt that the more time he could spend in the van looking at the scenery, the better. Still concerned about him, I stopped every hour to take him for a walk, watching him closely for anything out of the ordinary. When we reached Kamloops for the second time in as many days, I phoned Kim and told her that this time we'd be making it to Tofino. Not wanting to be on the road too long that day, we found a campground outside of Kamloops and settled in for the night.

The next day Princeton still appeared to be feeling good, and my earlier concerns were mostly put to rest. I continued to think maybe he'd had a touch of the flu or stomach upset and continued to keep a close eye on him. That night we stopped at Hope, planning to take the ferry over to Vancouver Island the next day. I had made plans to meet up with Gerrit for dinner that evening and wanted to be in Victoria by late afternoon.

Princeton enjoyed the ferry ride as much as he had the year before. Once again we left our vehicle and made our way to the bow of the ship and remained there until we docked. Princeton just loved having the ocean breeze wash over him, his eyes fixed on what lay before him. And as before I sat beside him on the steel deck of the ferry, and for almost an hour and a half we stared out onto the water. We both jumped a little when the ship's whistle blew as we approached the ferry terminal, and we headed back to the van and prepared to disembark.

When we reached the campground outside of Victoria we had stayed at a year ago, I was surprised to find it closed. A big steel gate blocked the entrance. Annoyingly, it was still listed online as available accommodation. I was disappointed, as our previous stay had been a lot of fun. Princeton had loved being allowed free run of the place, and he got along great with the owner's dog. And I'd had fun hanging out around the communal campfire in the evenings with the owner's daughter and her girlfriends who were visiting for a few days, drinking a little wine and smoking a little pot as she repeatedly raided her dad's store for supplies to make s'mores. Princeton only got to eat the graham crackers. He still considered marshmallows an insult, and I wasn't about to go through the chocolate thing again. When Princeton wasn't eating graham crackers, he'd sit with us around the campfire, wondering what the hell was so funny at times. During our nightly conversations, the owner's daughter mentioned that her father was considering closing the campground. He had owned it for several years and wanted to move on to something else. In the end, I guess that's what he did.

Unfortunately, when we discovered the campground had closed it was late Friday afternoon. The likelihood of finding another campground around Victoria was pretty much nil. I gave Gerrit a call to see if he could recommend something, and after contacting the other area campgrounds and discovering they were full, he didn't have any suggestions. There was, however, another option.

Gerrit met us a few minutes later and took us to a Walmart located close to downtown Victoria. Surprisingly, a dozen motorhomes and campers occupied the back of the parking lot. At a restaurant nearby Gerrit and I had dinner while catching each other up on our lives over the past year. After dinner I returned to the Walmart and parked in a relatively secluded spot. For someone who had routinely ridiculed other RVers whenever I saw them parked for the night at Walmart, I was becoming a regular user.

The next day I found a campsite near Victoria. I managed to reserve it for a couple of nights, allowing Princeton and me to hang around Victoria for two days. When Gerrit wasn't working he took us to places he thought we would enjoy. Otherwise we stayed in the campground, taking walks and relaxing. Although Princeton seemed fine, I was still concerned as to why he hadn't been feeling well during our first day out and didn't want him to overexert himself. We took shorter walks than usual (probably just as much for my benefit as for his—I was suffering chronic back and hip pain from leaning over him as I held on to his harness), and I made sure he rested frequently. We met a nice older couple the next stall over, and they invited us to share their lunches and dinner with them. It was a very relaxing and enjoyable couple of days, but knowing Cam and Kim were expecting us, we started driving to Tofino Monday morning.

As we approached Cathedral Grove, I wondered if I should keep my mouth shut and drive by without stopping. I wasn't really interested in spending a few hours having Princeton drag me along the trails, stopping erratically to investigate every damn plant or bug that caught his attention. Knowing how much he'd enjoyed it last year, however, I stopped and told him we could go for a *short* walk, this time on the side we hadn't visited last year. And that there would be *no* sitting on stumps posing so people could take pictures.

And, of course, our short walk became a *long* one. Princeton bounded through the trails, stopping at things I didn't even know were there so he could investigate them further. This time I didn't lift him onto any stumps and made sure we didn't loop in the opposite direction when we arrived back at the entrance. I explained to Princeton that things weren't going to look or smell any different regardless of how many times he went back to check them out. Ninety minutes later we were back on our way.

Kim and Cam had made arrangements with the owners of the wharf where their houseboat was located for us to spend as many nights there as we wanted, so as we drove into Tofino, I wasn't overly concerned about where we'd be staying. Although appreciative of the offer, I knew that Princeton would be happiest at the campground we'd stayed at before, and after spending the first night on the wharf, I was back at Green Point Campground early the next morning inquiring about no-shows. We managed to get a spot for each day we were in Tofino.

I've heard it said that visiting somewhere for the second time is never as exciting or enjoyable as the first—that the first time remains the most memorable regardless of how many times you return. In many respects I agree, but I also feel that if it's somewhere you truly love, each visit will be as special as the first. For me and Princeton, Tofino was such a place. The second time we were there, we did many of the same things, but it felt as if it were a continuation of our first visit. It was as if we had never left. From the dinners with Cam and Kim to the days spent at Incinerator Rock to the evenings hanging out with Troy at the campground store, everything felt as if we had done it just recently, not a year before.

In some respects our second visit was even better than our first. Although we would eventually do new things in Tofino, its familiarity made our stay easier for us. I knew how to get camping spots,

*When Princeton and I returned to Tofino, we once again
spent our days wandering its magnificent beaches.*
—Photograph by author

and this time managed to get one of the best sites available, overlooking the ocean, for multiple nights. We ate at many new places but also visited the restaurants we had really enjoyed a year before. And perhaps most importantly, I was already aware of Princeton's favourite places and could take the extra time finding similar places he would love.

Princeton again ran kilometre after kilometre on the sands of Long Beach, dancing in and out of the waves as they rushed to meet him. But this time I ran with him, holding up his back end by gripping his harness. We went back to Wickaninnish Beach several times to lean against the driftwood and watch the waves and visit the interpretive centre. The attendant who worked in the souvenir shop remembered us both from before and proudly told me of the new home he had just purchased in Ucluelet. We spent our evenings with Troy at the little store in the campground, Princeton reprising his role as guardian of the woodpile. More than once we visited the fish and chips place on the main street of Tofino, Princeton and I eating too many deep-fried dill pickles. And we made numerous visits to Chocolate Tofino, where Kim and Cam made sure we had our fill of freshly made gelato.

One place we spent more time at than we had the year before was Ucluelet. While Tofino is very touristy, Ucluelet's working-class feel makes it very appealing. It does have its share of trendy restaurants, boutiques, and coffee houses, and although it will probably become even more touristy, I hope some of its gritty persona survives. Another thing I liked about Ucluelet was its carwash. Tofino doesn't have anywhere to wash a vehicle, and Poseidon desperately needed a bath. While there I took the opportunity to revisit the aquarium, happy knowing that all the marine animals I had seen before had been carefully returned to the ocean and replaced with new ones.

Another place I really enjoyed visiting was the Amphitrite Point Lighthouse, located on the southern end of the peninsula close to

*The summer of 2015 would be the last time Princeton and I
would visit Tofino together.*
—Photograph by author

Ucluelet. It's easy to find; drive through Ucluelet and you'll find it a few kilometres outside of town. Several gentle trails wind around the area, and the views are fantastic. Compared to the sandy beaches of Tofino, much of the coastline is rugged and fairly rocky, with plenty of seabirds and marine animals to see.

Our last night in Tofino was a special one. We said goodbye to our friend Troy (he would be gone when we returned) and drove down to Incinerator Rock. It was windy and overcast; a storm was on its way. It was a little after nine, and I wanted to spend some time with Princeton sitting on the beach and watching the increasingly violent waves crash toward us before the gates closed at eleven. The beach was nearly deserted, and we found a perfect place to sit and watch the ocean. For nearly two hours we sat there, pressed together, feeling the occasional raindrop as darkness fell upon us. Although the ocean was now black and turbulent, it was just as breathtaking as it had been earlier in the day. I didn't speak to Princeton as we sat there. He knew there wasn't anything to say. Just being there together was enough.

Although our time together that evening was special, I also felt a sense of sadness. I had to be realistic and accept that Princeton's travelling days were drawing to a close. At seventeen, he had seen and experienced much more than most other dogs, but the wonderful times we had spent travelling together couldn't continue forever. Even if his health was otherwise good the following summer, I knew his mobility would inhibit us. As I sat there with him on that stormy night, I couldn't help but wonder if he had made it as far as he had because he wanted to do it for me. I've always believed that animals are much more aware of our feelings than we give them credit for. Princeton, especially, was always very aware of my feelings, whether they be anger, sadness, or joy. As I stroked the back of his head, I hoped he knew that I'd always tried to give him as much joy as he had given me. Finally I spoke to him, telling him how proud I was of him. I spoke of our travels and the things we had seen together. I told him that he was responsible for making my life that much more special. I told him what a tough son of a bitch he was, refusing to allow anyone to tell him when his life would draw to a close. But most importantly of all, I told him how much I loved him, and I thanked him for being my friend.

Princeton turned to look at me, then turned his head back toward the water. I think he knew we wouldn't be coming back here again. We watched the waves for a few more minutes before I lifted him and carried him back to the last vehicle in the parking lot. Neither of us looked back.

24

A Complicated Journey Home

FOR YEARS NOW I've had the unpleasant experience of passing kidney stones. Those who have had them know how "unpleasant" they can be. In my case, I know that something is about to happen because I start feeling some discomfort a few days before I actually pass them. Another sign I'm about to pass a stone is that my urine starts containing blood. I'll be standing at the toilet, taking a piss, and notice that my urine has a reddish tinge. That's when I mutter "Fuck" and prepare myself for the inevitable. So when I was squatting on the ground, checking tire pressures on Poseidon the morning we were departing Tofino, and noticed that Princeton's urine was red, I knew something wasn't right.

After muttering "Fuck," I went to him and checked him over. There were no interesting lumps or bumps, and he didn't appear to be in any discomfort. I went inside the van and felt his little bed. It was damp in several places. For whatever reason, he had urinated on it throughout the night. Within a few minutes I had packed up the van and we were driving toward Victoria.

As you know, the last thing Poseidon can be considered is fast. This time, however, it understood that it had to move with a little authority. I wanted to be in cellular coverage as quickly as possible so I could contact one of Princeton's veterinarians. Princeton was doing his best to look out the windows but spent most of his time being tossed around as I drove through the curves, the look on his face telling me he didn't understand what the problem was.

Once in cellular coverage I tried contacting each of Princeton's primary veterinarians. Drs. Kwantes and Fowler were away, and Dr. Marshall wouldn't be available until she came into her practice later that day. As we continued toward Victoria, my mother called me to see how we were doing. I told her of the problem Princeton was having and asked if she could help locate a veterinary practice in Vancouver that we could visit when we crossed over to the mainland. It was important to me to take the ferry to Vancouver instead of stopping in Victoria, knowing I could drive back to Edmonton in under twenty-four hours if I had to. My mother contacted my sister, and she managed to find a practice near the Horseshoe Bay ferry terminal near Vancouver.

Eventually, we made it to Nanaimo but had to wait for an hour before boarding the ferry. I let Princeton out of the van to see if he could pee. He was experiencing some discomfort when he urinated, and his pee was still reddish. Once we were on the ferry, we remained in the van so I could keep my eye on him. There would be no sitting at the bow of the ship, watching the ocean. The veterinary clinic my sister had located was about half an hour away from the ferry terminal. Upon arrival, I carried Princeton through the front doors and waited for the veterinarian.

When Princeton was first diagnosed with cancer, he was a regular patient of Dr. Kwantes. Occasionally Dr. Kwantes would refer Princeton to someone who had more experience with oncology or specific forms of medical imaging. As his treatments progressed, Drs. Marshall and Fowler became part of Princeton's medical team. They too sometimes referred Princeton to other veterinarians with more specialized fields of practice. Princeton and I had the opportunity to meet several veterinarians during the last few years of his life. Most of them always had his best interests in mind. There was always the odd one, however, upon learning that Princeton was an osteosarcoma survivor, who would make a diagnosis based solely on his history instead of considering any other contributing factors.

This was what happened at the veterinary clinic we were visiting just outside of Vancouver. The veterinarian didn't check Princeton's temperature or palpate him. He didn't listen to his heart and lungs. He instead wanted to know Princeton's history and, learning he had been diagnosed with osteosarcoma, told me that there was a strong possibility his urination issues were a result of cancer. I asked about a bladder infection or kidney or bladder stone but was told that these were unlikely. He recommended rushing Princeton to a twenty-four-hour emergency animal clinic in Vancouver for X-rays, an ultrasound, and admission for further observation. I remarked that a bladder infection can potentially demonstrate the symptoms Princeton was experiencing and that at least a urinalysis should be performed. The veterinarian finally agreed that a urine sample should be taken and sent to a lab for analysis. He then recommended an antibiotic shot.

As this was happening Dr. Marshall called me. She listened carefully as I explained Princeton's symptoms and demeanour. Without hesitation she said, "He has a bladder infection. I'm surprised he hasn't gotten one sooner. Lying around in the ocean probably introduced some pretty interesting things to his urethra. And I'm sure his mucking around in all the lakes and rivers you visited up north probably has something to do with it too."

She wanted to know where the closest drugstore was (across the street from the veterinary clinic) so she could phone in a script. The antibiotic she prescribed treated most types of bladder infections and would probably suffice until the lab report came back with details of exactly what sort of bug we were dealing with. I went to the drugstore, got the medication, and gave Princeton a pill before we left the parking lot.

Hearing Dr. Marshall's diagnosis and trusting her implicitly, I relaxed a little. Princeton, apart from straining when he urinated, seemed to be feeling fine. Nonetheless, I thought it was a good idea to find somewhere to camp close to Vancouver in case there was a problem during the night. I found a campground close to Squamish, about an hour from Vancouver, and although it was full, I was allowed to park in the visitors' area for the night. After eating cold spaghetti from a can, the two of us went to bed. Princeton fell asleep immediately and remained peaceful until he awoke about 3:00 a.m. for a pee. I took him outside and, using a flashlight, shone a light on his urine stream. It still had a reddish tinge—not much better than before. After falling back to sleep, he rested comfortably until morning.

The next time Princeton peed was about 8:00 a.m. His urine was still reddish but not as bad as it had been the day before. His bed had a few damp spots, but no worse than when we'd left Tofino. The veterinary clinic we had visited the night before promised to put a rush on Princeton's urinalysis and contact me immediately when the results were available. I was confident the antibiotic was already starting to work and decided that Princeton was well enough to head for home.

I kept a close eye on him, and during the few hundred kilometres we travelled that day, he seemed fine. By evening the colour of his urine was a light pink, and he wasn't straining to take a piss. The medication seemed to be working. The next morning I received a call from the veterinary office and was informed that Princeton's urine had tested positive for bacteria. Cultures now had to be grown to determine the type of bacteria involved and its susceptibility to various antibiotics. They promised to contact me with the results of the cultures and to forward the findings on to Princeton's primary veterinarians.

As Princeton's bladder infection was improving, I wasn't in the same hurry I'd been in before to get him home. We would be home tomorrow, and he would be off to see either Dr. Marshall or

Dr. Kwantes, but until then we could take our time and enjoy our trip back home. As we usually did, we stopped at lots of places where we could stretch our legs and Princeton could do a little exploring. One such place was somewhere I had always wanted Princeton to visit, and on the second-last day of our trip, I pulled into a parking lot beside the highway, opened the sliding door of the van, and said, "This is something you should see."

Mount Terry Fox is close to Valemount, British Columbia. It's dedicated to the young man I mentioned earlier, who was diagnosed with and later succumbed to osteosarcoma. "You're a survivor," I said to Princeton as we walked up to the plaque honouring Terry. "Not everyone, people or pets, is as lucky as you, but those who are, especially with osteosarcoma, should always be thankful for this guy."

I went on to explain to Princeton that he and Terry shared the same cancer, but unfortunately Terry had lost his battle. His spirit remains, however, and the hundreds of millions of dollars raised for cancer research over the past decades in honour of him have helped not only people conquer the disease, but animals too.

Princeton and I stood there in silence for a few moments. Maybe it was because of the seriousness in my voice, but Princeton seemed to understand that this was a special place. He remained where he was as I went back to the van and retrieved my camera to take a picture of him by the monument. It was one of the last photographs I ever took of him while we were travelling.

The last night we spent together in Poseidon will always remain one of my favourites. We found an abandoned turnoff alongside the highway, a few kilometres away from Jasper. I'm not sure what it was used for, but it was the size of about two football fields. I parked as far away from the highway as I could, next to an embankment. A family in a truck and trailer had decided to stop there too, but they were quite a distance from us. We sat outside the van, watching the occasional vehicle pass by on the highway. We had spent much of that summer away from the farm, driving on desolate gravel roads in the far north or splashing in the waves of the Pacific Ocean. We'd visited with old friends and made new ones. It wasn't always easy, but it was always worth it. We were adventurers, and we'd seen and done more together in the last few years than many people do in a lifetime. Both of us knew that our travels were coming to an end, but at that moment it didn't matter. All that mattered was that we were together.

Later that night, my hand on his head as I lay in my sleeping bag, the night silent except for the distant sounds of semi trucks on the highway, I told Princeton once more how wonderful and special it was to have seen and experienced so many places and things with him.

The next day we were home. A couple of pounds heavier, a bladder infection, and a sore back, so all in all, a pretty good trip. The first thing I did was make an appointment with Dr. Kwantes to discuss Princeton's bladder infection. He was due for blood work and radiographs of his chest anyway. By then the bacterial cultures from the lab in Vancouver had been completed and the results forwarded to Drs. Kwantes and Marshall. Apparently, a second organism was present that was resistant to the antibiotic Dr. Marshall had prescribed, so a new one was needed.

Both the X-rays and blood work were unremarkable. And because of his previous surgery, Princeton's liver enzymes were now within the normal range. A bladder X-ray was also performed, and that too was fine. Princeton's medication was changed to an antibiotic that would kill both types of bacteria found in his urine, and Dr. Kwantes recommended that another urinalysis be performed in two weeks.

Two weeks later I was chasing Princeton around the yard, holding a sterilized container up to his groin while he pissed and ran at the same time. For some weird reason, he now preferred to hop around and pee simultaneously. He could still stand on his own, but because of the weakness in his remaining rear leg, he found it easier if he was moving instead of squatting while urinating. As he ran, my job was to lift up his hindquarters with one hand and hold the container beneath him with the other. This meant, of course, that most of Princeton's piss ended up on my hand instead of in the container. After a few attempts, along with a stinky hand, I finally had enough urine to take to Dr. Kwantes.

A couple of days after I'd dropped off the urine sample, Dr. Kwantes phoned to say that there was no bacterial growth in Princeton's urine culture. He advised completing the full course of the antibiotic and didn't expect any additional problems. About two weeks after that, Princeton had yet another round of blood work performed. The results were even better than before. Not only were most of the values well within the specified parameters, but Princeton's liver enzymes were also the best they had been since 2012. Dr. Kwantes ended the conversation by stating that Princeton was doing far better than even he had expected.

25

A Wobbly Dog

UNFORTUNATELY, PRINCETON CONTINUED to experience muscle wasting in his remaining rear leg. All of us experience this as we get older, due to losing the ability to process protein as we age. Dogs are no exception. It was again recommended that Princeton get used to a dog cart or wheelchair, so I again tried to get him to use one. And as before, he hated it. After I strapped him in, he'd look at me with disgust, refusing to move. If I tried to lead him by his collar, he'd drop to his knees. If Princeton was to maintain his mobility, I would have to assist him.

Princeton still loved his freedom to go where he wanted but had to constantly rely on me to hold on to his harness to support his hind end. I didn't mind, except I was stooped over all the time. He still liked to run, so I had to run with him. Even at his advanced age, going up to the barns wasn't enough. He'd insist on running around the farm and occasionally onto the road in front of the farm. I started taking him to nearby parks just so he could have a change of scenery. Soon, however, I was having severe back and hip pain. I had suffered severe injuries to these areas earlier from a motorcycle accident, and being stooped over while either walking or running a couple of kilometres a day made things much worse.

However painful it was for me, it was all worth it if it made

Toward the end of Princeton's life, his new friend, BK,
would often be with him.
—Photograph by author

Princeton happy. He had spent a lifetime waiting for me outside of chicken barns while I was inside doing chores. The workday sometimes stretched into eighteen hours, even longer, and Princeton would be at my side without a complaint. As long as he was happy and otherwise healthy, there wasn't anything I wouldn't do for him. I would carry him if needed.

As time went on, however, Princeton was sometimes content to lie around and do nothing. Often he liked nothing better than to stretch out on the lawn and watch the day unfold. In 2014 another stray cat wandered onto the farm, and he and Princeton became close friends. They would often lie together on the grass for hours, watching me go from barn to barn or work around the farm. I named the stray BK and allowed him to live in one of the poultry barns. Barnie, the now self-appointed supreme ruler, who was no doubt a little jealous of the relationship, would often go to where Princeton and BK lay together and beat the crap out of Princeton's new friend. Barnie would then nuzzle up to Princeton for a few moments before wandering off to see if she could find something to kill. After she left, BK would return to a welcoming Princeton. I don't know why Princeton and BK liked each other so much, but I'm thankful for the relationship they had.

Princeton was using his John Deere Gator more frequently. I fabricated a canopy to cover the cargo area and placed a large orthopaedic doggy bed in it. He would sit in the back of the Gator as I drove around, proudly looking out at his farm. It reminded me of the times he would look out the windows of Poseidon as we travelled.

We also had to make a few changes whenever we went somewhere in the old pickup. Princeton was used to leaving the truck and visiting with everyone once we had reached our destination, but I now made him wait in the truck as his friends came out to see him instead. Without exception, they always did. I knew this bothered him sometimes, but I had to do what was best for him. I still wanted

Princeton to be active, but going to several places, in and out of the truck each time, was becoming difficult for him.

One place he refused to wait in the truck was the local PetSmart. Whenever I drove into the parking lot, he knew exactly where he was. We had been going there for a couple of years for cat food and other things, and all the staff knew him by name. They claimed him as their mascot, fussing over him when he hopped through the door. Because PetSmart has concrete floors and Princeton had difficulty walking on them, I would leave him up front by one of the cash registers. He'd sit there, beside the cashier, greeting everyone as they paid for their items. This wasn't because he wanted to meet everybody and see if they'd purchased anything interesting, but because of the doggy treats he received from the customers. PetSmart has a container of dog treats at each till that everyone is welcome to give to their dogs. Princeton, who never had a problem with anyone feeding him, would sit there as the customers gave him these treats. The staff often joked that he wouldn't want his dinner that evening. But he always did.

It was around this time that I started to wonder what life would be like without my best friend. What I was thinking was probably no different from what a lot of pet owners feel when their friends become old or sick. It's almost perverse that we spend years loving them, often making them a part of our family, only to spend the last part of their lives obsessing about their deaths when we should be celebrating our remaining time with them. I know I've been guilty of this, as I'm sure many others have as well. I told myself several times not to think as I did, to instead appreciate and enjoy the time we had left. Still, knowing I would be walking to my barns alone one day not only saddened me, but also frightened me.

Besides his mobility issues, Princeton was still very healthy. And just as importantly, his zeal for life was undiminished. The fire still shone brightly in his beautiful brown eyes, and I hoped he would be around for some time yet. It was important to me, however, to never see something within Princeton simply because I wanted it to be there. He had always trusted me to do what was best for him, and I reminded myself that the day would come when I would have to do what was best for him in a way much different from before. Until then, the two of us would continue on together as we had for the past sixteen years.

The fall was mostly uneventful. Princeton, now nearly completely dependent on me to help him walk, was still quite active. The days he wasn't relaxing with BK, we would easily walk over a kilometre. One November afternoon, while Princeton and I were walking around the yard, he suddenly rolled over onto his right side. He had been fine until then, even managing to run short distances by himself. After I stood him up, I noticed that his head was tilted to the right and it was impossible for him to stand on his own. I immediately rushed him into Park Veterinary Centre to see what was wrong with him.

Dr. Kwantes wasn't available, so Princeton was treated by another veterinarian. Sitting with him in the examination room, waiting for the doctor, I thought he was improving. His head remained tilted to one side and he was still unsteady on his feet, but he appeared much better than he had a little over an hour ago. After a complete examination, the veterinarian made a diagnosis.

Idiopathic vestibular disease (IVD), commonly known as "old dog vestibular disease" or "old rolling dog syndrome," is scary as hell to watch when a dog experiences it. Most pet owners confuse it with a stroke. One moment your dog is walking or running without a problem, and the next he's on his side, rolling around and unable to stand. Fortunately, most dogs recover completely within a few days. The disease affects a dog's balance, and the underlying cause isn't easily identifiable. The name itself sums this up; "idiopathic" refers to a disease or condition for which the cause is unknown, and "vestibular disease" refers to a sudden loss of balance. There are several theories about why this disease sometimes afflicts older dogs, the most commonly suggested cause being inflammation or nerve irritation within the inner ear, but the exact cause hasn't been confirmed. In addition to the falling over and head tilt, another common symptom is nystagmus, the rapid movement of the eyes back and forth. Princeton didn't have this symptom, but after checking with other veterinarians, the doctor who examined him discovered that some dogs that suffer from IVD never exhibit it.

The veterinarian went on to say that Princeton would likely recover. Occasionally, some dogs retain a slight head tilt but no other symptoms. She recommended taking him home and making him comfortable. The next couple of days he would need some assistance walking — something I was used to — but would probably then be back to his old self. I asked the veterinarian, who had never treated Princeton before but was certainly aware of him, her opinion of his health otherwise. "Him?" she replied. "He's fine. He's one of those dogs who goes on forever."

Within a couple of days, Princeton was indeed back to his old self. He had a slight head tilt, but being a three-legged dog who had to balance himself in a particular way, his head was always a little off-kilter anyway. Within a day he was walking as he had before the episode, which had done little to slow him down. The third night after the episode, he went to sleep on his bed without any indication that he was suffering from the disease.

Two hours later I was awakened by him barking furiously. I rushed to the entryway to see what was the matter. Princeton lay on his side, barking and yelping. He was kicking out and trying to lift his head. "What's the matter?" I shouted as I dropped to my knees to hold his head. He continued barking as I tried to soothe him. His eyes were darting back and forth, and I immediately thought he was having another IVD episode. I quickly dressed, placed Princeton into the truck, and rushed him to the emergency clinic.

He was given a complete physical examination. The attending

veterinarian felt that Princeton had once more succumbed to vestibular disease. It wasn't uncommon for some dogs to experience multiple bouts of it over a short period and then never again. The doctor recommended performing a CT scan of Princeton's skull and thorax to make sure we weren't missing anything. On the off chance that the episodes Princeton was experiencing were caused by a brain lesion, the CT scan would likely indicate this. I agreed and asked to have the procedure done while he was still in the emergency clinic.

A CT scan (computed tomography scan) creates cross-sectional images using multiple X-rays taken at various angles, which are processed by a computer. Because of these multiple images, CT scans usually provide more information than a regular X-ray. In Princeton's case, the CT scan might show any irregularities of his brain that could explain his recent behaviour. The following morning, he underwent the procedure, along with another blood analysis.

The results of the blood work were, as usual, unremarkable. Most of his values were well within the specified limits. They were outstanding considering how old he was. The preliminary findings of the CT scan indicated no significant abnormalities that could explain Princeton's symptoms. No lesions of the brain were noted, and another veterinarian who examined Princeton agreed with the first that he had probably suffered another idiopathic vestibular episode. Princeton was already showing signs of improvement, being able to stand on his own and eating anything the hospital staff offered him. He was discharged from hospital with an anti-inflammatory and antibiotic, and they told me someone would contact me once a specialist had further examined the CT scan results.

When Princeton returned home he was active and cheerful. His head was cocked to one side, but no more than when he had suffered his first episode of vestibular disease. For the next few days, I was nervous as hell, expecting him to have another attack. I'd watch him carefully, coming out from the barns every fifteen minutes to check up on him. During the night I'd get up every hour to check him, only to find him sleeping peacefully on his little bed. Each day I relaxed a little more, and after a few days, I was confident the worst was over.

About a week after Princeton was discharged, I received a call from the emergency clinic to advise me that the specialist had some concerns about Princeton's CT scan. He confirmed that there was nothing in the findings to explain why Princeton had experienced a vestibular attack, but he had discovered a left hepatic mass and two pulmonary nodules. I made an appointment with Dr. Sereda, the internist who had performed an ultrasound on Princeton the first time he had liver disease, to discuss the findings.

The first thing I asked her was why the liver mass and lung nodules weren't discovered earlier when another internist first looked at the CT scan, especially since neither was exactly insignificant and both were easily visible. She didn't know why, but regardless of the oversight, felt that they were significant enough to be of concern and should be investigated further. The mass on Princeton's liver could be anything, but she wouldn't know if his liver disease had returned without first performing a biopsy. Dr. Sereda thought the nodules in his lungs were most likely metastatic cancer, but Dr. Fowler, who had looked at the scans earlier, felt that they weren't cancerous at all and suspected pulmonary fibrosis. Dr. Sereda recommended performing an abdominal ultrasound and fine needle aspiration of both the liver mass and the lung nodules.

Surprisingly, I wasn't that worried about what Dr. Sereda had told me. Maybe it was nothing more than a gut feeling, but I was confident the nodules in Princeton's lungs and the mass on his liver weren't going to harm him. Most importantly, at least to me, was that the CT hadn't found any brain lesions. The rest of the CT scan had also found nothing out of the ordinary, and the blood work hadn't identified any problems either. Metastasis from a primary liver tumour is very rare, and since the rest of the scan hadn't discovered anything, I questioned how the nodules in Princeton's lungs could be metastatic disease. Princeton's osteosarcoma diagnosis had been about four and a half years earlier, and I was confident it too had nothing to do with the recent discoveries. I agreed with Dr. Sereda, however, that only an ultrasound and biopsy would tell us what we were dealing with, and I made an appointment with her for the additional tests. For now Princeton had recovered from his latest bout of vestibular syndrome and was back to normal.

Over the next few days, I spoke with Drs. Kwantes and Marshall to get their opinions of Princeton's CT scan. Both agreed with Dr. Sereda that a biopsy and ultrasound would provide the answers we were looking for. Dr. Kwantes went over Princeton's previous X-rays, and although the lung fields still appeared clear, he noted that there could possibly be cysts where the CT scan had found the nodules. This isn't to say that he had overlooked them, as it's far easier to notice something on an X-ray if you know exactly where to look. The cysts were also very tiny, only a few millimetres in diameter, and X-rays won't often yield abnormalities under a centimetre in diameter. This was actually welcome news; whatever the cysts were, they might have been there for some time and had remained static in size. Regardless of how long they had been there or how they originated, both he and Dr. Marshall thought they likely indicated pulmonary fibrosis.

In early December Princeton went in for a full abdominal ultrasound. He hadn't suffered any more vestibular attacks and remained active around the farm. The ultrasound would confirm the precise locations of the liver mass and lung nodules and determine if they had increased in size. Another ultrasound would be required during the actual biopsy to guide the needles Dr. Sereda would use to extract the tissue samples. It addition to determining the position and size of the liver mass, she noticed a small nodule on Princeton's spleen. She determined that the liver mass was in a position easily accessible for aspiration, but the nodules in his lungs would be difficult to access. Dr. Sereda made the decision to attempt to obtain a sample from Princeton's liver only, feeling that trying to obtain one from his lungs might do him more harm than good.

A few days later Princeton was back at Guardian Veterinary Centre for his biopsy. I told him that I loved him and would be there waiting for him when the procedure was over. He was taken away as I settled into one of the waiting room sofas. An hour later a technician came out and asked me to come to an examination room. Knowing that an hour wasn't long enough to complete the procedure, I immediately became worried.

"There's been a problem," Dr. Sereda said as she walked in a few minutes later. "Princeton reacted negatively to the sedative we gave him."

"What happened?" I asked.

"Once we administered it, he immediately started to bark and snarl."

She went on to explain that Princeton was fine now, but his behaviour had changed dramatically once the sedative was given. It was severe enough that she had administered naloxone, a drug used to block or reverse the effects of opioid medication, to Princeton as soon as his abnormal behaviour began. He was now resting comfortably, and Dr. Sereda expected him to be back to normal within a few hours.

The sedative she had administered was butorphanol, an opioid commonly used for pain control and as a component in anaesthetics. It's generally safe with minimal side effects and is tolerated quite well in dogs. Princeton had been administered the drug a couple of months earlier when he had to be sedated for his CT scan and hadn't had a problem. Although I can't say with absolute certainty, I'm sure he had received the drug for his previous surgeries as well. Why he had a reaction this time, no one could say, but everyone agreed that he should never be given the drug again, and special attention should be given to him whenever a sedative of any type was to be used.

Dr. Sereda offered an alternative to using a sedative: no sedative at all. She was confident she could perform an ultrasound-guided fine needle aspiration of Princeton's liver mass without it and he wouldn't be in any discomfort. She had allowed me to be involved in Princeton's previous ultrasounds and suggested that my comforting him would minimize his movements, allowing her to obtain a sample quickly and safely. Although she'd been reluctant to try to obtain a sample of the lung nodules, she mentioned that without a sedative this would be impossible. Not only were the nodules within the lungs, but their location made them difficult to access without going through tissue and bone. This is something Princeton would feel, and the feeling wouldn't be pleasant. The good news was that the latest ultrasound had shown the nodules hadn't increased in size, and I think Dr. Sereda now agreed with the other veterinarians that they might not be cancerous after all.

Six days after the first attempt, Princeton was back at Guardian for another try to aspirate the mass on his liver. I gently placed him on his back on top of a specially prepared platform, talking to him softly while Dr. Sereda prepared to begin. After his abdomen was shaved and sterilized, she guided the needle, using ultrasound, into the liver mass and collected a sample. If Princeton experienced any discomfort, he didn't show it. The only thing that bothered him was the alcohol applied to his bare belly, which made him sneeze occasionally. Once the procedure was finished, Princeton was placed on his feet and we made our way down to the reception area. He wanted to leave as soon as possible—not because he was upset over the procedure, but because as we rode the elevator down to the main floor I took his head in my hands, looked into his eyes, and said, "Hot dog." As far as Princeton was concerned, this more than made up for any unpleasantness he might have experienced.

Two days before Christmas I received a call from Dr. Sereda. She had the results from Princeton's biopsy. She mentioned that she was calling from home instead of the clinic, which worried me.

Why would she call from home? Were the findings that bad? Did Princeton need aggressive treatment immediately? I soon had my answer.

Dr. Sereda later told me she had called me from home because she knew I would be obsessing over the biopsy results. She was also excited over the findings: the results of the biopsy indicated no evidence of cancer. Nothing but normal, healthy liver cells. She was surprised by the findings, even suggesting that perhaps she had mistakenly inserted the needle through the mass and into the healthy liver tissue. As she is a board-certified internist with many years' experience, I found this hard to believe. I think she too considered this unlikely but was attempting to allow for any variable that could explain the results. She suggested that there was a very small chance Princeton was experiencing a hepatocellular carcinoma as before, but she considered this unlikely. And in the off chance he was, it was probably benign. His liver values were excellent, and she recommended that no further action be taken. If we wanted to, Princeton could undergo another ultrasound in six weeks to determine if the mass had increased in size or changed in appearance.

As he had done so often in the past, Princeton surprised everyone.

26

An Entirely New Problem

TWO DAYS LATER we celebrated another Christmas together. Princeton spent most of the day in my sister's kitchen, sampling everything on the menu. For a Christmas gift I bought him an oversized doggy bed. Princeton went through his beds often, requiring a new one every couple of months. He never wore them out but destroyed them by tearing the stuffing out of them. Every so often I'd find him sitting on his bed (or what was left of it), surrounded by big chunks of foam rubber. For reasons I never understood, he always looked extremely pleased with himself whenever he did this. He never ate any of it, but once he'd started systematically taking one apart, it was basically finished. His new one was extra large with cushioned edges and a tough outer layer, and I hoped it would last until at least the summer.

One night in early January I was awakened by a loud banging. Realizing the sound was coming from the entryway, I rushed in to check on Princeton. His feet were hitting the wall as he thrashed around on his bed. I dropped to my knees and held him until the thrashing ended about a minute later. When it was over he got up on his own and went to the door, wanting to go outside. I helped him down the steps where he urinated and then rolled around in the snow. I took him back into the house and laid him upon his bed and sat with him. This episode was similar to his two vestibular episodes except for one important detail: he had experienced a loss of consciousness. During Princeton's vestibular attacks he was aware of what was happening to him, and he barked because he was frightened, not understanding why his balance was gone. This was different. This time I knew he had experienced a seizure, as he had remained silent during the attack and appeared confused when it was over. But he seemed to be feeling okay, so I thought I'd wait until morning to take him to see Dr. Kwantes.

At about 5:00 a.m. I was awakened once more. Princeton was having another seizure. When it was over, he failed to recover as quickly as he had a few hours before. I loaded him into the truck and rushed him to the emergency clinic. The attending veterinarian performed a physical examination and took blood for analysis. She recommended keeping him there for observation before she decided what further testing might be required. I had to return home to check the barns but would return within a couple of hours. Before I got back to the clinic, Princeton suffered a grand mal seizure. The veterinarian who had seen Princeton earlier that morning witnessed it. There was no question that we were now dealing with an entirely new problem.

When I returned, the veterinarian and I discussed Princeton's seizures in detail. The doctor suggested that most dogs his age who suffer from cluster seizures are suffering from brain cancer. She recommended an MRI to try to determine if this was true of Princeton. Another option was a palliative approach: no more testing but medication to control the seizures. I had no problem with an MRI, except that the procedure required Princeton to be sedated to control his movements. He had reacted violently the last time he was sedated, and no one could say that he wouldn't have the same reaction again. Sending him home with medication without trying to determine what was causing the seizures wasn't an option for me. Sure, Princeton was a very old dog now, but he was still healthy and relatively active. What confused me most, however, was why a CT scan, performed less than two months earlier, hadn't detected any sort of brain lesion. I realize an MRI often offers more precise imaging, but I thought the CT scan would have revealed something.

I decided that I needed to take a couple of days to think about what would be the best course of action. For the last sixteen years I had always done what was best for Princeton, and now was no exception. Should I offer him palliative care, hoping the seizures weren't a result of a brain lesion? Or should I risk his health and allow him to be sedated for an MRI? I wanted to speak to Drs. Kwantes, Marshall, and Fowler to see if they could offer any insight. The veterinarian currently dealing with Princeton's seizures agreed this was a realistic approach, and in the meantime prescribed some anti-seizure medication for him.

Princeton was discharged from the clinic with the medication and a little bell attached to his collar. While he was in hospital, a nurse attached it to his collar to alert the staff if he started to shake from a seizure. He would wear this little bell for the rest of his life, even when he no longer needed it. The medication prescribed to control his seizures was Keppra, an anticonvulsant. Originally developed for human use, it is now sometimes used to treat seizures in dogs and cats. An advantage it has over other anti-seizure medications such as potassium bromide and phenobarbital is that it doesn't appear to influence kidney or liver enzymes. Although Princeton's liver enzymes, which had been elevated in the past, were now within normal limits, Keppra was the safest choice. The primary side effects are upset stomach, behavioural changes, and drowsiness. In both people and animals, however, side effects depend on the individual. Some will experience few or no side effects, while others will react negatively to the drug.

I felt concerned and frustrated. Princeton had recovered from his vestibular issues, and his veterinarians were no longer that concerned about the liver mass and lung nodules, but here was something else to worry about. It would have been easier if we knew what was causing the seizures, but further testing was required for a proper diagnosis. Worse, Princeton reacted negatively to Keppra. He stumbled around and was often lethargic. If I tried to make him walk, he would either refuse or stumble over. I moved his bed into the living room and in front of the TV, hoping he would have some stimulation while I was in the barns. The day after he returned home, he suffered another seizure. A few days after that, he experienced another. As miserable as I felt for him, I'm sure he felt much worse. I've always accepted what several veterinarians have told me throughout the years—that an animal's quality of life should be considered when making any decision for them—and it terrified me knowing that Princeton was suffering. There was, however, one thing I felt might be causing the seizures, but I found myself alone in my opinions.

Throughout the nearly seventeen years Princeton and I were together, he always received the best medical care I could provide for him. This was true not only of him, but also of my other animals. I provided my animal friends access to excellent veterinarians, but I also educated myself about their conditions and familiarized myself with various treatment modalities. Whether this was learning about renal disease in cats or osteosarcoma in dogs, I would spend days at a time reading assorted case studies and talking to people who could educate me about specific diseases and treatments. Additional information was available online and at libraries, including those at colleges and universities.

Whenever one of my animals suffered a disease or ailment, familiarizing myself with their affliction allowed me to ask knowledgeable questions about the disease and treatment options. Except for a handful of veterinarians I've dealt with over the years, most accommodated my questions and didn't have a problem sharing their knowledge and experiences. Because of this, when a decision had to be made about the health of one of my pets, I usually felt that I was part of the process instead of merely a spectator. This was especially true of, but not limited to, Drs. Marshall, Fowler, Sereda, and later, Cockwill. But no one was more accommodating and receptive to my input than Dr. Kwantes. Starting with Sierra, the cat I eventually lost to renal failure, Dr. Kwantes patiently answered every question I had and took the time to educate me on the disease and treatment options. Often he'd prepare for me a list of topics I was to study on my own, and we'd discuss them in detail at the next appointment. This continued with Princeton. For the last few years of Princeton's life, Dr. Kwantes and I would often discuss his care, each of us carefully listening to and considering the input of the other. Not only did this allow me to understand and appreciate what Princeton was facing, but it also gave me the confidence and initiative to investigate Princeton's illnesses or treatments on my own.

Because of my insistence on educating myself, I questioned the drug prescribed for his incontinence. I felt that, however remote the chances might be, the medication could be contributing to his seizures. Before I go further, I want to state that most of Princeton's veterinarians always did what they thought was best for him, and any medications prescribed were always intended to help him in the best way possible. Most veterinarians make their diagnosis and recommend treatments based upon their training and experiences. Sometimes a diagnosis is wrong or a treatment unsuccessful, but this is to be expected. Medicine isn't always a cut-and-dried science, and animals, like people, often respond to illnesses and medications in different ways.

As dogs age, they often develop bladder leakage. This is common, and various medications are available to combat this problem. Starting when he was around sixteen, Princeton would sometimes have little accidents while sleeping. Unless he was suffering from a bladder infection, these pee puddles were usually very small. Occasionally, when he raised himself from his bed each morning, I'd see a damp spot, usually no more than a couple of inches across.

In the winter of 2015, he was prescribed Propalin in the hopes it would reduce the frequency of these accidents.

Propalin is usually prescribed for female dogs, but there's some evidence that it's also successful for treating incontinence in male dogs. The active ingredient in Propalin is phenylpropanolamine. Phenylpropanolamine is no longer available in Canada and the United States for human use, as it may lead to an increased risk of stroke in young women. Interestingly, the exact mechanism of phenylpropanolamine isn't fully understood, but it's thought to stimulate the alpha adrenergic receptors, which triggers the release of norepinephrine, a substance similar to adrenaline. When Propalin is administered to dogs and cats suffering from urinary incontinence, it's the stimulation of these alpha adrenergic receptors that increases the urethral sphincter tone of the animal, decreasing involuntary urine leakage. Although the drug is considered effective and safe for cats and dogs, some side effects have been reported. These include increased heart rate and blood pressure, restlessness, decreased appetite, and in severe cases, collapse.

When I first researched Propalin, much of the evidence confirmed that most dogs experience few of the reported side effects. However, some pet owners suggested that their dogs reacted violently to the medication. These reactions included, but weren't limited to, seizure activity. Although I believed then (and still do) that the drug is generally safe, I found it outside the realm of mere coincidence that Princeton had suffered multiple seizures while taking the drug. When I discussed this with Princeton's doctors, including his regular veterinarians and those who had seen him in emergency, everyone felt that Propalin had little to do with his seizures. Their experiences with it had always been favourable, and most thought his seizures were related to a brain abnormality.

So here I was, agonizing over a decision I would have to make. Take a chance and have Princeton sedated for an MRI, expecting to find a brain tumour, or continue to think that something else was contributing to his seizures. The only thing I knew for sure was that Princeton was miserable. He was loopy because of Keppra and had lost interest in doing anything. After he suffered his second seizure when he returned home from emergency, I discontinued Propalin, and Princeton had yet to experience another. Although this was promising, I couldn't (and still can't) unequivocally claim that the drug had been responsible for the seizures. Princeton had also been on Keppra for some time, and if the seizures were caused by a brain lesion, then perhaps the anticonvulsant was working. I'd wait and see how he did over the next week or two before I made any decisions.

For the next week I let Princeton spend his nights in the living room. I slept on the couch beside him, hoping the bell attached to his collar would awaken me if he had a problem. He was still behaving oddly because of Keppra but experienced no further seizures. When the next week began, we continued sleeping together in the living room, and gradually I became less concerned that another seizure would occur. After the end of the second week, I held off on the MRI, and with the blessing of his doctors, decided to slowly wean Princeton off Keppra. He was weaving around like a drunken sailor because of the drug, and this was no sort of life for him. If he experienced a seizure as the dosage of Keppra decreased, then I could assume the Propalin had nothing to do with them and would take the chance to have him sedated and the MRI performed.

Over the next several weeks, Princeton, Murray the cat, and I spent our nights in the living room. Murray would alternate between sleeping with me on the couch and snuggling up to Princeton on his bed. Every few days I decreased the dosage of the anticonvulsant until Princeton was no longer taking it. We continued sleeping together for another week, and I prepared myself for the sudden ringing of Princeton's bell to alert me to a seizure. The ringing never came. The fogginess that had surrounded Princeton for nearly two months lifted, and the fire returned to his eyes. I moved back into my bedroom, and he returned to the entryway. He never experienced another seizure for as long as he lived.

Were Princeton's seizures a negative reaction to Propalin? No one, including me, can determine that for sure. What I can claim is that once I stopped giving him Propalin the seizures stopped. They never returned, even after discontinuing Keppra. Regardless of whether it was Propalin or not, the important thing was that Princeton remained seizure-free. For the rest of his life he might have experienced occasional bladder leakage, but this was far better than administering a drug he might have reacted negatively to.

Another treatment I discontinued when Princeton started to experience seizures was chiropractic visits. He often had his back and neck adjusted during his visits, and although I was doubtful that these adjustments were responsible for his seizures, I thought it was appropriate to discontinue any treatments that, however unlikely, might have led to his seizures.

Although Princeton would eventually recover from his seizures and Keppra usage, the experience had taken a toll on him. In the past, whenever he'd overcome a health issue, he bounced back almost immediately. This time was different. He recovered slowly, relying on me much more than he had before. At his age, and with what he had already gone through, I shouldn't have expected anything different, but it was still difficult seeing him struggle to regain his steadiness and ability to walk. He hadn't been very active over the last couple of months, which made his hindquarters even weaker than before. For me, the hardest part of his recovery was watching him try to understand why things didn't work as well as they once had. For the remainder of the winter and throughout spring, however, Princeton worked hard and his mobility returned to where it had been before the seizure activity. By late spring we were going for our regular walks, still visiting various local parks so he could experience a change of scenery. Throughout his recovery one thing never changed: his attitude. After the fogginess of the anticonvulsant left him, he was as bright as ever. Soon he was pulling me along as he ran, stopping only when he discovered something he wanted to see or smell. He was happy. And I was happy he was still with me.

Although Princeton had nearly fully recovered by late spring, I knew that our travelling days were behind us. Still, I was hopeful we could take some day trips together in Poseidon, but I didn't want to take him too far in case he had a medical emergency. Princeton tired easily now too, and I wanted him to relax and enjoy whatever time he had left at the farm, where he had spent nearly his entire life. His recent seizures had been not only hard on him, but also emotionally difficult for me. Princeton was very old, and although he was fine now, I knew it wouldn't always be this way.

Except for the time I lived in an apartment that didn't allow animals, I've always had a furry companion. Throughout this time I've learned one indelible truth about pet ownership: we usually out-live them. And when the time comes that their lives are more pain-ful than joyous, we have to bestow that one final gesture of love and let them go. It's the price we pay for the companionship and un-conditional love our pets give us, and the sadness and anguish we feel when we make the decision to help our pets end their lives is beyond description. Seeing them draw their last breath as we hold them in our arms is the last part of the journey we share together, and the memories of that shared life are all that remain.

For nearly seventeen years Princeton and I had been inseparable. If he wasn't with me, I felt incomplete. I was a better person with him than without him. I was an impatient, workaholic, often self-destructive person, and he was a compassionate, thoughtful, trust-ing, and loving dog who made everything okay. It's human nature to feel sorry for ourselves from time to time, but being with Princeton made me realize I was the luckiest guy in the world. Life was pretty damn good when we were together. If the days were long and things didn't go my way, it didn't matter—I had Princeton. I knew he wanted to continue our journey together, and for now we would, but I also wanted him to know that when his situation became too tiresome or painful for him, I would find the strength to let him go his own way and carry on without him.

One spring evening, as Princeton and I walked to the end of the driveway to close the gate, I dropped to my knees and embraced him. I whispered in his ear not to worry about anything. When the time came, probably not for a while, we'd both be okay. He seemed satisfied with that.

27

Fading Fire

PRINCETON CONTINUED BEING his happy self as summer rolled around. As he had done the fall before, he was often content to lie upon the grass and watch me work or to ride around in his John Deere Gator. Most evenings, after chores, we'd go for rides in the Gator and end up several kilometres from home, stopping only when we found something new to see. I'd unload Princeton from the box, and we'd spend a little while looking at all the new and fascinating things. Princeton's eyesight and sense of smell were still as acute as ever, and he loved going to places he'd never been to before. Going home in the darkness, I'd wind out that little Gator as Princeton sat grinning on his bed behind me, his head stuck out the side of the box as we sped along, savouring the night air as it entered his nostrils. I'd pull into the driveway, close the gate behind us, and drive to the barns to check the birds. Princeton, instead of waiting for me outside the doors of the barns as he'd done nearly all his life, waited in his personal mobility vehicle. After nearly seventeen years of working hard, Princeton was enjoying his retirement.

It was a Saturday evening in June when I first noticed the mass on Princeton's gum line. I had just finished mowing the grass, and Princeton was joyfully rolling around on the freshly cut lawn. As he rolled from one side to the other, barking at things that weren't there, I went to give him a belly rub. Princeton, in doggy heaven, had forgotten what he was barking at and lay there quietly, his tongue hanging out of his mouth. As I continued to scratch his belly, I noticed a black mass along his lower right gum line. I had gotten into the habit of checking Princeton's teeth every few weeks and knew it hadn't been there the last time I checked. So I did what everyone would probably do and poked it. It was hard but didn't seem to be bothering him. But it bothered me, and not wanting to wait until Monday when Park Veterinary Centre was open, I decided to take Princeton to Guardian Veterinary Centre to have it looked at.

The growth in Princeton's mouth was thought to be an epulis, a benign tumour that frequently afflicts middle-aged to older dogs. It's a rather disgusting-looking growth that usually appears on the gum tissue. Princeton's growth was a couple of centimetres in diameter and black in colour. Although this was not life-threatening, the attending veterinarian suggested having a biopsy performed and having the growth removed, as it would increase in size and interfere with Princeton's eating. The vet also said that Princeton appeared to be in remarkable shape considering his age and previous health concerns. Princeton sat on the floor looking up at us as we discussed him, probably thinking he had better things to do, like riding in the Gator on a warm Saturday evening instead of sitting in a clinic when there was nothing wrong with him.

When we returned home Princeton continued rolling around on the freshly mowed grass and barking at imaginary beasties. I planned to phone Park Veterinary on Monday to set up an appointment with Dr. Kwantes to have a biopsy performed to make sure the lump was nothing to worry about. I was probably being overly cautious but wanted to make sure nothing was wrong with Princeton. As I would find out later, however, something was very much wrong with him.

A couple of days later, he went to see Dr. Kwantes for a biopsy. He had a complete checkup including X-rays and blood work and once again was declared to be clinically healthy. Not only that, but during the last few weeks Princeton's strength in his rear leg had increased, making him less dependent on his harness. The X-rays of Princeton's lungs looked good, unchanged from the previous radiographs. Dr. Kwantes, aware of the location of the nodules discovered from the CT scan, said they hadn't increased in size. He agreed the growth was likely nothing more than an epulis and scheduled an appointment to remove it and have it analyzed. Princeton made it through the surgery without a seizure or any other problem.

I was driving with Princeton when I received the call from Dr. Kwantes. We had just finished eating hot dogs from Des's cart and were heading home to perform the late-afternoon chores. I had been dealing with Dr. Kwantes for nearly twenty years, and when I answered the phone I could tell whatever he had to say wasn't good. He began our conversation by asking if I had some time to discuss the results of Princeton's biopsy.

After pulling into the nearest parking lot and looking at Princeton as he sat beside me, I asked Dr. Kwantes to continue.

"I received the lab results from the mass we removed from Princeton's mouth, and I'm afraid the news isn't good," he replied. "The growth isn't an epulis at all. It's a malignant melanoma."

I didn't say anything, the word "malignant" consuming my thoughts. Sensing my silence was a response, he continued. "The prognosis for dogs with oral melanoma is poor. Princeton's is very aggressive, the mitotic index at over forty."

I sat there for several moments, still unable to say anything. I reached over and touched Princeton's head, slowly moving my hand behind his ear and starting to scratch. He always loved that so much.

"What are our treatment options?" I finally replied.

Dr. Kwantes went on to explain that treatment options were limited. If the entire mass was removed with good margins, six months' survival wouldn't be unrealistic. If surgery wasn't performed, probably two months at best. Radiation therapy was also an option, with about a third of dogs treated surviving up to a year. Unfortunately, chemotherapy hadn't proven successful for treating oral melanomas, and so wasn't recommended. He then mentioned that a recently introduced vaccine, combined with surgery, had shown promising results.

"I'm sorry, Terry," he said before the call ended.

For almost half an hour I remained parked, sitting in the truck with Princeton and scratching him behind his ear. I felt a gamut of emotions ranging from sadness to anger, but it was a sense of helplessness I felt most of all. It all seemed too much. Over the past few months, I had seen Princeton make a remarkable recovery from something we, his caregivers, might have caused. Before that he had overcome his liver problems without so much as a whimper. Five years earlier he had fought and won his battle with a deadly cancer, giving up a leg in the process; no one except me had expected him to win. And through all of it, he demonstrated a resilience and upbeat quality that everyone who knew him came to admire. Whenever anyone had put a limitation on him, he always proved them wrong. Princeton was everyone's "wonder dog." But now there was this. It wasn't right. It wasn't fair. It wasn't fair to Princeton, me, or anyone else who loved him.

Fuck you, cancer. Leave my friend alone.

Oral melanoma is the most common oral tumour in dogs. Like all cancers, it originates from a dog's own cells, this time from the skin cells that make the skin pigment melanin. It can affect any dog, but dogs with dark pigmentation (dark skin and gums) seem predisposed to the disease. And older male dogs stand a greater chance of developing melanoma. As Dr. Kwantes had said, the prognosis for a dog suffering from oral melanoma is poor. It's an aggressive cancer, and even if the original tumour is removed, it often spreads to other parts of the body, including the lymph nodes and lungs. Most studies have also determined that in over half the dogs with oral melanoma the cancer moves into the jawbone.

Tumour size appears linked to survivability, even when the mass is removed. This is probably because of the aggressive nature of the disease. Survivability is better in dogs with a smaller tumour treated aggressively than in dogs with a large tumour that has metastasized. Princeton's melanoma was almost two centimetres in diameter and was thought to have spread to one of his lymph nodes but not anywhere else, placing him in either the Stage II or Stage III category. Princeton's melanoma wasn't apparent from looking at his face, and it didn't appear (yet) to have any bone involvement. Both Drs. Kwantes and Marshall agreed that if Princeton was to have a chance of survival, any treatment would need to be performed quickly.

The first thing to do was to find the melanoma vaccine. Dr. Kwantes was the first to mention it and, although he had yet to use it himself, said it appeared to have some benefit. "Vaccine" is actually a misnomer, as it's not really a vaccine but a treatment that's becoming increasingly commonplace in fighting cancer: immunotherapy. For many years, the standard protocol of cancer treatment has been chemotherapy. Chemotherapy drugs have evolved over the years and have been responsible for saving or prolonging the lives of many people and animals battling cancer. Without these drugs, many people and pets would not enjoy the quality of life they have today. As successful as they have been, there are sometimes harmful, even life-threatening side effects. Chemotherapy drugs work by killing fast-growing cancer cells, but they don't distinguish between such cancer cells and fast-growing normal cells, and damage to healthy cells can result. Immunotherapy, on the other hand, uses the body's immune system to seek and destroy cancer cells.

The immune system of people and animals protects the body from diseases and infections. In addition to attacking germs and other foreign material, it attacks abnormal cells. Many of these abnormal cells are cancer cells, so the immune system prevents them from spreading. Some cancer cells, however, have the ability to hide from the immune system because they look and behave like normal, healthy cells. Immunotherapy not only boosts the body's natural defences, but also helps it identify these unhealthy cells. We hoped the melanoma vaccine would help Princeton's body destroy the cancerous melanoma cells and prevent the disease from spreading.

How it does this is really quite remarkable. Dogs have a specific tyrosinase enzyme responsible for melanin synthesis. When a dog suffers from oral melanoma, this enzyme is found in both melanoma cancer cells and in some normal, healthy cells. Since it's present in normal cells, the dog's immune system doesn't attack the cancerous cells, which aren't considered a threat. To stimulate the dog's immune system to attack the cancerous cells containing this enzyme, the dog is injected with human tyrosinase enzyme. Although human tyrosinase is very similar to canine tyrosinase, a dog's immune system will identify it as a threat and actively attack the human enzyme. And because the two enzymes are nearly identical, canine tyrosinase is also targeted, destroying the melanoma cancer cells. Side effects are minimal—usually the loss of some pigmentation. The vaccine is usually administered over several weeks, and to date the results have been promising. I soon discovered, however, that as promising as the vaccine was, obtaining it was a different matter altogether.

The vaccine is available for use only in veterinary clinics that specialize in oncology. Although Princeton's earlier osteosarcoma was treated by Drs. Kwantes and Marshall, neither one specialized in oncology nor had direct access to the vaccine. Both tried exhaustively to procure the vaccine but were unsuccessful. I contacted Dr. Fowler, who said that he could acquire what we needed. Dr. Marshall reached out to Dr. Cockwill, a specialist also working at Guardian Veterinary Centre, and he agreed to be involved with Princeton's case.

In mid-June Princeton visited Guardian for an evaluation. I had decided that if the disease hadn't metastasized and his chances of recovery were good, I would proceed with whatever treatments were recommended. If the cancer had spread and the prognosis was poor, I would elect to use palliative care, making Princeton as comfortable as I could until the disease had destroyed his quality of life. Once that happened, I would make sure he wouldn't suffer anymore.

Princeton seemed in good health and spirits when he was examined. Except for the melanoma, which had grown back remarkably quickly, he didn't show any other signs of the disease. Everyone was surprised by how well he seemed to be feeling, considering six months earlier many had written him off because of his seizures. Dr. Fowler suggested a full-body CT scan as well as a skull CT to determine whether metastasis had occurred and the melanoma had invaded Princeton's jawbone. Depending on the results, a choice would be made to remove the tumour, perform a mandibulectomy if needed, administer the first round of the melanoma vaccine, or instead adopt a palliative approach. Dr. Fowler suggested that the sooner we started, the better Princeton's chances would be. He thought the following day would be best for the CT scans.

On June 17, Princeton was back at Guardian. Still concerned about his reaction to the sedative months earlier, the doctor adopted a specific protocol for him. The sedation went fine, and soon a complete CT scan was performed. As I had done before, I paced anxiously in the reception area, waiting for the results. Eventually, Dr. Fowler came out to speak to me.

Mostly, Princeton's results were good. There were no signs of metastasis from the oral melanoma, and the nodules in the lungs (there was still no consensus on what they really were) had remained static. The only concern was the bone involvement with the melanoma. A small portion of Princeton's lower jaw would need to be removed to ensure proper margins when the melanoma was excised. Dr. Fowler assured me this would not interfere with Princeton's eating or drinking and wouldn't even be visible unless someone peered into his mouth. He also wanted to remove one lymph node. He expected the surgery to be successful and Princeton to recover completely from the anaesthetic. Once the surgery was finished, Dr. Cockwill would administer the melanoma vaccine. The removed tissue would then be submitted to a lab for further analysis. I agreed to the surgery and went back to pacing.

Shortly after lunch Dr. Fowler returned to inform me that Princeton had made it through the surgery without a problem. He had excised the entire mass with good margins, also removing a portion of Princeton's jaw, and the vaccine was administered. Princeton was already awake, looking around to see where I was. As I was escorted to the recovery area, two of the nurses said to me how amazed they were by how quickly Princeton came out of the anaesthetic considering his age. I didn't expect anything less. He was, after all, Princeton.

He stayed overnight in hospital and went home the following day. He would have to return to Guardian in two weeks, this time under the care of Dr. Cockwill, for a checkup and another dosage of the melanoma vaccine. Dr. Fowler submitted the portion of the jaw that was removed, along with the submandibular lymph node, for further analysis and expected the results in about a week. He assured me he would contact me once the analysis was completed.

For the following week Princeton didn't seem to have any problems. He was on soft food until his jaw healed, but since that included daily hot dogs, he didn't seem to mind. Looking at him, it was impossible to tell he'd had part of his jaw removed. Even when I looked into his mouth, which I did all the time now, his lower jaw didn't look that much different than it had before, except a few teeth were missing. Within a day he was mostly back to his old self, walking around the farm and going for rides in the Gator. He slept a lot, but I suppose that given his age and what he'd just experienced, that was to be expected. A week and a half later, Dr. Fowler received the results from the tissue samples and phoned me to discuss them.

Princeton's mandible mass was as previously diagnosed: oral

melanoma. It was malignant and highly aggressive. The mass had been completely excised, but the margins were rather tight, less than one millimetre in the soft tissue portion and three millimetres in the bone. The lymph node wasn't quite as easy to analyze. It did contain pigmented cells, but they didn't have the same cytological (cell) appearance as the cells within the tumour. Submandibular lymph nodes also act as a draining site for non-cancerous pigmented cells. Because of this, the pathologist couldn't determine if the swollen lymph node indicated metastatic disease. The results of the report, combined with that of the CT scan, failed to find any evidence of metastasis, making most of us cautiously optimistic that Princeton had a little more quality time left. We all knew that the prognosis of dogs suffering from oral melanoma wasn't good, but we hoped the surgery, combined with the vaccine, would allow him to continue on his journey for as long as he wanted to.

Two weeks after his surgery, Princeton hopped into Guardian for a checkup and the second round of the melanoma vaccine. He seemed to be feeling good and, surprisingly, was walking more on his own than he had been lately. His checkup and blood work were both good, and my only concern was that he had been wetting his bed more than usual. Instead of the tiny wet spot each morning, sometimes he had emptied his bladder completely. I always checked on him every few hours, and when I entered the entryway where he slept, I could tell by the look on his face if he'd had an accident. Princeton was a proud doggy, and he was disappointed with himself if he was unable to hold his pee. If this happened I would carry him outside, hold him up to see if he wanted to urinate further, and tell him that it wasn't his fault. Knowing he had a history of bladder infections, I made an appointment for a urinalysis.

It turned out Princeton had another bladder infection. An antibiotic was prescribed, followed by another when the lab report indicated the first one wouldn't be successful in treating the infection. Princeton responded favourably to the second antibiotic, but something else was causing me concern: for the first time in all the years we had spent together, through the good times, the misadventures, and the illnesses, the fire in Princeton's eyes was slowly ebbing away. The liveliness and intelligence in those eyes was sometimes replaced by a look of fatigue. Princeton was satisfied to spend much of his time lying on the grass with his friend BK. I would often sit by them both, scratching Princeton behind the ear as he laid his head on my lap. We'd often sit there for hours as I stroked his fur and talked to him. One summer evening I fell asleep as I lay beside him, awakening late at night with the stars above me and Princeton's face next to mine. Lifting him up and holding on to his harness as he took a short walk and peed, I knew that the journey we'd embarked upon nearly seventeen years before would soon come to an end. I left him on the grass and turned and walked away from him. I didn't want him to see me cry.

As the summer went by, Princeton had both good days and bad days. There were days when he was alert and bouncy and moved around with enthusiasm, and days when he was content to do nothing more than sleep. He had lost some of his appetite, and some days he would only eat things like boiled turkey or chicken. He never lost his love of hot dogs, however, but the days of bounding joyously up to Des's cart were over. He'd remain in the truck as we drove to the cart, waiting patiently for me to bring him back his favourite meal. He received another melanoma vaccine injection and another lymph node was removed. Except for the other swollen lymph node, the disease hadn't seemed to progress.

I've been told that a responsible pet owner knows when it's time to help a beloved pet move on. That it's the final act of love we can give them, and that when the time comes, we will release them from their suffering. I often thought about the talk I'd had with Princeton in the spring when I promised him I wouldn't let him suffer. Nor would I, however, end his life prematurely. I've known people who have had a pet euthanized simply because they were unwilling to care for them when it got to be too much work, all the while claiming that they did it for the welfare of the animal. I've always believed that end-of-life care is part of being a pet owner, but it's also important to acknowledge when our care is making our pets more miserable than they already are. I didn't want my emotions to cloud my judgment about what was best for Princeton. I asked both Dr. Kwantes and Dr. Marshall, now Princeton's friends as well as his veterinarians, to tell me if my love for him ever interfered with my judgment. If my desires and hopes ever caused me to see what wasn't really there. If my hope that somehow Princeton and I would have a little more time together wasn't fair to him. Both accepted, and for now the best any of us could wish for was that he would be comfortable for whatever time he had left.

By August I knew that Princeton wouldn't be with me much longer. He was uncomfortable, now suffering from spondylosis, which had caused some of his vertebrae to fuse together. He was often immobile and depended on me to help him urinate and move around. There were times, however, he seemed like his old self. A look of excitement would appear on his face whenever I said "hot dog" or "Timbit," his eyes bright and clear as I scratched him behind his ear while we rode in the truck to get him one of his favourite treats. Other times he and I would lie together in the living room, a smile on his face as I spoke to him. If I stopped petting him, he would grunt and nuzzle me until I started again. There were times he'd be waiting for me when I came into the house from doing chores, obviously happy to see me, knowing we would be spending some time together. I knew in my heart that Princeton wasn't ready to leave just yet.

One of the most difficult things I had to do for Princeton as he neared the end of his life was to make arrangements for his crema-tion. I didn't want to be contacting crematoriums after he had passed. It was important to me to find someone I could work with, someone who would understand that Princeton was more than just a dog. I wanted them to understand that he was my everything. I chose the same place that had cremated my cat Sierra in 2012, and they agreed to assist me as soon as I made the call that I needed their services.

Something else I did was to remind Princeton of what I'd said to him in the spring: that in time, I would be okay without him. I would continue to make him proud. When people asked how the name Black Dog Farms Inc. came about, I told them that it was because of a very special dog. I also told everyone that I was only an employee and Princeton was CEO of the company. And although he's gone now, I still tell everyone the same thing. As the company ventures into other things, I'll always remember Princeton as the boss. Sometimes, even now, I ask him his opinion about a business decision I have to make as if he's standing beside me. Lastly, I promised him his memory would provide the inspiration for something I've always wanted to do: write a book. His inspiration is far greater than my talent as a writer, and I hope whatever literary shortcomings I have demonstrated here will be eclipsed by the wonderful stories he provided.

28

A Journey's End

THE TRAGICALLY HIP (commonly referred to as "the Hip") are a Canadian rock band that began their career in the eighties. Over the years it's often been said that they defined what it's like to be Canadian. As a proud Canadian in my early fifties, I've been fortunate to enjoy their music for nearly thirty years. If I was at a house party in the late eighties or through the nineties, the Hip was always on the stereo.

There were five members of the group, the most recognizable the lead vocalist, Gord Downie. Sadly, Gord died of brain cancer on October 17, 2017. He was diagnosed with the terminal disease in 2015 and given a grave prognosis. The band made the formal announcement of Gord's cancer in May of 2016. Shockingly, they also announced that they would be touring that summer. It would be their last tour. The final concert was on August 20, 2016, in Kingston, Ontario, the band's hometown.

The concert was broadcast by CBC in its entirety without commercial interruption. It was a remarkable finale for an even more remarkable group that represented the best Canada had to offer. Over one-third of Canada's population watched the concert that evening. Princeton and I were among them.

The night of the Tragically Hip's last performance was the last good night Princeton and I shared together. We snuggled side by side, he lying on his doggy bed and I lying beside him. He was alert, and much of the pain he had been experiencing during the last week had disappeared. His eyes were bright and clear, and the two of us watched the Hip perform. Princeton was never really a big TV watcher, even when he lived in the living room during his seizures, but maybe because I was so interested in the concert, his eyes rarely left the screen. As we lay on the floor, he put his head across my chest and continued to watch the program as I scratched behind his ear. As old as he was, his eyesight hadn't diminished, and I'm sure he could see Gord Downie's emotions as he performed with his bandmates for the final time. If a particular song reminded me of some detail in my life, I'd tell Princeton about it. He'd lift his head from my chest, smile, look at me with his wonderful eyes until I was done speaking, and turn back toward the television. For nearly three hours, nothing bothered him. He wasn't sick. He wasn't in pain. He wasn't old. It reminded me of the nights we had shared together in Poseidon, happy to be together and not worried about anything at all.

Princeton died August 28, 2016, shortly after 4:00 p.m. It was a Sunday, sunny, but not too warm. The kind of day Princeton liked most. I was with him when he passed, as was Dr. Fowler. I know with absolute certainty that the world flickered briefly, like the flame of a candle before it goes out forever, when it realized that one of its most special creatures would no longer be a part of it—that the life of a wonderful, gentle, beautiful, and intelligent being had ended. Three days later Princeton was cremated. The following morning, the day of my fifty-first birthday, the ashes of my friend were returned to me.

Princeton's final day began with my rushing him into Guardian Veterinary Centre very early in the morning. The night before, he was noticeably uncomfortable, at times barking loudly as he lay on his bed in the house. I originally thought it was because of his spondylosis and gave him a powerful painkiller, which failed to make him feel better. At around 4:00 a.m. I loaded him into the truck and drove him to Guardian. The veterinarian on duty performed a short examination and took an X-ray. She felt that Princeton's discomfort was gas, as his intestine was bloated. She suggested that I leave Princeton at the clinic for the day since he had an appointment with a specialist the following morning. I asked what was causing the gas, but she couldn't give me a definitive answer. Hoping to gain a little more insight, I decided to take him home to rest until another veterinarian came on duty later that morning.

I took Princeton back a few hours later to see the other veterinarian, who performed another examination and took additional radiographs. His diagnosis was that Princeton was suffering from a blocked intestine. The only way to correct the problem and alleviate Princeton's pain was to perform immediate surgery. The second veterinarian, much more sympathetic to Princeton than the first, asked me to carefully consider if putting him through this procedure was fair to him. Princeton was suffering, and even if the surgery was successful, it wouldn't help him with his other problems.

By then Dr. Fowler had arrived to check up on the patients he had performed surgery on the day before. He looked at the radiographs and agreed there was a blockage in the intestine, most likely a foreign body. He also asked me to consider if the surgery was in Princeton's best interests. Having known Dr. Fowler for nearly three years and witnessed how compassionate he was toward his patients, I asked what he thought I should do. He replied that he couldn't answer that for me; the decision was up to me. He also explained that there are no right or wrong decisions in a situation like this. All he asked was that whatever decision I made was made carefully and for the right reasons.

Even now, I question whether or not I made the right decision. The remainder of Princeton's life was now measured in weeks, if not days. He would not get better. He would not magically return to his youthful, healthy self. What I thought about most, however, was whether it was right to euthanize Princeton, knowing that what was causing his pain was correctable. But there was also the possibility that he would not recover from the surgery, and whatever I had hoped to achieve through it would make him worse off than he already was. I asked to spend some time alone with Princeton. Together, we would make the decision.

I explained to Princeton that if he had the surgery, the pain would go away. If he didn't, the pain would go away soon too. The difference was that if he had the surgery, there was chance he would still be here. Life, however, would still be short for him. I told him that he was my best friend, and I loved him more than anything or anyone I had ever loved before, but I didn't know what to do. I asked him if he had any fight left in him. When he looked into my eyes, I knew he was asking me the same.

Dr. Fowler remained at the clinic to perform the surgery. "I'll see you soon, sweetheart. When you wake up, I'll be there," I said to Princeton when the nurses arrived to take him to the operating theatre. He looked at me with his lovely brown eyes, smiled, and licked the side of my cheek. He continued to smile at me as he was wheeled away.

As I stood outside the clinic, I continued to think about the decision to have the surgery performed. Princeton would pass soon, but I wanted it to be from old age and not because of something he might have eaten. He was a survivor. Each time any of us thought he wasn't long for this world, he'd bounce back. He'd bounce back this time too, and although he'd pass away soon, it would be on his own terms. When I walked back inside Guardian, the veterinarian who had made the diagnosis approached me and asked if he could see me privately. It was then that I knew my journey with Princeton had come to an end.

The doctor explained that things had been going well when Dr. Fowler started the surgery. Princeton was doing fine under the anaesthetic, and there weren't any complications. But soon Dr. Fowler discovered that Princeton's intestine was not blocked by a foreign body but had collapsed entirely. The entire length of it was dilated and greenish. The intestine was dead, likely because of a blood clot. Nothing could be done.

As we spoke in an examination room, I rose from my chair and walked toward a window. I stood there, looking through the window as the doctor continued telling me that nothing more could be done for Princeton. After a few moments he said that he was sorry. I could tell by the tone of his voice that he meant it. He asked if I would like to have Princeton brought out from the anaesthetic for a few moments so I could say goodbye. He wouldn't be in any pain. No, he might not be in pain, but he'd be confused knowing I was upset. I wanted his last memory of me to be the one in which we smiled at each other as he was wheeled away for his surgery.

I asked to be taken to the operating theatre to be present while Dr. Fowler performed the euthanasia. The first thing I noticed was how good the sutures looked where Dr. Fowler had stitched up Princeton—good enough for him to be sent home as if nothing were wrong. It's odd how we look at things as we try to combat our grief. As Princeton lay peacefully on the operating table, Dr. Fowler told me how sorry he was. I knew it was a difficult time for him too. I stood there for a few moments before approaching my friend. As I stroked his fur, I said, "I love you, Princeton. Thank you for being my friend. I love you, Boo. I promise I'll always keep your truck. And our van."

Turning to Dr. Fowler, I told him that it was time. Before he administered the barbiturate, I remarked to him how difficult it must be to put animals to sleep.

He paused before responding, "The hard ones are the ones who still have a chance. You always gave Princeton a chance." Whenever I'm missing Princeton I think of what Dr. Fowler said to me and I feel a little better.

A moment later Princeton received the barbiturate, stopping his heart immediately. His strong and courageous heart. I stood there, watching Princeton's electrocardiogram, or ECG. It continued to pulse, the electrical system within his heart not accepting that his heart muscle had stopped forever. The technical term for this is electromechanical dissociation. More than anything, this is what I'll remember about the moment Princeton died: the last few seconds of electrical activity on the monitor before it fell silent. And then, for the first time in seventeen years, I was alone.

No one said anything as Dr. Fowler and I took Princeton by gurney from the second floor of the clinic down to the first floor and out to the truck. The nurses and staff turned away as we passed by them. Princeton was well liked by most everyone there, and I wasn't the only one who was upset. It was important to me to bring Princeton home and not leave him at the clinic for the crematorium staff to pick up. I didn't want him to be alone in some cooler. I wanted him to be at home. I would take him to the crematorium myself when the time came. Dr. Fowler again expressed his sympathies and helped me place Princeton in the truck, then stood at the rear entrance of the clinic and watched as I drove away.

Before reaching home I stopped at a convenience store and purchased eight bags of cubed ice. Once we were home I felt very much alone. I opened the rear door of the truck and looked at Princeton's lifeless body for several minutes. I spoke to him softly as I carefully stroked his fur, telling him how wonderful it was to have known him. I thanked him again for being my friend and told him that there would never, ever be another like him. Finally, I told him how much I loved him, and regardless of how much time passed, I would always cherish the love he had given me and would never forget the time we had spent together.

Suddenly, I felt a gentle nudge from behind. I turned around and there was Grover, my neighbour's dog.

Grover is black like Princeton and also looks as if he has some

Lab in him somewhere. He's a great dog who is loved by his owners, especially Doug. Grover is a bad dog sometimes, whose hearing can be described as "selective," and he likes to wander off Doug and Sherry's property. Sometimes I can hear Doug yelling for him in the evenings, but Grover doesn't return unless he feels like it. Other times he wanders over to my farm to see if he can bother the cats or pick a fight with the goat. This only happens about once every couple of months. When he does come to visit, he always has a sheepish look on his handsome face. Grover, it seems, understands that he's not supposed to be here. He usually keeps his distance and trots off toward his home when I tell him to.

Gone was Grover's usual sheepishness now, replaced by a peaceful quality and understanding. I fell to my knees and gave him a hug. He remained motionless as my tears spilled onto his fur. After a few moments I rose to my feet and rested my hand on Grover's head. He looked at me, turned away, and very slowly walked toward the barns. I watched as he walked by the front of the first barn, the second, and then turned to walk along the small driveway between the second and third barns. Soon he was gone from view as he headed to the far end of the barns.

I turned back to Princeton and spoke to him for another minute or so before carrying his body inside the garage. By then Grover had come back into view and was rounding the far corner of the fourth barn. He walked in front of all four barns, eventually stopping and sitting in front of the first. We looked at each other. The route he had taken was the same route Princeton and I had taken during the last walk we'd had together the night before. Grover and I continued looking at each other for several minutes until he got up and trotted down the driveway, heading for home.

Some people claim everything happens for a reason. That our fate is predetermined and we are here only to live our lives as best we can within the confines fate has placed upon us. I don't believe this. I've always thought life is what you make of it, that we are free to choose our own destinies. I also think, however, there are things in this world we have yet to understand. Perhaps we aren't meant to. Instead, we must accept and embrace moments regardless of how fantastic they may seem.

Grover's visit was one of those things. Without reservation, I believe his retracing of the last steps Princeton and I took together the evening before his death had been Princeton's way of telling me he was all right. That he had no regrets. And neither should I. That although our journey may have ended, our time spent together was beyond compare, and the wonderful memories we have of one another will never fade.

Thank you, Princeton. Thank you for everything.

The next morning I contacted the crematorium I had made the arrangements with previously and was told I could bring Princeton in Wednesday morning. It was two days away, but my friend John, who manages a division of a poultry-processing company, supplied me with a large cardboard crate and a quantity of shaved ice to keep Princeton's body cool until the time of cremation.

During the next two days, I frequently went into the garage to check on Princeton. I'd ask how he was doing. If he was okay. If he needed anything. I spoke to him as if he were standing beside me, waiting to start our day. I wished him good morning and left the lights on in the garage each night so he wouldn't be frightened. Princeton allowed me to say what I wanted to him, including my goodbyes.

I told very few people of his death. Soon, however, everyone knew he had passed. Dr. Kwantes was away from his practice, but I texted him the evening Princeton died. I contacted Dr. Marshall Monday morning. Except for telling them and a few close friends, I chose to deal with Princeton's death the way I usually do when it comes to something personal: alone. But within a few days, I started to receive calls from people I hadn't told. Veterinary clinics that might have seen Princeton only once or twice reached out to me and offered their condolences. Other friends and acquaintances started calling to extend their sympathies. Most everyone cried along with me as I told them about how Princeton had died. He was loved by almost everyone who knew him, and I wouldn't be the only one who would miss him.

For several weeks numerous sympathy cards arrived in the mail. I still have them, as each one is special. There's one card, however, that remains my favourite. It was given to me by the staff at Park Veterinary Centre. Before Dr. Kwantes signed his name to the card, he wrote something that took me aback when I first read it. A couple of months later, he confessed that at the time he didn't know what to say and finally decided to write what he truly felt. It wasn't a condolence, just one poignant sentence: "It has been an honour."

It was. For both me and Princeton.

I brought Princeton to the crematorium a little before 4:00 a.m. Wednesday morning. I had requested a private cremation, not wanting his ashes to be mixed with those of any other animals. The proprietor allowed me to place Princeton into the cremation chamber and start the furnace to begin the process. I left a few minutes later, wanting to sit alone outside and wait for it to be over. After several hours the cremation was finished, but I wouldn't be able to pick up the ashes until the following day. That was fine, as the important thing was I'd been able to be with Princeton until the very end. I knew he would have wanted that.

I've always found it comforting to receive the ashes of any of my pets, but I'm always surprised by how little actually gets returned. It's basically bone and small amounts of minerals. Where did the rest go? As I sat outside of the crematorium, watching the heat leave the chimney, I knew that whatever was leaving would go on to eventually become part of something else. Everything around us, including ourselves, is comprised of atoms, and whatever left that morning would become something very special. Because it was once part of Princeton.

The first few days following Princeton's death remain a blur. It was a busy time of year for the farm, and plenty of things needed attention. I would start early in the morning and work until late, often not bothering to eat. I hoped that the harder I worked, the less I would grieve over Princeton. It didn't work. For almost seventeen years he had been beside me, sharing in the day's activities. He was not only my constant companion, but also my helper. I would always take the time to explain to him what things were and what they did. Many times I'd kneel on the shop floor while he sat beside me and show him whatever I was repairing. I would carefully explain to him what it did, showing him all the parts while I disassembled it and put it back together. Each morning, while driving home from coffee and Timbits, I told Princeton everything we had to do that day. He would sit across from me, watching me as I explained what needed to be done. When we arrived home he'd jump from the truck, trot off a few steps, and wait for me, eager to get on with the day's work. Working until I was exhausted didn't lessen the pain but instead made me think even more of the things we'd done together.

Each night when I walked into my house, I would carefully step over Princeton's bed and dishes, still in the entryway. For nearly two weeks they remained there. I just couldn't bear the thought of moving them. Sleep, when it did come, was always restless. For weeks I would awaken suddenly, thinking I had heard Princeton's bell or his feet kick the wall, only to realize a second or two later that he wasn't there. I'd often catch a glimpse of something outside the barns or around the yard, and for a brief moment I'd think it was Princeton. I like to think maybe it *was* him, his spirit making sure I was okay. I wasn't the only one who missed him, as both Barnie and BK spent much of their time looking for him. Barnie still does. The goat also seemed to understand that something wasn't right. She would often walk to where he usually was, only to discover that he wasn't there. One of the saddest moments was when she came up to the Gator when it was out of the garage and looked into the back of it, hoping to see Princeton. She lingered and then turned and walked away, and never looked for him again.

A small part of Princeton that I carried with me seemed to help a little. A few days after his death, I had a jeweller friend make a pendant for me. It's Princeton's dog tag set into a sterling silver mount. The tag still has our engraved names and phone number. I got it for him the third week after I brought him home, hoping it would help him if he ever got himself lost (and as you know, it did). Before my friend placed the tag into the mount and attached a stainless steel chain, I placed some of Princeton's fur between the two pieces. I wear the pendant today, never removing it unless necessary.

As the weeks went on, I continued to hear from people expressing their sympathies and asking how I was doing. We'd spend several minutes talking about Princeton, how special he was and the wonderful life we'd had together. The three primary veterinary clinics that had taken care of Princeton, Park Veterinary Centre, the Edmonton Holistic Veterinary Clinic, and Guardian Veterinary Centre, all kept in touch, everyone wondering how I was and if there was anything they could do to help. Throughout the years I had gotten to know many of the staff of each clinic, several of whom always did their best for Princeton. Besides Dr. Kwantes, Dr. Marshall, and Dr. Fowler, there were other veterinarians, receptionists, technicians, and nurses who often went out of their way to help me and Princeton. A few weeks after his death, I asked each of his primary veterinarians how I could thank them and their staff for their help and support over the years.

The first to reply was Dr. Fowler of Guardian. He, and most of the staff, knew Princeton as the hot dog dog. Whenever he'd had an extended stay at the clinic, I would always visit Des and pick up a hot dog to take back for Princeton. Even when he was there for only a checkup, we usually went for a hot dog when the appointment was over. This was probably why Princeton liked going to Guardian. Dr. Fowler thought the best way to thank him and his staff and to honour Princeton's memory would be something related to hot dogs. So one late-September afternoon, Des brought one of his carts to the clinic and set up at the back door.

For two hours each of the staff came out to be treated to hot dogs and soft drinks, courtesy of me and Des. Everyone looked through a photo album of Princeton's travels I had placed on Des's cart, and they smiled and laughed and asked questions when they came to certain photographs. Most everyone at Guardian knew Princeton was a traveller, but few realized he had visited so many places. I also displayed a framed picture of Princeton and Des sitting together, taken the day of Des's wedding the summer before. Although the weather wasn't the greatest, everyone had a wonderful time. Some staff members came even though it was their day off to have a hot dog and share their memories of Princeton. Others returned several times to have another hot dog and look through the photo album again. It was a wonderful way for everyone to celebrate Princeton's life and to reflect upon what he meant to each of them. Thank you, Des.

Today, a framed picture of Princeton, lying on a beach in Tofino, hangs on the wall behind the reception desk at Guardian.

The second clinic to respond was the Edmonton Holistic Veterinary Clinic. Dr. Marshall and the staff thought for nearly a week before deciding that a framed picture of Princeton would be the best way to honour him. They knew Princeton not only as a survivor, but also as a dog with a gentle demeanour combined with a strength and toughness rarely ever seen. They wanted a picture that exemplified these special traits. I went to the clinic one day to share several pictures with the staff and see which one they preferred. Soon they chose one and I was off to see my friend Emily at her gallery to have it framed. Admittedly, I had misled Dr. Marshall and her staff a little, only wanting to get an idea of the sort of picture they wanted; I wanted to choose the picture because I wanted it to be a surprise. Emily, as usual, did a phenomenal job, and about two weeks later,

I presented a large photo of Princeton with museum-quality framing to the staff. Princeton was pictured against a log on the sandy beach in Tofino, looking every bit his age, his muzzle and the fur around his eyes greying, but with a look in his eyes of intelligence and strength. He looked magnificent. Everyone cried. I did too.

The picture hangs in Dr. Marshall's office, above her desk, and if she ever leaves the clinic, everyone has decided the picture will go with her.

Dr. Kwantes took the longest to decide, probably because he was particularly fond of Princeton. Eventually, he said that the best way to honour Princeton's memory would be for me to supply lunch for the staff when they had a meeting. Not just any lunch, but lunch provided by Tim Hortons. Like Dr. Fowler, Dr. Kwantes always associated a particular food with Princeton, this being his other favourite snack, Timbits. Whenever Princeton had had a checkup, Dr. Kwantes told me that I shouldn't be feeding him so many Timbits—not because of any real health concerns but because Princeton was a little too porky. I always told Dr. Kwantes that I would do as he said, but after each visit to his office, Princeton and I would somehow find ourselves in the Tim Hortons drive-thru ordering Timbits before we went home. Dr. Kwantes knew exactly what was going on.

One afternoon, several months after Princeton's death, I delivered a platter of sandwiches, soup, and chili to Park Veterinary Centre for their staff meeting. And, of course, lots of Timbits.

Earlier I had presented Dr. Kwantes with a small framed picture of Princeton for his office. It hangs on his wall, and he tells me he can feel Princeton looking down at him. It was taken just outside the town of Princeton, British Columbia, on our way to Tofino.

29

A Very Special Dog

I DON'T SLEEP much anymore. I've always had trouble sleeping, but since Princeton's death my insomnia has become worse. In fact, every word of this book was written when most everyone else is sleeping. When the nights are particularly long, I often get out of bed and walk outside onto the deck. Princeton's doghouse still sits beside the door. When I look out at the darkness that embraces my farm, I can sometimes see a dark shadow, just for a moment, off in the distance. It's only there momentarily, a bouncing black blur, and then it's gone. Maybe it's there because I convince myself it's there. Maybe it really is. Either way I don't care, because each time I see it, I smile.

I've heard people claim that something loved never dies because memories continue forever. In some respects I agree, but I have always believed that it goes much deeper than that. Princeton lives on in my memories and also in the way I live my life. My dog made me a better person. Not only was he my friend and companion, but he was also a family member and business partner. The longer he was with me, the more I realized I was the luckiest guy in the world. For nearly seventeen years I went to work with my best friend. How many people can say that? When people and things pissed me off, it was Princeton's gentleness that made me realize there wasn't anything to be angry over. As a pair we were inseparable, capable of dealing with whatever challenges came our way. Princeton taught me to see things as he saw them. The world to him was a special place, to be lived in and cherished. He also taught me that even the most seemingly insignificant things and briefest moments can offer the greatest happiness.

This is how Princeton continues to live on. This is how he will remain with me.

Looking back now, I understand why so many others felt such affection for him. Although he had several challenges later in life, his determination and happy demeanour never left him. A few months after Princeton's death, I asked Dr. Fowler if he expected to ever meet another dog like Princeton. Dr. Fowler, a surgeon and educator who has cared for more animals than any other veterinarian I know of, answered immediately: "No. Princeton was different." Throughout his career he knew of perhaps one or two other dogs who had come close to surviving osteosarcoma as long as Princeton had, but none had possessed his attitude. He was a survivor, but his attitude made everyone want to cheer for him.

When I asked Dr. Marshall the same question, her reply was nearly the same. She considers Princeton to be a "once in a career" sort of dog. A dog who remains in your thoughts long after he passes. She again mentioned that Princeton was the toughest dog she'd ever known. Nothing could defeat him.

Dr. Kwantes and I talked about what had made Princeton so special. He also said he'd never experience a dog like Princeton ever again, but added something else: Princeton was indeed very special, but the bond between him and me even more so. It allowed us to overcome any hardship presented to us. Whatever it was, we went through it together. When Dr. Kwantes told me this, I thought back to the times when Princeton was going through his osteosarcoma and liver problems, to the nights I'd sit with him and tell him to take from me whatever he needed. I had taken Princeton's gentleness and compassion before, and I wanted to give him the same in return. I'm sure much of this sounds overly sentimental, but I'd like to think that at least some of what Dr. Kwantes told me has some truth to it.

I haven't gotten another dog and probably won't for a while. In time I may adopt another, but it will never fill the deep hole left behind by Princeton. Nor should it. I want that hole to remain open forever. That place was Princeton's. I subscribe to the belief that your departed pet sends you another one when you're ready. When I'm ready for another dog, Princeton will send him (or her) to me. Whenever I think of another dog, I envision an old dog walking slowly up my driveway, needing a home. When the time comes, I'll know it.

Princeton's old pickup, the one I purchased specifically for him and promised I would keep forever, is about to be removed from active duty. It still runs well, but having travelled close to 750,000 kilometres, the body has gotten a little rough. I intend to restore the body and drive it occasionally. It was Princeton's truck and it needs to be treated far better than the battered old farm truck it has become. Poseidon, the faithful old camper van and third member of our travels, now sits in the hay shed. Like the old F-150, I promised Princeton I would keep it. Not long ago I walked by it, laid my hand on its hood, and said, "I miss him too." In time I'll use it again, maybe even with another dog, but for now its travelling days are behind it.

Lately, I've been thinking of all the spare parts and tools I still have packed in it. What did I use during our travels? One lousy fuel filter. Princeton and I travelled nearly sixty thousand kilometres in Poseidon, and except for the time we got dirty fuel, we never had a problem. Sometimes we travelled in temperatures so hot, Princeton couldn't get out of the van because the asphalt was too hot for him to walk on. Poseidon would just burble away, keeping us in air-conditioned comfort. Other times we camped in sub-zero temperatures and depended on its little furnace to keep us warm and comfortable.

Whether we found ourselves in remote locations without a soul around or driving the winding road to Tofino, Poseidon always took care of us. It knew it was responsible for the welfare of a very special dog.

That's my story of a remarkable dog. A dog who was with me for a third of my life. A dog who will remain in my memory and continue to influence my life until I die. He will always remain my best friend, and I hope I did everything I could for him. I've never considered myself religious—I'm more agnostic than anything—but if we do go somewhere when we pass, I want to go where Princeton went. I'd be happy with that.

Epilogue

O N THE ONE-YEAR anniversary of Princeton's death, I awoke early. I was between growing cycles, and the barns were empty. After taking care of the cats and the goat (but not letting her out of the barn), I got out the keys to Princeton's old F-150. After filling both fuel tanks, I drove to Tim Hortons. At the drive-thru I ordered a tea and a Timbit. The Timbit I placed on the passenger seat, alongside my pendant, which I had placed there earlier. I started to drive.

Considering it was the anniversary of Princeton's death, I didn't feel as upset as I thought I would. The past year had been a difficult one. I continued to miss Princeton terribly, some days being worse than others. Today was different. As much as I longed for him, I also felt a sense of excitement. It felt as it had in the past, when we awakened and prepared ourselves to leave in Poseidon for however long we wanted.

We were off. Once on the highway I started driving west, heading out of the city. I didn't have any idea where we were going, but it felt like the right direction to take. I kept the radio turned off, and after a while started talking to Princeton as if he were beside me, looking out the windshield, excitement on his face.

I didn't speak of where we were going but instead of all the wonderful trips we had taken together. I spoke to him about all we had seen. What we had experienced and the people we had met. The ocean and the mountains. The open highways and little towns we'd passed through. The places we'd stayed for the night.

I told him what a wonderful dog he was and how lucky I was to have known him. I apologized to him for the times I wasn't as understanding as I should have been. I told him how sorry I was, and that I should have done more for him. Or that maybe I had done too much.

Four hours later we drove past Snaring River campground, where we had stayed a few times. Then the Jasper Park Lodge, where I'd first seen how easily Princeton could embrace being pampered and coddled. And then into Jasper itself, the town where we had walked along the sidewalk together, often the focus of people who wanted to know more about the old three-legged dog.

We had been driving for close to five hours, but it felt as if we had only just left home. We stopped at the rest areas we had visited and purchased fuel where we had stopped several times before. I kept speaking to Princeton as we drove through Jasper and continued our drive west. It was late afternoon then, but I didn't feel like stopping. After nearly seven hours of driving, I pulled into a rest area Princeton had been particularly fond of. I reached over, took the pendant from the passenger seat, and placed it around my neck. I got out of the truck and headed toward the open field Princeton had loved romping through. I walked through the field, turning around once to look back at our old truck.

After about fifteen minutes I walked back to the truck, got in, and sat there for a while, not saying anything to Princeton. Finally, I turned to where he had sat for all those years and asked him what he wanted to do. Should we go farther? Or should we go home? Whatever he wanted, it didn't matter to me. Minutes later we were back on the highway, heading in the direction we had come from.

February 16ᵗʰ, 2018, to February 4ᵗʰ, 2019.
The year of the dog.

Acknowledgments

WHEN I STARTED to write this book a few weeks after Princeton died, it was in complete secrecy. As I mention in the book, I started to do so because of a promise I had made to him, along with a personal desire to one day write a book.

My words were never intended to be read by anyone. I planned to make my manuscript as good as possible, but once completed it would remain with me, never to be shared. Weeks after Princeton's death, however, I continued to hear from people offering their condolences and inquiring how I was doing. Often my well-wishers and I would talk for several minutes about Princeton and the experiences we had shared together. And without fail, everyone mentioned how special Princeton was. How much of an inspiration he was. And how the relationship we shared was beyond compare.

The manuscript was in its infancy then, and although I still intended to keep the completed work to myself, I began to question if I had the right to do so. And more importantly, whether Princeton would have agreed with my intentions. As time went on and the manuscript grew, I wondered if perhaps I was being selfish. Maybe Princeton's story should be shared. And I should feel honoured to be the one to tell it. Eventually, I decided to tell a few people what I was doing as they slept. With their encouragement, I began to seek out individuals who could help me make my book the best I could so I might one day share it. It is these people, friends and professionals alike, I wish to thank.

First, there are three veterinarians, Dr. Kwantes, Dr. Marshall, and Dr. Fowler. Princeton visited many veterinarians throughout his life, but after his passing, it was these particular veterinarians who not only encouraged me to share Princeton's story, but also continued to educate me in various facets of veterinary care. Each read the manuscript in its infancy, and I'll always be grateful for the care they provided to Princeton and the support and input they offered to me after his death.

I also thank my other beta readers, Kim Shaw and Trent Filthaut. Kim returned my manuscript with sand from Tofino in its pages. She read much of it on the same beaches Princeton and I had enjoyed so much. She apologized about the sand; I thought it was a lovely touch. Trent was not only an early reader, but also my IT guy. My understanding of computers is limited, and he assisted me on several occasions in making sure my manuscript was properly formatted and the contents protected.

I want to acknowledge my editors, Caroline Kaiser and Susan Fitzgerald. I thought the dreaded red pen from my school years was a thing of the past. Apparently not. Both offered excellent suggestions and provided polishing where needed, but they also reassured me that what I had written was actually worth reading. It's difficult for me to accept any sort of compliment, and I'll always be thankful for their kind words. Both also offered suggestions beyond the writing process and helped to make the transition from manuscript to a published work a reality.

I thank Cam Shaw for allowing me to share with him my vision for the front and back covers of the book. He then used his talents to design a beautiful exterior. He and Kim are not only my friends, but were Princeton's as well. I know Cam's design is a tribute to the dog who made our friendship possible.

David Moratto did an outstanding job designing the interior of the book. He openly shared the design process and always took the time to answer my many questions. I'm very grateful for David's talents and patience.

I would also like to take this opportunity to thank the other people who eventually learned of what I was doing in the middle of the night. All offered support and, at times, suggestions. Of note are Terri Y. and Mark Trick. Terri gave her usual support and love, not only during the writing of the manuscript, but before and after as well. Mark was always up for a beer when I needed a sounding board.

And, of course, thanks to my mother. She may not have been involved with the writing of Princeton's memoir, but she provided something else that contributed to its existence: instilling in me the belief that anything is achievable, even if the road isn't as smooth as we would like it to be.

Thank you all.
—TERRY FONG, AUGUST 2018